# THE BEGINNING OR THE END

# THE BEGINNING OR THE END

## HOW HOLLYWOOD—AND AMERICA—LEARNED TO STOP WORRYING AND LOVE THE BOMB

GREG MITCHELL

THE
NEW
PRESS

NEW YORK
LONDON

Requests for permission to reproduce selections from this book should be made
through our website: https://thenewpress.com/contact.

Published in the United States by The New Press, New York, 2020
Distributed by Two Rivers Distribution

ISBN 978-1-62097-573-2 (hc)
ISBN 978-1-62097-574-9 (ebook)
CIP data is available

The New Press publishes books that promote and enrich public discussion and
understanding of the issues vital to our democracy and to a more equitable world.
These books are made possible by the enthusiasm of our readers; the support of a
committed group of donors, large and small; the collaboration of our many partners in
the independent media and the not-for-profit sector; booksellers, who often hand-sell
New Press books; librarians; and above all by our authors.

www.thenewpress.com

Book design and composition by Bookbright Media
This book was set in Janson Text and Akzidenz Grotesk

Printed in the United States of America

10 9 8 7 6 5 4 3 2 1

History is often not what actually happened, but what is recorded as such.

—*Henry L. Stimson, Secretary of War, 1940–1945*

# CONTENTS

# CAST OF CHARACTERS

**Carter Barron:** MGM's representative in Washington, D.C.

**Jerome Beatty:** Magazine writer who wrote original "Top Secret" story for Wallis

**Roman Bohnen:** Character actor, likely Communist, slated to play Truman

**Niels Bohr:** Top Danish atomic physicist who fled to Sweden

**Vannevar Bush:** Head of federal office overseeing science work

**Al Cohn:** Former screenwriter who sold Hal Wallis on atomic bomb movie

**James B. Conant:** President of Harvard who advised on use of bomb against Japan

**Bob Considine:** Well-known magazine writer, Hearst columnist, author

**W.A. Consodine:** Groves aide, military adviser at MGM for movie

**Hume Cronyn:** Actor picked to play Oppenheimer

**Brian Donlevy:** Well-known actor who took role of Leslie Groves

**Tom Drake:** Young actor who played ethical scientist Matt Cochran

**Albert Einstein:** 1939 letter to FDR alerted him to ability to make atomic bomb, later criticized use of weapon

**Enrico Fermi:** Led chain reaction experiment in Chicago

**General Leslie Groves:** Military chief and overall director at Los Alamos

**David Hawkins:** Former Oppenheimer aide, tech adviser to movie

**Walter Lippmann:** Nation's most renowned opinion columnist

**John Lee Mahin:** Well-known screenwriter hired by MGM to tweak Wead script

**Sam Marx:** MGM producer, former story editor for studio

**James K. McGuinness:** Former MGM screenwriter now exec, right-wing activist

**J.J. Nickson:** Activist scientist in Chicago

**J. Robert Oppenheimer:** "Father of the Atomic Bomb" (wife: Kitty)

**Tony Owen:** Hollywood agent, husband of Donna Reed

**William "Deke" Parsons:** Armed Hiroshima bomb on way to target

**Ayn Rand:** Novelist and screenwriter for Hal Wallis

**Donna Reed:** Young actress, former student of Edward Tompkins

**Charles Ross:** Truman press secretary, former newspaperman

**Robert Smith:** Screenwriter hired by Wallis to salvage Rand script

**Charles Sweeney:** Pilot of Nagasaki bomber, adviser to MGM

**Leo Szilard:** Famed physicist who tried to halt use of bomb against Japan

**Norman Taurog:** Director of movie whose best films were behind him

**Paul Tibbets:** Pilot of *Enola Gay*

**Edward Tompkins:** Young Oak Ridge scientist, former teacher of Donna Reed

**Audrey Totter:** Actress who played Groves's secretary Jean O'Leary

**Robert Walker:** Actor who portrayed roguish fictional Groves aide Colonel Jeff Nixon

**Hal B. Wallis:** Very successful producer, now with Paramount

**Frank "Spig" Wead:** Screenwriter, famous for military flying exploits

**H.T. Wensel:** Physicist picked by Groves to replace Tompkins as tech adviser

# A BRIEF CHRONOLOGY (APRIL 1945–OCTOBER 1945)

**April 12**: President Roosevelt dies.

**April 25**: President Truman is finally told about the bomb
project.

**May 7**: Germany surrenders to the Allies.

**Early July**: Plans set for use of bomb, Szilard petition
protests this.

**July 16**: Successful test of the first atomic bomb at the
Trinity site.

**July 26**: Potsdam Declaration calls for unconditional surrender
of Japan. Truman gets Stalin's agreement to attack
Japan by mid-August.

**August 6**: Hiroshima devastated with "Little Boy" bomb.

**August 8**: The Soviet Union declares war on Japan.

**August 9**: Nagasaki attacked with "Fat Man" bomb.

**August 14**: Japanese emperor announces surrender.

**September 2**: Japan formally surrenders as the U.S. occupation
begins.

**September–October**: Thousands of Manhattan Project scientists form associations and call for international control of atomic energy.

**October 25**: Dr. Edward Tompkins from Oak Ridge writes his former student Donna Reed in Santa Monica.

# PREFACE

With its costly drama *The Beginning or the End* finally completed in early January 1947, including a critical new scene ordered by the White House, MGM dared to screen it for atomic scientists in Chicago. Legendary studio chief Louis B. Mayer had once called it "the most important" movie he would ever make. Now, after dozens of revisions and deletions ordered by President Harry S. Truman and the military, how would it fare with some of the men who helped create the revolutionary weapon that had been deployed against two Japanese cities seventeen months earlier?

Leo Szilard, who played a key role in developing the bomb and then tried to impede President Truman from using it, attended the preview in the city's Loop with nuclear chemist Harrison Brown, a veteran of the Manhattan Project's top-secret site at Oak Ridge, Tennessee. During the screening, scientists around them erupted in laughter at the broad Italian accent of the actor playing Enrico Fermi, whose atomic chain reaction in Chicago paved the way for creating the new weapon. They chuckled at miscast Hume Cronyn's valiant attempts to mimic J. Robert Oppenheimer, the now-famous scientific director at Los Alamos. Then they turned sullen as the pro-bomb message of the film became clear, with General Leslie R. Groves, overall director of the Manhattan Project—played by Brian Donlevy—portrayed as a dashing hero. The scientists had no clue that the movie studio had secretly granted Groves script approval, which he had fully exercised, and then some.

Harrison Brown found it profoundly disorienting to see so many former colleagues on the silver screen. The factual errors upset him. He considered the tacked-on love story insipid in the extreme. The ear-splitting noise accompanying the Fermi chain reaction sounded like the Walls of Jericho falling; almost as bad were the flashing lights and buzzing bells. He was particularly outraged by repeated references to leaflets being "showered" over Hiroshima warning of an imminent atomic attack; nothing of the kind occurred. And then the movie didn't even bother to depict the assault on Nagasaki, which he found nauseating. To top it off, the fanciful ending seemed both silly and overly optimistic about a nuclearized future.

As the screen went dark and the lights came up, the MGM representative, in from Hollywood, asked audience members for comments. Nearly all remained silent. Leo Szilard, meanwhile, beat a hasty retreat, slipping out a side door, down an elevator, and out to Brown's sedan parked on the street nearby. There Brown would find him crouched on the floor between the front and back seats as if in penitence or afraid to be recognized. "If our sin as scientists was to make and use the atomic bomb," Szilard would later admit, "then our punishment was to watch *The Beginning or the End.*"

In the following pages, I trace what might be called "The Making and Remaking" of this would-be Hollywood epic, from its genesis, when it was inspired by the scientists' warnings, to the pro-bomb celebration—dictated by the Pentagon and White House—that it eventually became. There are many wild, unlikely, and entertaining stops along the way (as befits any Inside Hollywood account), but this story also charts an extremely significant turning point. For a moment it appeared that a nuclear arms race and the earth-shattering threat it represented—still very much with us today—might be slowed, or even stopped in its tracks, only

to be refueled by wide-ranging official efforts to shape media coverage and public opinion. Seventy-five years later, this country's
"first-strike" nuclear policy remains in place. The atomic attacks
on Japan continue to be endorsed by most Americans and, by all
evidence, the vast majority of those in the media and in key posi-
tions in the government (no matter who is president). This can
only encourage, or at least enable, a pre-emptive strike by any
nuclear power today. A recent survey of three thousand Americans
by You Gov and the *Bulletin of the Atomic Scientists* found that more
than a third would support a nuclear strike on North Korea—even
if it killed a million civilians there—if that country tested a long-
range missile capable of reaching the United States. The *Bulletin*
in early 2020 moved the hands of its famous Doomsday Clock to
100 seconds before midnight, the closest ever.

In the end, this book offers not only deep reconsideration of the
use of the first nuclear weapons against two Japanese cities, but
an urgent warning about secrecy, manipulation and suppression as
threats to the planet accelerate today.

—*Greg Mitchell*

# 1

# The Donna Reed Show

The letter addressed to Mrs. Donna Owen arrived at her ocean-front Santa Monica home on October 28, 1945. The return address revealed that it came from her beloved high school chemistry teacher back in Denison, Iowa, when she lived on a farm and was still known as Donna Belle Mullenger. She had stayed in touch with handsome young Ed Tompkins for a few years after graduation, but then he suddenly vanished, without explanation, and had not responded to any of her letters.

This seemed odd. Tompkins had deeply influenced her outlook on life a decade earlier when she was an aimless sophomore, after he gave her a copy of the popular Dale Carnegie self-help book *How to Win Friends and Influence People*. In short order her grades soared, she secured the lead role in the high school play (Ayn Rand's *The Night of January 16*), and she was voted Campus Queen. "I think anyone that had him for a teacher would agree with me that he was the most interesting teacher we had," one of Reed's classmates would later relate, "and he had a good sense of humor that made classes fun." Donna Belle wanted to become a teacher herself but her parents could not afford a major school, so she enrolled in low-tuition Los Angeles City College. After appearing in stage productions there, the honey-haired beauty attracted the attention of talent scouts, leading to several screen tests.

Signed by MGM to a seven-year contract at the age of twenty, she appeared in her first movie, *The Get-Away*, billed as Donna

Adams. Many supporting roles followed, with her name changed to one she hated, feeling it had a dull, harsh sound that didn't reflect her personality: Donna Reed. Still, she secured roles in *Shadow of the Thin Man*, *The Picture of Dorian Gray*, and *Apache Trail*, and married her makeup man. She graduated from Mickey Rooney's love interest in *The Courtship of Andy Hardy* to John Wayne's object of desire in John Ford's *They Were Expendable*. She could play mid-western wholesome in her sleep, but some directors felt her range was narrow, and MGM had a flock of other young actresses to draw on. Along the way she became a popular girl-next-door pinup for homesick GIs, and personally answered many of their letters. She got divorced and in June 1945, still only twenty-four years old, married her agent, Tony Owen.

Then, that autumn, she signed with RKO for perhaps her biggest role yet, as Mary Bailey, wife of James Stewart in Frank Capra's *It's a Wonderful Life*, after Ginger Rogers turned it down as "too bland." At the same time she finally discovered what had happened to Ed Tompkins. A newspaper story revealed that he had been sworn to silence for several years after joining thousands of others in helping to create the first atomic bomb at the Manhattan Project site in Oak Ridge, Tennessee. After reading the article she sent him another letter, this time care of Oak Ridge.

Now she had received a reply. Opening the envelope, she unfolded a typed, single-spaced, two-and-a-half-page letter from Dr. Tompkins. The tone, given their formerly close relationship, was surprisingly formal (despite its "Dear Donna" salutation), and urgent. "The development of atomic explosives necessitates a reevaluation of many of our previous modes of thought and life," he began. "This conclusion had been reached by the research scientists who developed these powerful new explosives long before August 6, 1945." That, of course, was the day the first atomic bomb exploded over the city of Hiroshima in Japan, killing more than

125,000, the majority of them women and children. Three days later, Nagasaki met the same fate, with a death toll reaching at least 80,000.

The day before Reed received the Tompkins letter at her modest beach house, more than ninety thousand locals had gathered in the Los Angeles Coliseum to witness a "Tribute to Victory." It featured a re-creation of the bombing of Hiroshima, narrated by actor Edward G. Robinson. A B-29 bomber, caught in searchlights, dropped a package that produced a large noise and a small mushroom cloud. The crowd went crazy. Americans, weeks after the Japanese surrender, remained nervous about atomic energy, however. Scientists, political figures, and poets alike were sounding a similar theme—splitting the atom could bring wonderful advances, if used wisely, or destroy the world, if developed for military purposes. Atomic dreams, and nightmares, ran wild. "Seldom, if ever, has a war ended leaving the victors with such a sense of uncertainty and fear," warned radio commentator Edward R. Murrow, with "survival not assured."

Now, in the rather dense letter to his former pupil, Dr. Tompkins explained that the scientists' initial "excitement" and pride in what they had accomplished were now subsumed by soul-searching. Until the Hiroshima blast, many of his colleagues were unaware they had been working on a munitions project. Others had signed physicist Leo Szilard's futile petition asking President Harry S. Truman to hold off using the weapon against Japan. In any case, a large number were now opposed to building new and even bigger earth-shattering bombs.

Tompkins revealed that thousands of Manhattan Project scientists had formed associations in Oak Ridge, Chicago, Los Alamos, and New York to deliver their warnings and "to foster thought and discussion which can lead to adoption of international control of atomic energy." Contrary to claims by military leaders and politicians, there was "NO possibility" that the United States could maintain a monopoly on production of these weapons. The so-called secret of the atomic bomb was known internationally. The Soviets, for example, would surely build their own model within a few years. Finally, there could never be an effective defense against these weapons, and "a hundred long-range rockets carrying atomic explosives could wipe out our civilization in a matter of minutes."

In light of all this, it was imperative that effective international controls be established as soon as feasible. But what did Donna's old chem teacher want *her* to do about it? Tompkins reported that the new associations were showering elected officials in Washington with leaflets, lobbying influential reporters and commentators, and preparing a major book. This was "a good start but much remains to be done," he noted. It seemed to him "there would be a large segment of the population that could be reached most effectively through the movies." His final paragraph featured an explicit pitch:

> Do you think a movie could be planned and produced to successfully impress upon the public the horrors of atomic warfare. . . . It would, of course, have to hold the interest of the public, and still not sacrifice the message. Would you be willing to help sell this idea to MGM? Or if not, could you send us the names of the men who should be contacted in this matter? We would be not only willing but anxious to offer our technical advice in the preparation of the script and settings. . . . You can, no doubt, think of many forms which such a picture could take.

Never inserting even a hint of personal familiarity from their days in Iowa, or asking about her life or career, Tompkins concluded with the plea, "Will you give the whole matter your consideration and perhaps discuss it with others at the studio? I'd appreciate hearing your reaction to the suggestion as soon as possible."

Just days later, Tompkins fired off a second letter to "Mr. and Mrs. Tony Owen." He had polled his peers at Oak Ridge and found they were eager to wander down the road to Hollywood, but not quite blindly. Tompkins boldly proposed that the celebrity couple fly east to Oak Ridge at their own expense the following week to discuss the project, with no time to waste. Together they could hash out a scenario for "a very good picture with a lot of public appeal"—and then catch a short flight to Washington to gain the approval of the Manhattan Project director, General Leslie R. Groves.

Well, that was a lot for Donna Reed, or anyone, to digest. Just seven years earlier the same man had been delivering quite a different lecture in a rural classroom. Fortunately, she told Tompkins in a brief phone call, her husband was quite willing to carry the ball. Tony Owen, a slick, fast-talking dynamo, was thirteen years her senior. A native of New Orleans and Chicago (real name: Irving Ohnstein), he had served as vice president of the Detroit Lions pro football club after brief careers as an actor and as a newspaper reporter. Following a stint in the military, he settled in Los Angeles and secured his first clients as a talent agent.

When he finished reading the Tompkins missives, Owen started calling producers to gauge their interest, if any. Having not heard from Donna again, Tompkins called her at home. She related that her husband had learned from studio insiders that it might be a simple matter to get such a movie produced if the military signaled its approval—and if exclusive dramatic rights for key figures in the story could be obtained. Reed warned Tompkins, however, that Hollywood studios were reluctant to make any pictures with "political repercussions." When he told her that scientists were already sketching scenarios for a script, she advised that surely any of them would be "completely rewritten" by the studio.

Tony Owen, meanwhile, called his friend Samuel Marx, a top producer at MGM, where Reed was still under contract. Marx agreed to meet him the next day for breakfast at the swanky Beverly Wilshire Hotel. There he would find Owen in a highly animated state. Owen displayed the letters to his wife from Tompkins, which the producer found fascinating. Marx offered to take Owen to meet with Louis B. Mayer, one of the most powerful men in town and the studio chief since the 1920s, straight away. So they raced their automobiles to the studio lot in nearby Culver City. Mayer knew Owen well, had even attended his recent wedding.

As it happens, MGM had expressed some interest in an atomic bomb film nearly two months earlier, with Japanese victims of the attacks still smoldering in the ruins. On August 9, just hours after the strike on Nagasaki, MGM's Washington representative, Carter Barron, phoned the chief of the Pentagon's Feature Film Division to discuss the possibility of an exclusive movie about the bomb project. Five days later, Barron wrote the same man to reveal that MGM was "now working" on a movie tentatively titled *Atomic Bomb* and would appreciate any useful "information or material." The heroine would be a physicist associated with the genesis of nuclear fission, Lise Meitner, who had fled Germany for Sweden in 1938. But nothing came of Barron's interest and the idea seemingly expired.

The bomb soon made its first appearance in a Hollywood movie from a far lesser studio, albeit in a cameo role. A minor RKO movie called *First Yank into Tokyo* had been rushed into release in mid-September with a slight shift in plot and a tacked-on ending. *First Yank* told the improbable story of an American pilot, Major Steve Ross, who undergoes plastic surgery to look Japanese so that he can infiltrate a brutal POW camp in Tokyo and rescue an American scientist. In the original script the scientist possessed secrets about a revolutionary new gun; in retakes that was changed to the atomic bomb. Ross's other motivation: his girlfriend was also held by the Japanese. Somehow he managed to free both the scientist and the girl, then led them to a U.S. submarine off the coast. Realizing he can't go home "looking like a Jap," he returned to shore to help former Korean prisoners kill some of the "yellow monkeys." A new ending traced a warplane in flight while a narrator explained that "a group of scientists made untold sacrifices so that this B-29 could make its bomb run over the heart of the Japanese empire, bringing final and terrible retribution." Then the narration dissolved into the U.S. national anthem.

Two other completed movies also bluntly added Hiroshima references before release. The spy thriller *House on 92nd Street*, directed in semi-documentary style by Henry Hathaway and featuring an introduction by J. Edgar Hoover, the FBI director, focused on Nazi agents in New York attempting to penetrate a secret wartime project known as "Process 97." Now dialogue was added to link that to the atomic bomb. A lower-budget movie, *Shadow of Terror*, pictured an American scientist carrying a secret formula to Washington, D.C.—later to be revealed as nuclear in nature—who is threatened by foreign agents.

Now MGM was being handed, via Donna Reed and Ed Tompkins, a unique entry point to a far more ambitious cinematic bomb project. To date the studio's main reference to the new weapon was crowning its newly signed starlet Linda Christian "The Anatomic Bomb," leading to a full-page photo of her in a swimsuit in *Life* magazine.

In his massive office at MGM, sitting behind his pure-white oval desk in the sprawling Thalberg Building, Louis B. Mayer greeted Marx and Owen. The actress Helen Hayes once called Mayer "the most evil man I have ever dealt with in my life," yet hailed MGM as "*the* great film studio of the world—not just of America, or of Hollywood, but of the world." Sam Marx considered him ruthless, an unprincipled pirate, but like others recognized that Mayer's deceptions and bullying—not to mention his eye for talent and understanding of movie audiences—proved pivotal for the studio. Mayer, no intellectual, tolerated "social issue" pictures but loved escapist entertainment. Among MGM's greatest films were an inordinate number of musicals, from *The Wizard of Oz* to *An American in Paris*.

Listening to the atomic bomb pitch, Mayer grew excited. Now in his early sixties, overweight and white-haired, King Louis remained vigorous, vulgar, tyrannical, and, as always, quick to judge. With little prompting, he promised that if the necessary approvals and rights were gathered he would consider an epic film on this subject his top priority for 1946. He would budget at least $2 million for it, a lofty sum for that time. It might one day be "the most important movie" he would ever film (and MGM had made *Gone with the Wind*), perhaps in the vein of his 1943 film, *Madame Curie*, but more topical. This was a man, born in Minsk and raised in Canada, so patriotic he falsely claimed he had been born on the Fourth of July—the actual date was July 12—and for years staged an elaborate studio picnic that day to mark the occasion.

Eager to rush forward, Mayer urged Owen and Marx to seek clearances that very minute, straight from the top—"from the horse's mouth," as he put it. "Let's call President Truman himself," he suggested. Mayer was a rock-ribbed Republican, but the studio titan believed Truman would surely accept his call. It took some persuading, but Owen finally talked him down from that idea. Instead, Mayer ordered Marx to call the studio's representative in Washington, Carter Barron, to find out if White House and military approvals were likely to come.

The following day Barron assured Mayer on this score, but

added that to make sure of that, Marx and Owen should visit Oak Ridge and Washington as soon as possible to gauge the mood of scientists and generals, and gather background information. Mayer ordered Marx to "take the *Starwind*" (MGM's private plane) and "come back and tell me what you find." Tony Owen informed Dr. Tompkins by telephone that Mayer was "very enthusiastic," citing that $2 million budget, and "in sympathy" with the ideas the scientists wanted to promote. The only other studio expressing interest in such a film was United Artists. MGM, however, seemed willing to spend more money, although unlike UA it could not promise the scientists a share of the profits. Tompkins told Owen that they might be willing to "forego royalties if an exceptional picture could be made."

On November 4, Marx and Owen took off for Tennessee in the studio's DC-3. Marx had seen and done a lot in Hollywood over the past fifteen years, but this promised to be one of his wildest rides yet.

Irving Thalberg, Hollywood's "boy wonder," had hired Marx, a tall, dark-haired tailor's son who had just emerged from Columbia University with literary ambitions, as MGM's story editor in 1930. It didn't hurt that he was distantly related to the Marx Brothers. Sam supervised, and partied with, the likes of F. Scott Fitzgerald, William Faulkner, Anita Loos, Moss Hart, and Ben Hecht. It was an era when top-shelf writers from the East flocked to L.A. to be pampered and paid. Dorothy Parker accepted the job after reportedly advising, "All I need is a room to lay my hat and a few friends." Herman Mankiewicz, who would write *Citizen Kane*, had invited Ben Hecht to L.A. with the immortal line, "millions are to be grabbed out here and your only competition is idiots." Playwright S.N. Behrman contributed the quip, "It's slave labor and what do you get for it? A lousy fortune!"

Sam Marx secured the film rights for such MGM classics as

*Grand Hotel*, *Tarzan the Ape Man*, *Mutiny on the Bounty*, and *The Thin Man*. Commented *Fortune* magazine: "More members of the literati work under him than it took to produce the King James version of the Bible." Assignments didn't always pan out, however. Marx, for example, brought F. Scott Fitzgerald back to Hollywood from the East to script a movie based on the popular book *Red-Headed Woman*. Fitzgerald, drinking to excess, was not able to execute a first-class screenplay, and was soon sent packing. Anita Loos took over and the film became a smash hit while establishing Jean Harlow as a sexpot star. Loos was favored by Marx for any sort of "shady" script, feeling confident she could supply "the delicate *double entendre*" that might get past the censorship board.

When Marx assigned William Faulkner the script for the next Wallace Beery movie the writer asked, "Who's he?" (Faulkner would create stories or scripts for MGM and other studios for many years.) Marx nearly had a chance to work with another celebrated writer, William Saroyan, who offered to tackle Franz Werfel's novel about the Armenian genocide, *The 40 Days of Musa Dagh*, but MGM dropped the project under pressure from the Turkish government. It also killed another "political" Marx project, Sinclair Lewis's *It Can't Happen Here*.

Turning to producing, Marx helmed the popular *Lassie Come Home*, several Andy Hardy films, and the war picture *Yank on the Burma Road*, among others. At one point he left Mayer to work for Samuel Goldwyn and Harry Cohn at other studios, then returned to MGM. He was also known as one of the men who discovered the body of Paul Bern, Jean Harlow's husband, who had committed suicide (though many suspected murder). His barroom stories about 1930s Hollywood were colorful to say the least. Yet in 1945 he was still only forty-three years old.

Now Marx, along with Tony Owen, would be greeted at the Oak Ridge airport on a blustery morning by Ed Tompkins and three associates. Tompkins, he found, was rather tall, thin, boyish, and wore rimless glasses. The four scientists approached the men from Hollywood with outstretched arms. "We are very happy that you are here!" Tompkins exclaimed. "We hope you can tell the world the meaning of the bomb, because *we are scared to death*."

Unbeknownst to all of them, however, MGM was not alone in lurching ahead to make the first atomic epic. Hal B. Wallis, producer of *Casablanca*, *The Maltese Falcon*, *Sergeant York*, and others far weightier than anything Sam Marx ever managed, had been pursuing the idea at Paramount since late September. By the time MGM got moving he had already engaged a well-known magazine writer, Jerome Beatty, to supply a treatment for a film tentatively titled *Manhattan Project*.

The writer Wallis hoped to recruit to pen the script, however, was a woman under contract to work for him six months out of every year. This was the controversial novelist Ayn Rand. She had already written two screenplays for Wallis. Earlier that year her *Love Letters* had earned four Oscar nominations. It told the story of a man (Joseph Cotten) falling in love with an amnesiac woman (Jennifer Jones) who may have killed his soldier friend. Bosley Crowther of *The New York Times* slammed her script as a "mucky muddle," but it proved to be a box office hit. Rand's breakthrough 1943 novel *The Fountainhead*, meanwhile, was back on the bestsellers list—it had once been rejected by twelve publishers—and slated for a major Warner Bros. movie. Its main character, a highly individualistic architect named Howard Roark, reflected her strong, anti-socialistic views. And she would be free to tackle this atomic bomb script starting in December.

Wallis and Rand had been friends for years, even though he did not share her political philosophy. She affectionately called him "the Boss." On leave from the studio, she was currently living at the Essex House off Central Park in Manhattan with her husband, a painter, Frank O'Connor. When Rand, born in Russia as Alisa Zinovyevna Rosenbaum, had arrived in New York in 1926 at the age of twenty-one, she had shed "'tears of splendor" on viewing the famous skyline. In the autumn of 1945, however, the manager of the Essex House apparently viewed her as a possible scam artist. He wrote to Wallis (addressing him as "Wallace") to check on her financial wherewithal. "Miss Rand," Wallis happily replied, "is the author of the bestselling book *The Fountainhead*, and she is now under contract to me as a screenwriter. Her contract here is for a long term, and I should say that the O'Connors were an excellent credit risk."

Now her next assignment under that contract, to compete with the MGM epic, promised to be Wallis's *Manhattan Project*. The first "nuclear race" of the postwar era was on.

# 2

# From Oak Ridge
# to the Oval Office

When the two Hollywood hustlers, Sam Marx and Tony Owen, arrived at Oak Ridge, *Time* magazine had just labeled the atomic scientists *The Guilty Men*. "Appalled by their miracle, they rushed from their laboratories into the political fray" to oppose the new federal and military plan to control atomic research, the story observed. "They huddled in private, wrote and talked to Congress, cried in the press that something must be done. Some of them, convinced that the nationalization of atomic research would be a fatal error, even talked of violating the Army's security regulations to force a showdown."

That week three physicists had authored a major piece for *Life* magazine on the moral responsibility of scientists to prevent any further use of nuclear weapons. The headline blared, "THE ATOMIC SCIENTISTS SPEAK UP: Nuclear Physicists Say There Is No Secrecy in Atomic Bomb and No Defense Against It." Therefore, the activists concluded, "the bombs must be outlawed by international agreement." Albert Einstein, meanwhile, had written an article for *The Atlantic* declaring that since another major war was "inevitable" the secret of the bomb "should be committed to a World Government" and the United States should immediately announce its readiness to do so: "We shall not have the secret very long."

The cinema-scientist summit in Oak Ridge convened just as the legislative initiative backed by President Truman, the May-Johnson bill, faltered. It called for creating a nine-member Atomic Energy Commission consisting of five civilian and four military members with broad powers similar to those executed by the Manhattan Project—from acquiring property to conducting research and regulating security. Most of the activist scientists instantly objected to the strong military presence on the commission. A full-time administrator and deputy administrator might also come from the military and dominate the wonky, part-time commissioners. The scientists also flagged the secrecy provisions, which called for penalties of up to ten years in prison and $10,000 fines for security breaches. They had accepted onerous military control and secrecy in creating the first atomic bombs; no longer.

While the debate raged the bill languished. In the weeks since Hiroshima, *New York Times* military reporter Hanson Baldwin warned, "the world has made little progress toward either international security or international morality. They have been weeks of confusion and divided counsel, of lack of leadership, of claims and contradictions—and all the while the atomic bomb has clouded the skies of tomorrow."

In this atmosphere, the first published fictional response to Hiroshima appeared in *Astounding Science Fiction*. A sketch written by Theodore Sturgeon entitled "August Sixth 1945" expressed the ambivalence felt by many sci-fi writers: pride at having predicted the creation and use of an atomic device but also acute apprehension about future "plot" twists—their specialty, after all. Sturgeon declared that man learned on August 6 "that he alone is big enough to kill himself, or to live forever." The legendary editor John W. Campbell had rejected it as a story submission so it was published on the letters page.

On the evening of their wind-blown arrival at Oak Ridge, Sam Marx and Tony Owen met with a large group of activist scientists. It was, in part, an "illegal" assembly, because some of the scientists were not supposed to fraternize with those from certain other top-secret areas. Marx, who kept a kind of journal for his trip, would observe, "They told us enough about the bomb—what had been done with it and what the future was—that Mr. Owen and I saw here the possibilities for the most important motion picture ever attempted." He was troubled, however, by the hatred for the military, even for General Groves, displayed by some of the scientists, who complained about excessive security that kept them confined to the site, and in some cases away from their families, for months or years. More than that, they resented that Washington seemed mainly interested in atomic energy's potential use in war. They felt double-crossed. Marx found them rather noble in their idealism but far too self-important, even arrogant.

The following morning the visitors from L.A. were given a full tour of the enormous site. While they were not allowed inside many of the facilities for security reasons, they were able to take photographs outside. The scientists had posted a large sign outside one lab declaring, "Dawn of Peace, Let's Make It Forever." It became apparent to Marx that the scientists and the Army had quite different outlooks. The military did not believe in international control, nor that the Soviets could catch up with America any time soon, especially if the United States built even more powerful weapons. To calm their fears about military control of the MGM movie, the Hollywood duo invited Tompkins and a young colleague to accompany them to Washington. The newsletter of the Oak Ridge scientists nevertheless reported that the overriding aim of the trip was "to get General Groves' approval for a full-length story on atomic energy."

First stop was a disheveled fourth-floor walkup office on Vermont Avenue in Northwest D.C., headquarters for the newly formed association representing disparate groups around the country, the Federation of Atomic Scientists (FAS). It was a wild scene:

phones ringing off the hook, activists dashing in and out, frenzied discussions in the hallway. It housed one desk, a few chairs, one telephone, and a very noisy typewriter, plus an almanac, copies of the *Congressional Record*, and files collecting recent speeches. When they weren't convening in corners or searching for documents the scientists often had to sit on the floor. The single bathroom was unmentionable. A scientist visiting from Ohio would report to a friend, "The office is a dumpy suite of rooms. . . . Furniture very meager. The secretary is very good, works about 70 hours a week, is terribly overloaded. . . . So far she hasn't been paid. No one has got any money. . . . Politically it looks haywire, too. . . . I admire the spirit but it is a hell of a way to do things."

Marx and Owen, after their cordial welcome at Oak Ridge, discovered amid this chaos even more anger directed at the military and rampant distrust for any Hollywood saga and, therefore, them. The activists they met seemed to want only their side of the story told. Marx and Owen moved to escape the tension before Tompkins played peacemaker. This left the matter of cooperation with the filmmakers at least an open question.

Next up: meeting General Groves at the War Department. He had built the Pentagon across the river in Arlington, Virginia, a few years earlier, but his two-room office was still in D.C. Groves was now a national celebrity, credited as the key player in creation of the atomic bomb, along with the scientific chief, J. Robert Oppenheimer. His appearance—trim moustache and obese figure over his six-foot-three-inch frame—was therefore familiar to the two men. Groves liked to say, in defending the killing of so many in Hiroshima and Nagasaki, that it was like being a surgeon: sometimes you must spill a lot of blood when you cut out a tumor. As the general spoke to them, in this typically belligerent way, it became even clearer to Marx the trouble that might lie ahead, for the future of arms control and for his movie. "The scientists are for sharing everything we know with all people of the world," Marx would write (in something of an exaggeration), "and the Army is for holding onto the head start that we now have" (which certainly was not). Groves went even further, advocating that if any other country not a close ally of the United States started to create atomic weapons we should "destroy its capacity" to do so.

With the understanding that the Army's view would be strongly featured in the picture, Groves said he would be "very happy to cooperate with MGM even to the use of his name in connection with this story," Marx recorded. Later, at dinner with Groves and his wife, Marx revealed that MGM was considering Clark Gable to portray him. Mrs. Groves happily announced that if that happened she definitely wanted to play herself in the movie.

While Marx found the meetings with Groves productive, the Oak Ridge Association's newsletter was not impressed. Dr. Tompkins, it reported, had found Groves eagerly promoting ideas he wanted in the film and making an overall "poorer impression" than other military leaders he met. The writer joked that Groves "would like a shot of the scientists sitting on his knee to show that all is rosy between them."

More private meetings and dinners for the Hollywood visitors followed, with: Groves's secretary Jean O'Leary (who was famous for keeping the general's secrets); Colonel W.A. Consodine, the close Groves associate and head of the Counter Intelligence Corps; and General Thomas Farrell, who on the tiny Pacific island of Tinian supervised the use of the bomb against the Japanese. All of them promised MGM "full and complete cooperation," as Marx put it in his report, but an Army publicity specialist warned that this would hinge on permission from Secretary of War Henry L. Stimson and/or President Truman. He also insisted that negotiations over the movie must be kept from the public.

Marx then went to Capitol Hill, where he met with Senator Brien McMahon, a freshman from Connecticut, who was conducting investigations into military and civilian uses of atomic energy, possibly leading to legislation. McMahon also offered support for the MGM project. Because of what he considered the "religious implications" of the new weapon, Marx took advantage of Archbishop Francis Spellman's trip to Washington (from his New York home) to query him at length in his hotel room. Spellman had learned about the Manhattan Project from President Roosevelt, who kept it hidden even from Vice President Truman. Later he flew to Tinian to bless the bomber crews after the destruction of Hiroshima and before the attack on Nagasaki. "He told me that his church deplores the use of any weapon which would kill innocent women and children," Marx wrote for his journal, "but he believed that in wartime any weapon that could end the war should be used."

This was a sentiment quite at odds with, among others, one of the leading Catholic magazines, *Commonweal*. It had opined that victory in the war had been "defiled. . . . The name Hiroshima, the name Nagasaki, are names for American guilt and shame." Japan was essentially defeated when we dropped the bombs without warning "to secure peace, of course. To save lives, of course." The editors found it "disturbing that there has been so little public protest" in America about the use of the bomb. It was tragic that the bomb was employed, but just as worrisome that Americans "have tacitly acceded to its use." Of all the casualties in the two cities, an estimated 90 percent were civilians.

Criticism of the use of the bomb remained scattered but persistent. "How can the United States in the future appeal to the conscience of mankind not to use this new weapon?" asked Richard

L. Strout of the *Christian Science Monitor*. "Has not the moral high ground for such an appeal been cut away from our feet?" The conservative editor of *U.S. News*, David Lawrence, had lamented, "Surely we cannot be proud of what we have done. If we state our inner thoughts honestly, we are ashamed of it." Would the MGM movie take up this challenge?

The public, in any case, remained worried if not terrified. A Gallup poll found 69 percent calling the creation of atomic weaponry "a good thing"—but more than one in four felt it was likely that it would one day "destroy the entire world." Spellman's view of the years ahead was similarly divided. "Just as we now think that everything before the discovery of fire was the Dark Ages," he told Sam Marx, "I feel that in the future we will think anything before the discovery of atomic energy was the Dark Ages." On the other hand, there might not be much of a future. "This bomb fulfills the third prophecy of the Old Testament," Spellman warned. "Man will destroy himself by fire. I hope your motion picture can work to avert such suicide. You had better hurry!"

Then, in a historic coup, MGM's man in Washington, Carter Barron, managed to secure a November 19 meeting for Marx and Owen with President Truman at the White House, with the understanding that it would be strictly off the record. Dr. Tompkins would not attend, as he had returned to Oak Ridge, which surely would not bother the president. Truman's recent confrontation in the Oval Office with a far more prominent atomic scientist had left him with nothing but bitterness.

Three weeks earlier he had met Robert Oppenheimer, who had steered creation of the new weapon at the Los Alamos laboratory in New Mexico, for the first time. After the usual pleasantries between the former haberdasher and the world-famous physicist, Truman asked Oppenheimer to guess when the Soviets would develop their own bomb. Oppenheimer, who privately felt it would not take long, claimed he did not know. Truman knew better, predicting: "Never!" Truman also seemed to confirm Oppenheimer's worst fear, that the United States intended to bully the Soviets with their new weapon instead of working for detente and arms control.

The usually confident Oppenheimer, far out of his element, grew nervous, reflective, finally muttering, "Mr. President, I feel I have blood on my hands." Truman, according to his own story, replied, "The blood is on *my* hands—I ordered using the damn thing—let me worry about that." Other accounts would vary, with some claiming the president mocked his visitor by offering him a handkerchief. (In Oppenheimer's version, Truman simply advised that any blood could easily be washed off.)

Truman would later instruct Acting Secretary of State Dean Acheson, "I don't want to see that son of a bitch in this office ever again. He didn't set that bomb off, I did. This kind of sniveling makes me sick." Truman privately referred to Oppenheimer as that "cry-baby scientist." After talking with the physicist, Secretary of Commerce Henry Wallace would observe in his diary, "I never saw a man in such an extremely nervous state as Oppenheimer. He seemed to feel that the destruction of the entire human race was imminent." Oppenheimer confided that many of his colleagues at Los Alamos no longer had the heart to work on terror weapons, fearing it would eventually lead to the slaughter of tens of millions or perhaps hundreds of millions of innocent people.

Marx and Owen were no doubt a bit on edge themselves, striding into the White House for the 11:45 appointment, but the casual Truman soon allayed their fears. The sit-down was supposed to last fifteen minutes; it stretched to fifty. Marx was impressed with Truman's affability, calmness, and intelligence, as he filled holes in the atomic narrative the MGM producer had pieced together from others. Truman's manner reminded him of an unheralded tennis player who finally gets his big chance at Wimbledon—and then plays way over his head. Truman's only failing was telling bad jokes.

Some of Truman's bomb-related anecdotes appeared tailor-made for a movie. There was that time, for example, when he was a U.S. senator on a committee investigating government expenditures. This took him to the gates of Oak Ridge, where millions of federal dollars were being poured into some kind of mysterious war project. When he was barred from entering he called FDR and demanded an answer. Roosevelt advised him to forget about this "very special place" for now. When Truman became his vice president, FDR still did not inform him about the bomb project and he died in April 1945 before scheduling that talk.

Marx had already formulated a scenario for his movie, which he had not yet shared with the scientists but was happy to sketch for the president. It would cover every phase of the bomb's conception and development and eventual use against Japan. Truman responded enthusiastically, going so far as to verbally grant permission for the studio to proceed. As they were exiting, Truman stopped them at the door and asked if they had titled their movie yet, and was told no. "Make your film, gentlemen," he urged, "and tell the world that in handling the atomic bomb we are either at the beginning or the end."

"Mr. President," Marx replied, "you have just chosen the title of our film."

Two days later, MGM's Barron wrote Truman that before Marx and Owen returned to L.A. they wanted him to know that his "gracious" chat at the White House "was the supreme inspirational climax of the widespread research activities they have been involved in." After ticking off all the key people they had met, with special attention to General Groves and Archbishop Spellman,

Barron declared, "We are happy to advise you that they all believed the motion picture industry could do a great service to civilization at large if the right kind of film could be made . . . although always within the bounds of government approval." Barron thereby granted nearly unprecedented (in peacetime) official control.

But Barron wanted to make sure that Truman would also allow the studio to portray him making some of his key decisions. (An unwritten rule in Hollywood required this when depicting sitting presidents.) To this end he stressed that the movie would not only perform "a great service" but potentially reach a very wide audience. "We are, of course, anxious to put entertainment into this film, rather than concentrate on its document phases, for it is our belief that only for solid entertainment does the world sit in theaters and listen. They go to school for education and to churches for sermons. We want them to come into theaters and to be entertained." Yet MGM would always depict the president "with dignity," even in scenes of "drama and excitement."

In his reply, Truman confirmed that it was "a pleasure to discuss the Atomic energy program" with his visitors. Anxious to exploit Truman's endorsement, Barron informed the Pentagon's publicity chief that the studio had now titled the movie *The Beginning or the End*, which had been "suggested by the president during our conversation with him."

Marx would also soon meet with Robert Oppenheimer. The two had known each other slightly growing up in New York City, with Marx just two years older. Oppenheimer said he would consider being portrayed in the film but only if Marx agreed to visit him at his home in California in the spring—he had just resigned his Los Alamos position to return to Cal Tech—to show him a script. Asked what sort of payment he might demand, Oppie (as he was known to friends and colleagues) replied that even with the war over it was still hard for his wife to buy nylons, so if Marx brought a few with him when he visited that would be sufficient compensation.

In Manhattan, Marx threw a party in his suite at the Waldorf with plenty of booze and music. Paul Tibbets, the pilot of the *Enola Gay* who released the bomb over Hiroshima, and other military men attended. A woman asked if it was true that the Hiroshima bomb was deployed via parachute. Marx, bursting with newfound expertise, told her that was not correct—but technical devices to record the strength and heat of the blast *did* float down by parachute. With this, one of the other party guests cried, "I'll be damned, I dropped those instruments, and I'm still not allowed to tell anybody, and here comes a man from Hollywood who now knows all about it and nobody's stopping him from talking about it!"

Marx did suffer a temporary setback, however, when Albert Einstein made it known he had no interest in receiving the producer, or discussing his putative movie, at his Princeton office. Still, for Marx and Owen, their sojourn in the East clearly would end as a mission accomplished. They seemed to have gained White House approval. While some of the activist scientists reserved judgment, others promised to send along pages of background information. Ed Tompkins had agreed to relocate to Los Angeles for several weeks to serve as technical adviser to the movie (and renew his acquaintance with Donna Reed). MGM had also offered a top consultant position to General Groves, who implied he would embrace it.

The scientist-military balance for the MGM epic appeared fair on paper, but it was far from that. Unlike Tompkins, Groves was promised a hefty fee—and he had been assured that he could exercise close to veto power over anything in the script.

Whether Leslie Groves would ever allow the scientists' views to gain proper respect appeared doubtful. After all, he had recently asserted, "The atomic bomb is not an inhuman weapon." The startling long-term dangers posed by the new weapon hardly fazed him. After the first explosive test at the Trinity site back in July he had projected no "damaging effects" from radioactive materials on the ground in any atomic detonation over Japan. Even after the bombings he trivialized the alleged effects of radiation on Japanese victims, declaring them nothing but a "hoax" and "a good dose of propaganda." Groves also repeatedly called for the United States to build more bombs while keeping atomic secrets tightly under its control. He believed the Soviets were incapable of making their own weapon for at least another decade, maybe much longer.

Now, in widely reported congressional testimony, he estimated that while 40 million Americans might perish in a nuclear attack, the survivors would retaliate and win the war. When asked about reports of twenty thousand or more dying in Japan in the weeks after the atomic bombing, he finally admitted that "radiation disease" was indeed real, but predicted that many in the atomic cities would overcome it. As for those who would not: doctors had assured him that before they died these patients did not experience "undue suffering." In fact, he added, "they say it is a rather pleasant way to die."

Beyond that, there seemed to be little chance that Groves would allow in the MGM movie much, if any, criticism of the decision to use the two bombs against Japan. He had been intimately involved in every phase of that decision, including targeting (aim for the center of the city with a high altitude blast for maximum effect) and scheduling (as soon as possible, if not sooner). He briefed Truman on all of this, shaping his ultimate approval. Groves even helped write the president's prideful official announcement of the strike on Hiroshima, which was identified as a "military base," not a large city. He then played a crucial role in pushing forward the second atomic mission before Japanese leaders had a chance to respond to the first, ordering local commanders to put planes in the air as soon as weather conditions allowed. "I didn't have to have the president press the button," he later revealed, an act that contributed to the demise of at least 80,000 civilians in Nagasaki. Concerning the use of both bombs, "There wasn't anything I didn't interfere with," Groves would boast.

That included the conscience of J. Robert Oppenheimer whenever the charismatic but often conflicted Los Alamos chief expressed doubts about dropping the bomb. Groves would call Oppenheimer "brilliant" but "like so many of these scientists, he needed someone with a strong character to manage him." That might also be said (and for months was said, by others) of President Truman. Now Groves was determined, at the fullest extent, to "interfere with" and thereby "manage" the emerging MGM movie epic.

# 3

# The Race for the Bomb (Film)

While MGM was nailing down approval from President Truman and General Groves, Hal Wallis was rushing ahead at Paramount. He did not know about the competing project, so it's possible MGM remained in the dark about Wallis's entry. If true, this was an impressive display of secrecy in notoriously loose-lipped Hollywood, almost on the level of the Manhattan Project itself.

The genesis of the Paramount opus could be traced to a lunch in a U.S. Senate office building back in September. Gathered around the table were two of the pathfinders for the new weapon, J. Robert Oppenheimer and Ernest O. Lawrence (inventor of the cyclotron at the University of California in Berkeley); and Senator Warren Magnuson, whose state of Washington hosted the massive Hanford plutonium production site. Joining them was an outlier, a man named Alfred Cohn, but he had a rather amazing résumé himself. After leaving Cleveland as a young man, Cohn managed a newspaper in Galveston, Texas, eventually moving to Hollywood, where he wrote dozens of scripts for silent movies. He later adapted the story for the first talkie, Al Jolson's *The Jazz Singer*. He wrote best-selling books. Then he changed hats again, becoming the chief collector at the Port of Los Angeles—and finally one of five members of the commission that oversaw the L.A. Police Department, a post he continued to hold in 1945 at the age of sixty-five.

In this position he also served as a key city liaison with one of its leading industries, the movie business.

So here he was in Washington lunching with three even more notable gentlemen. Cohn took the opportunity to float the idea of a major motion picture on the greatest invention of the century, if not all time. The two scientists were not necessarily opposed. Excited, Cohn arranged to meet Hal Wallis that very night for dinner on board the legendary train *The 20th Century Limited*, heading west, to pitch the idea. Wallis bit, and soon drew up a contract that would pay Cohn a tidy sum to help lay the groundwork for the picture. Cohn hoped to engage Clarence Brown, director of *National Velvet* and *Anna Karenina*, but he had just committed to making *The Yearling* for MGM.

On November 9, Cohn wrote to an old friend, Truman aide Matthew J. Connelly, informing him that he was helping Hal Wallis create a film "which I fully expect will be one of the greatest moving pictures ever made." His first movie project in years, "and undoubtedly my last," it would trace the story of the A-bomb from its inception to its "reception" at Hiroshima. He wanted to open the scenario with Truman announcing the success of that mission, so Cohn wondered if there was footage of the president delivering the news. He promised to observe any security requirements for this "thriller," which would be "packed with drama and adventure."

But Cohn went further, relinquishing in advance (as MGM had) what might be called "final cut" of the picture. He had received assurances that General Groves and Dr. Vannevar Bush, head of the U.S. Office of Scientific Research and Development, "will cooperate," he told Connelly, and "of course we are giving them veto power over anything that goes into the picture." Connelly replied that while he was very interested in this movie, any footage or portrayal of the president would have to be cleared with Truman's press secretary, Charles Ross.

Now, at the end of November, Cohn notified Connelly that he'd be arriving at the Mayflower Hotel in D.C. in a few days and hoped to see him. Everything was going well on his picture, "despite the efforts of MGM, of which I am now fully informed." Cohn doubted that L.B. Mayer's studio "will go through with their project," but it wouldn't matter to him if they did. In fact, at this point, Paramount was ahead of MGM in some ways. Jerome Beatty, the writer Wallis had hired to pen the story for the film—still titled *Manhattan Project*—was presently completing a lengthy manuscript. And Wallis had just secured the services of scriptwriter Ayn Rand. She would be returning to the payroll, at the impressive rate of $750 a week, from her annual six-month sabbatical at the end of December. Wallis had planned to assign her a gangster movie, *I Walk Alone* (starring his recent discoveries, Burt Lancaster and Kirk Douglas), but now he would happily shift her focus to the invention and use of the atomic bomb.

By now, MGM had learned of the Wallis challenge. On Thanksgiving, Louis B. Mayer instructed Sam Marx to return to New York that very night—holiday be damned!—and secure a quick go-ahead for his film from Nicholas Schenck, president of the studio's parent company, Loew's, Inc. Mayer privately referred to his boss, with whom he had long battled, as "Mr. Skunk." Within days, however, Schenck expressed enthusiasm and promised to provide the pick of MGM's top stars for the film. From the Waldorf, Marx wired Dr. Tompkins on November 30 that he had achieved a "final okay from MGM executives." Now he would be "going ahead on largest possible scale. Hope your group will cooperate and assist as exclusively as possible. Hope you know I would not ask this if didn't feel it important for all of us."

One week later, Hal Wallis went public with *his* movie, four years to the day from the Japanese attack on Pearl Harbor (was this coincidence?). In a press release he announced the "immediate production" of a high-budget, $1.5 to $2 million "dramatized historical account of the development of the atomic energy project from 1939 to V-J Day." Every effort would be made to secure the cooperation of the leading military and scientific contributors to this saga. His aim would be to acquaint audiences around the world with the vast effort to create and then use this "unendurable" weapon.

Now MGM had no choice but to announce its picture. On December 10 the headline in *The New York Times* read, "Atomic Bomb Films Listed by 2 Studios." MGM was calling its entry *The Beginning or the End*, and falsely claiming that it had been in preparation for three months, not five weeks. The script would be written by Bob Considine, the well-known Hearst reporter and coauthor of the recent bestseller *Thirty Seconds over Tokyo*. Marx had met him in New York and liked everything about him. An unnamed MGM exec called it "our most important venture of 1946." Wallis, meanwhile, was clearly trying to force MGM to panic or perhaps even drop out of this race by claiming a cast would be chosen within days and that Paramount had rearranged its entire movie schedule to make facilities available for "immediate" filming.

Less than a week later, the *Times* returned with a feature piece topped by a classic header worthy of *Variety*: "Hollywood Atom Sweepstake." The two studios were in a "Race to Produce First Film History of the Atomic Bomb." Louis B. Mayer was quoted calling his project "the most important story ever filmed" but allegedly wished his rival well. The *Times* judged the race even at this point, with both sides willing to spend $2 million and secure cooperation from the true-life players. Paramount claimed to have earned an okay to film at Los Alamos, Oak Ridge, and other Manhattan Project sites.

Marx, for his part, adopted a pose of high-mindedness by contending MGM was hoping to aid "world harmony" while dramatizing the "human element." Tens of thousands of Manhattan Project workers and military personnel hailed from all backgrounds and several nationalities, and if they could work together, "why shouldn't it be possible" for everyone "to pull together to create a better world." He endorsed the One World concept (which must have surprised most of the activist scientists he'd met) and claimed that he wanted to "impress that thought on the public and do it in a manner that won't sound preachy."

Promising to cast the movie "big," Marx tossed around names like Clark Gable and Spencer Tracy. Groves's wife, he boasted, had already contributed one line of dialogue for the script: Upon learning of her husband's secret bomb work she had exclaimed, "My God, I'm married to Flash Gordon!" Marx admitted that winning the race for an A-bomb epic was important but MGM would never compromise quality "for the sake of speed. This film has got to be better than good." Still, he'd have to wait on Considine, who had not yet begun to write.

Over at Paramount, Jerome Beatty completed his 240-page draft of the *Manhattan Project* story. It was neatly typed but was, in truth, a rush job, with long passages from news reports or interviews inserted verbatim without comment, and with few real scenes or dialogue. It was more like a nonfiction book than a movie treatment, although perhaps that's all Wallis—with his eye on Ayn Rand to write the actual script—really wanted.

It opened in Berlin in 1938 with early German nuclear research, from which top scientists Lise Meitner, Otto Hahn, and others exit. Niels Bohr, the great Danish physicist who knew a lot about the Nazi program, flees to Sweden. Their counterparts in the United States go to work, and General Groves, "who has a way about him—a way of getting things done," arrives to manage

them. An extreme secrecy apparatus allows no instance of sabotage. Finally, after 190 pages, Beatty reached the Trinity test site
and then Tinian, and finally Japan. And if Hitler had won the race?
"We are mighty lucky," Beatty affirmed in closing. "We were on
God's side."

Back in Los Angeles, Sam Marx, confronted by the Hal Wallis
project, knew that a high-stakes race for an A-bomb picture had
become all too real. With little time to reflect, Marx wrote a colorful summary of his recent travels and expanded his early, fact-laden
outline for the movie to nearly fourteen pages. This scenario was
similar in many ways to Beatty's story, with strong justification
for the bombing of Japan (but exposing the human tragedy there),
while also highlighting the scientists' warnings about controlling
the atom.

It also proposed a scene showing the *Enola Gay* crew returning
to Tinian after the bombing. Doctors rush forward to examine
their eyes for possible damage after being exposed to the fireball
over Hiroshima. "To hell with the eyes, Doc," one replies, concerned about radiation effects on an equally important part of the
body, "look further down!"

The Marx sketch stood in stark contrast to the one-thousand-
word unsolicited treatment recently sent to him by Oak Ridge
activists. The Oak Ridge scenario was apocalyptic in the extreme,
while placing the scientists and their concerns front and center.
This was clear right from its "prolog," with a statement that what
followed was not fantasy but based on facts, forecasting what would
happen if the scientists' pleas were not heeded. Set two years in
the future, it would follow an activist leader from discussions in
the FAS office ("this must be sincere," the scenario instructed) to
dinner at home with his family. The next day, when this scientist
testifies before Congress, the chairman of the House committee

mocks him as an "alarmist" and claims that our defenses would keep us safe.

Sure enough, later that day, bombs go off in major cities across the United States—apparently set by saboteurs. Soldiers lie dead in the streets. Fires rage everywhere. (This was reminiscent of the recent *Life* story, "The 36-Hour War," which vividly depicted, with realistic illustrations, thirteen U.S. cities under atomic attack.) Our scientist hero manages to escape Washington with most of his family before the city is totally destroyed. A global nuclear war ensues. Survivors stagger across the American countryside, doomed. The social fabric breaks down. Shootings and lootings break out. "Civilization has died" across the globe. The scenario closed with the activist lecturing his family that "if the world had listened to" the scientists "this would not have happened. They did not realize the danger."

Back in the real world of 1945, the cultural anthropologist Margaret Mead and her husband Gregory Bateson had informed the scientists' association in New York that they wished to contribute ideas to any upcoming films. Mead had been profoundly affected by the atomic attacks on Japan, which she considered a defining moment in human history. When the bombings occurred she had been working on a book called *Learning to Live in One World* about the postwar era. Disturbed by the invention and use of the bomb, Mead had immediately destroyed nearly every page of her manuscript as hopelessly out of date. Instead she began gathering information on reactions to the atomic bomb, seeking to understand how humans might cope in a world in which they could now destroy themselves. This would shape her work for the rest of her life.

The leader of the New York scientists, Richard D. Present, told a colleague at Oak Ridge that Mead and Bateson, who had experience in "public opinion research and psychological attitudes," were "very interested" in the creation of films related to the bomb but were "skeptical about the way Hollywood will handle the social implications." He added, "It is of course not enough to have a scientist as mere technical adviser just to see that Spencer Tracy knows the difference between a neutron and a radio tube."

# 4

# FBI vs. Oppie

At Paramount, Hal Wallis had changed the name of his picture from *Manhattan Project* to *Top Secret*. He still hoped to snag Ayn Rand for his script, but she remained skeptical that he would accept her conditions. For her to proceed, the man she called "the Boss" would have to firmly agree that nothing would be added to her script that "clashed with my political ideas." Also, she must be allowed to interview Robert Oppenheimer, General Groves, and other key figures.

Perhaps to her surprise, Wallis agreed to all of this. Even so, she wanted to lay out her concept for the film in detail so there would be no misunderstandings, as she set to work at her home outside Los Angeles in the rural San Fernando Valley. Celebrities had just started moving to the area about twenty miles from the movie studios, lending it the nickname "Valleywood." The sprawling two-story ranch house, designed by modernist architect Richard Neutra, was built in 1936 for famed director Josef von Sternberg on thirteen acres of remote meadow in Chatsworth. It featured an aluminum facade with rounded edges and industrial windows offering views of the Santa Susana Mountains. An artificial stream with drawbridge wrapped around the front of the residence almost like a moat. The house had only one bedroom for residents and another for visitors but three separate garages for automobiles, including an oversized one for a Rolls-Royce. Tropical fish swam in the pond on the second-floor deck. Neutra told friends that Sternberg ordered that none of the bathroom doors should have locks—to prevent his party guests from finding a secure spot to commit suicide during the depths of the Depression.

Rand had purchased the home in 1943 after selling *The Fountainhead* to Warner Bros. Her husband, Frank O'Connor, brought in peacocks to roam the grounds and planted alfalfa and gladiolas for commercial sale. Rand despised Los Angeles but loved the steely skyscrapers of Manhattan, so this shiny ranch—and distance from Hollywood—appealed to her. As for the three garages: she did not drive.

Now she set to work on a lengthy memo she titled *An Analysis of the Proper Approach to a Picture on the Atomic Bomb.* Any such attempt, she wrote, "can be the greatest moral crime in the history of civilization—unless one approaches the subject with the most earnest, most solemn realization of the responsibility involved, to the utmost limit of one's intelligence and honesty, as one would approach Judgment Day—because that is actually what the subject represents." The atomic bomb, however frightful, was merely an inanimate object. "Whether it's used and how it's used," she typed, "will depend on the thinking of men. The motion picture is a most powerful medium of influencing one's thinking. To use such a medium on such a subject lightly or carelessly is inconceivable. If there is any reason why this picture cannot be made honestly—it is better not to make it at all."

Rather they must be motivated by one simple fact: It involves the life or death of mankind and "this picture could be an opportunity seldom offered to any man. It could be truly an immortal achievement, an event of historic importance and a great act of patriotism." But she had barely begun. Work on the memo would extend for many pages, and several days.

———

Shortly after the "blood on my hands" meeting in the Oval Office that so irritated the president, Robert Oppenheimer left Los Alamos with his wife, Kitty, and two young children. His family moved back to their Berkeley home while he settled in a friend's guesthouse in Pasadena where he would assume his new duties at Cal Tech. In letters to friends and colleagues Oppenheimer repeatedly expressed explicit, other times veiled, misgivings about his role in building the bomb. He referred to losing much of his "sanity" as his work neared its climax. To Ernest O. Lawrence back at Berkeley he voiced "profound grief" and "profound perplexity" over Truman's postwar demands for secrecy and for going full speed ahead in assembling a nuclear arsenal.

When Oppenheimer accepted a high honor from the government in a ceremony at Los Alamos he declared that any "pride" must be "tempered with a profound concern. If atomic bombs are to be added as new weapons to the arsenals of a warring world, or to the arsenals of nations preparing for war, then the time will come when mankind will curse the names of Los Alamos and Hiroshima." That same day everyone who had worked on the weapon at Los Alamos received a round, sterling silver pin with a large *A* and a small *BOMB* inscribed on it.

Delivering a farewell address at Los Alamos, Oppenheimer continued to defend the making if not the dropping of the bomb. The research was an "organic necessity," he argued, adding: "If you are a scientist you cannot stop such a thing. If you are a scientist you believe that it is good to find out how the world works . . . that it is good to turn over to mankind at large the greatest possible power to control the world and to deal with it according to its lights and values." Elsewhere, his public mutterings, while inconsistent, perhaps delphic, continued to suggest a troubling lack of commitment, in the eyes of many in the government and military, to helping design far more destructive weapons.

The FBI, therefore, resumed its efforts, begun during his Manhattan Project days, to find out if he was, as suspected, a card-carrying Communist or at least sympathetic to the aims of the Communist Party (CP). This was no small matter, since everyone recognized that the Soviets were hell-bent on building their own atomic bomb. Oppenheimer knew he was vulnerable. To a professor friend that autumn he confided, "I am worried about the wild oats of all kinds which I have sown in the past." One major problem was that his younger brother, Frank, a particle physicist deeply involved in the bomb project at Berkeley and Los Alamos, had indeed been a Communist Party member in the late 1930s. And after Hiroshima, Frank helped found the scientists' association at Los Alamos.

Another red flag: Robert's wife since 1940, Kitty, had also been a CP member. On top of that, Oppenheimer even while heading the bomb project seemed to renew his affair with Jean Tatlock, yet another former Communist. This drew special attention from investigators at Los Alamos, already alerted when he admitted on his security clearance form that he had once been "a member of just about every Communist Front organization on the West Coast." Tatlock, targeted by the FBI with phone taps and other surveillance, and suffering from clinical depression, committed suicide in 1944 not long after Oppenheimer spent the night with her in San Francisco, while two FBI agents sat outside in their car.

Now, in November 1945, J. Edgar Hoover circulated a three-page summary of Oppenheimer's vast FBI file to President Truman and his secretary of state. It revealed that CP leaders in San Francisco had been overheard referring to Oppie's past ties to the organization and their wish to reactivate them. Phone taps had found party members boasting of his CP membership but little hard evidence emerged; most of them were simply spreading rumors meant to reflect glory on—and opportunities for—the party. Going forward

the surveillance methods would be expanded to once again target
Oppenheimer himself.

Just before Christmas, Bob Considine turned in his film treatment
to MGM, covering well over one hundred pages. Writing quickly
to deadline was never a problem for the prolific Hearst reporter,
columnist, and radio host. Hanging in the den of his nine-room
apartment on Fifth Avenue in Manhattan was an autographed picture of William Randolph Hearst inscribed to "A great writer on
any subject, from his envious associate." The publisher, now in his
early eighties, quite ill and holed up at San Simeon in California,
was no longer much of a political or journalistic force, but the writer still followed the generally conservative Hearst line.

Considine might bring an unusual perspective to the MGM
project, however. As a war reporter he had come to welcome any
new weaponry or tactic that might speed the end of the slaughter.
So he was shaken when, on a visit to General Groves's office shortly after the atomic bombings, he found an unnamed "fine looking old scientist" in an outer room, slumped behind a desk. When
Considine asked him a routine question or two, the man began
weeping without shame. "I wish to God," the scientist murmured,
"we had never found the way to make this bomb."

Now Considine proposed for the MGM movie's prologue the
following, to be spoken by a portentous newsreel-type announcer
or printed on the screen "against a musical background of weird
sorcerer's music": *This is the story of those human beings who won
the grim race and produced the atom bomb in time to spare millions of
lives . . . perhaps your own. This is the true story of the birth of a bomb
that shook the world and made men realize for the first time in history
that they must live together in Peace . . . or perish in undreamed-of horror. This is the moment of man's true beginning . . . or his end.* So in the

very first words the notion that the bomb spared "millions of lives" was expressed as an article of faith.

Like the Marx scenario for the movie, Considine's story covered the early work on the bomb and Roosevelt's approval. Then a fictional character, young scientist Mark Weber from the University of California, tells his wife they must relocate so he can work on a secret project. He joins Enrico Fermi, who is about to conduct his controlled chain reaction at the University of Chicago's Stagg Field. Weber develops qualms when he learns that this wondrous breakthrough may lead to creation of a revolutionary weapon of war.

The scene shifts to the Pentagon, where General Groves "is strong-faced, good-looking . . . inclined to be a bit stocky" (a kind portrayal, to be sure). With him is an aide, Colonel Jeff Nixon, a "jaunty, good-natured . . . hero type." Groves's secretary complains that Jeff has kept her up until 3 a.m. A top general hires Groves for the "biggest job in the war." Groves asks him about the scientists. He replies, "They're a different breed. . . . I don't think any of them really want to make a bomb." When Groves meets Oppenheimer, however, we see that the physicist is "handsome, gentle, quietly efficient." But when another scientist patiently tries to explain nuclear fission, Colonel Nixon responds that until then he thought "physics was just a plural of Ex-Lax."

Months later, FDR at Warm Springs in April 1945 worries that the bomb will probably cost $2 billion by the time it's tested, meaning it might soon be known as "Roosevelt's Folly." Then he dies. Truman, now president, is finally told about the bomb and that it will shorten the war if it works. He offers his full support. At Trinity the bomb test succeeds. A young scientist tells Oppie he wants to quit working on such a weapon; if not allowed, he insists on riding the first bomb down when it is dropped (as actor Slim

Pickens would later do in *Dr. Strangelove*). So at this point, the scientists' moral issues are at least respected, even in the hands of Considine, the Hearst scribe.

At Potsdam, Truman tells Soviet leader Stalin they will soon drop a new bomb on the "Japs" so the Russians better enter the war soon. Stalin replies, "You crazy Americans, you're always inventing something!" Groves receives a wire signed by sixty scientists (in real life, the July petition circulated by Leo Szilard) who want Truman to explicitly warn the Japanese about the bomb to speed their surrender—or at least drop it on an "uninhabited island." Another general mocks these ideas and wants the bomb used as soon as possible.

The action shifts to the pilots on Tinian. Mark Weber, the one leading character concerned about using the weapon, nevertheless agrees to arm the bomb when it eventually heads for its target. But in practicing there's an accident, he is exposed to radiation, and he dies. Simply a martyr—or punished for questioning the mission?

On Tinian, the *Enola Gay* crew is briefed. A chaplain blesses them. Bomb and bombers head for Japan. Back at the Pentagon, Groves paces. Pilot Tibbets releases the bomb. A gray, swirling mushroom cloud rises over the doomed city. *Enola Gay* crew members are struck dumb, but express no obvious regret. A Japanese pilot flies over the city which is "so still and dead . . . It is as if a gigantic blow torch had been applied to it." The movie would end with a U.S. plane soaring over the same wasteland, while above the aircraft "there is a ray of blue sky and sunshine that typifies the world's desperate ray of hope."

While Hal Wallis, after commissioning a scenario from Jerome Beatty, hoped to switch to Ayn Rand for his screenplay, Sam Marx planned to stick with Bob Considine. The MGM studio executive overseeing the project, James K. McGuinness, had other ideas.

Yet another New Yorker who fled to Hollywood to find fame and fortune in the 1920s, McGuinness had contributed to more than a dozen screenplays, most quite forgettable. Notably, however, he had written the story for the Marx Brothers' classic *A Night at the Opera*. Although it would end up bearing little resemblance to the final film, he could dine out on that for years, and did. By 1942, he had assumed an executive post at MGM and did little writing, while narrating the war documentary *The Battle of Midway*.

McGuinness was a large man, born in Ireland, with a Clark Gable moustache, a heavy drinker married to a baroness. His friend, the hardboiled writer James M. Cain, author of *Mildred Pearce* and *The Postman Never Rings Twice*, claimed he never saw him stone sober. Cain would watch him with his feet up on his desk at MGM beating a cadence on the soles of his shoes with a riding crop. "He was a genuine snob, too," Cain observed. "Never lunched at the studio. Always ate at the club." (McGuinness once said, "In this world some people will ride and some will walk. I'm gonna be one who rides.") Another writer, Budd Schulberg, would remark, "I suppose some people thought McGuinness was charming—but some people thought Goebbels was charming."

He was also known as one of the most conservative figures in town, deeply opposed to the Screen Writers Guild (first organized in the 1930s), and a fierce anti-Communist. He believed that some writers—traitors or "Quislings" in his view—had been directed by Communist Party bosses, under orders from Moscow, to paint America in a poor light. McGuinness, in contrast, wanted films to be "pure entertainment." Sam Marx, who was more liberal by nature, despised him.

Now, over Sam's objections, McGuinness asked his friend Frank "Spig" Wead to write the script for *The Beginning or the End*. Wead, a Peoria native and famous flying ace who had just turned fifty, was an interesting fellow but a very poor fit for this project, Marx believed, even though he had two Oscar nominations to his credit. His most recent work: the war drama *They Were Expendable*, directed by John Ford, with Donna Reed in a supporting role. Before that he had written *Hell Divers* with Clark Gable and *Ceiling Zero* starring James Cagney. Wead was no hack, but his main interest remained the military, which did not trouble the ultra-patriotic McGuinness.

Sam Marx, on the other hand, felt Wead was as unsuited as anyone in Hollywood to deliver a tough-minded picture on the atomic bomb. He could write conflict, action and battlefield violence, but could he capture the work of scientists, not to mention the deep moral issues raised by the bomb and its use? Especially since he seemed to be under the sway of James K. McGuinness.

# 5

# Saboteurs and
# Bridge-Playing Wives

A Navy flyer and aviation pioneer, Frank "Spig" Wead had turned to screenwriting around 1930 after a crippling spinal injury seemed to end his military career. He still managed to re-enlist after Pearl Harbor and as a commander supported carrier-based operations in the Pacific. While war raged in 1944 he wrote a popular magazine article with the evocative title "We Plaster the Japs." Among the Japanese-held islands his operations would assault was Tinian, the future U.S. bomber base. (His exploits would be portrayed by John Wayne in *The Wings of Eagles*, directed by John Ford.) It's fair to say that he hated the enemy, had even witnessed deadly kamikaze attacks on U.S. ships. Now, little more than a year later, how would he treat the decision to annihilate 200,000 Japanese with two bombs?

Wead started his work for MGM with a memo, delivered on New Year's Eve, that outlined several issues and opinions related to the bomb, such as, "There is no advantage in the possession of many atomic bombs. The advantage lies with the nation which strikes first—contrary to all American basic feeling." Having read the Bob Considine draft he offered specific ideas for additions or changes, large and small. Somehow, for example, he knew that the letters *BPW* on a scientist's application to work in the Manhattan Project meant "Bridge-Playing Wife." He imagined a new scene with Oppenheimer walking in the desert with colleagues after the Trinity test. He spots a turtle and picks it up, addressing it this way:

"Well, how did you survive today my little one? Did you wear dark glasses?" He places the turtle in his pocket, planning to give it to his son as a present. Then, contemplating the new weapon's threat to all life on earth, he puts the turtle down and lets it crawl away.

On a more serious note, Wead admitted that many scientists did have misgivings about building the new weapon, and observed, referring to the fictional Mark Weber character, "There is a great story in this guy developing this bomb against his will." But he added: "His name should be distinctly American. Mark Weber is not." Too Jewish or German? He also proposed that instead of dying in a freak nuclear accident, Weber—or whatever his new name might be—should contemplate blowing up the Los Alamos lab to halt future atomic progress! Talked out of sabotage by Colonel Jeff Nixon, he commits suicide as his only form of protest. Finally, Wead pictured a scene with military officials from the United States, Canada, and the United Kingdom touring Hiroshima after the bombing, with each one imagining it as his own home town.

Despite his military orientation, Frank Wead's memo at times supported the views of the scientists over those of the Army, and its tour-of-Hiroshima scene even suggested some criticism of the use of the bomb (or at least it vividly pictured its result). But would any of that survive a close read from the movie's chief consultant, General Groves? Knowing his history of throwing his considerable weight around, one had to wonder.

Leslie R. Groves's entire life had revolved around the military. Born in Albany, New York, the son of a U.S. Army chaplain, he grew up mainly in Alta Dena, California. After graduating fourth in his class from West Point in 1918, he joined the Army's Corps of Engineers. By 1940, now a major, he was a key consultant on military construction sites, from depots and hospitals to air bases and munition dumps. A year later he was put in charge of building the giant complex in Virginia for forty thousand employees that would soon become known as the Pentagon.

A year after that, with this record for getting things done and reputation as a stickler for details, he was put in charge of the top-secret Manhattan Project with the rank of brigadier general. Hoping instead for a posting abroad close to the front lines, he was unenthusiastic at first but relented when told, "If you do the job right it will win the war." Groves would take charge of nearly every aspect of the project, including construction, technical development, security, and then planning for use of the completed bomb. Primary research would be conducted at Columbia University and the University of Chicago, while the main project sites were built at Los Alamos, Hanford, and Oak Ridge.

In October 1942 he hired Oppenheimer to run the scientific side against the advice of some who raised concerns about his lack of achievements (no Nobel Prize) and past links to the Communist Party. In Oppenheimer's favor was his willingness to spend several years living and working in a remote location. "I was appalled by his ignorance of American history, military history, anything pertaining to operations of this kind," Groves would later recall. On the other hand, "Oppenheimer's great mental capacity impressed me, I think, when he told me that he had learned Sanskrit just for the fun of it. . . . I was also very cognizant of one other thing and that was that there was nobody else. . . . The whole basis of it was that there wasn't a better man" despite his "very bad" security status. Groves personally cleared him on that score.

Ernest O. Lawrence, who knew Oppenheimer from Berkeley, had warned that there were other concerns about the man. Lawrence made "quite a point of this," Groves told an interviewer in 1965. "He said that 'The average Jew had no moral principles on a lot of scores.' He said, particularly with respect to sex life, 'You cannot trust them at all.' He said, 'You take somebody that you think has been happily married for thirty years and you find him in bed with his stenographer.' That was a shock to me, but I learned to agree that that was so."

A U.S. Army engineer named Kenneth Nichols, a top Groves aide on the Manhattan Project, would offer this frank assessment after the war:

> First, General Groves is the biggest S.O.B. I have ever worked for. He is most demanding. He is most critical. He is always a driver, never a praiser. He is abrasive and sarcastic. He disregards all normal organizational channels. He is extremely intelligent. He has the guts to make difficult, timely decisions. He is the most egotistical man I know. . . . .He abounds with energy and expects everyone to work as hard or even harder than he does. . . . He ruthlessly protected the overall project from other government agency interference. . . . I have had the opportunity to meet many of our most outstanding leaders in the Army, Navy and Air Force as well as many of our outstanding scientific, engineering and industrial leaders. And in summary, if I had . . . the privilege of picking my boss I would pick General Groves.

Groves was no romantic. When Secretary of War Stimson struck Kyoto off the target list for the first atomic mission, Groves repeatedly tried to get him to change his mind. Kyoto was Japan's historic and cultural capital, known for its beauty, and its utter destruction would make it harder for the Japanese to accept an American occupation, Stimson reasoned. On top of that, it hosted relatively few military operations—and its population of perhaps 1 million dwarfed that of other targets, guaranteeing vastly inflated civilian casualties. Groves cared little about any of that. In his view its size promised a better snapshot of the enormity of the bomb's destructive force. He wouldn't stop pushing for its spot on the target list until Stimson got Truman to affirm his ruling. (Later Groves would admit, "Events have certainly borne out the wisdom of Mr. Stimson's decision.")

When asked by a superior, as the bomb neared readiness, whether the United States should rethink the need to deploy it against reeling and surrounded Japan, Groves scoffed at the notion. As he later recounted, he could see "no reason why the decision taken by President Roosevelt when he approved the tremendous effort" should be changed at all. Many of the scientists who argued otherwise had escaped from Nazi Germany and once Hitler was routed "they apparently found themselves unable to generate the same degree of enthusiasm for destroying Japan's military power."

As the first reports of the success of the Hiroshima mission arrived in Washington, General George Marshall warned against feeling too much gratification, given the certainty of a large number of casualties. Groves replied that he was not concerned about that, given what happened to American POWs on the "Bataan Death March." He then took no steps to slow the Nagasaki mission to give the Japanese a reasonable chance to quit. Groves had always been the prime advocate for a "one-two" punch to shock the Japanese into surrender. After Hiroshima, in fact, he moved up the second mission two days, to August 9, despite forecasts of bad weather. (If not, it's possible that the second mission would have been canceled as Japanese surrender became more likely.) When clouds obscured the primary target, Kokura, this sent the Fat Man bomb to ill-fated Nagasaki.

Now, nearly four months later, the "meddlesome" Groves's promised role with the MGM atomic bomb movie became formalized. On the final day of 1945, he wrote and signed a letter of agreement with MGM's parent, Loew's, Inc., which was accepted a few hours later by the studio's fixer in D.C., Carter Barron. (This meant that Groves would not be signing the other movie contract he had received, from Hal Wallis Productions.) Having thrown in with MGM, Groves promised that he was not only authorizing the studio to use his name and "impersonation" by an actor but was also offering his "best cooperation" with this movie project. "Also, you may ask and receive from me in writing, my comments and approval as to your script and dialogue and the treatment you propose for actual persons," he promised. He would do this "with the appreciation that some dramatization and fictionalization may be required for your picture purposes and I will not unreasonably withhold my written approval."

Note the two references to "approval."

Groves also mandated that he would never be asked to disclose anything still secret about the bomb. Moreover: "Nothing which would violate security rules will be included in the picture." Also: "I understand the picture will be subject to War Department approval before issuance"—so make that *three* approvals.

The contract closed: "In full consideration of the foregoing, you agree to pay me the sum of Ten Thousand Dollars not later than December 31, 1945." (This equates to roughly $130,000 today.) Well, that would be fast work, since he and MGM's Barron only signed this agreement on December 31, 1945.

Borrowing liberally from the Considine story and his own memo, Frank Wead now submitted to Sam Marx a fifty-one-page outline. He pictured Truman deciding to use the bomb against Japan after a brief visit to the Oval Office from, among others, Groves, Fermi, and Colonel Nixon. They watch as he goes to the window and looks out at the Washington Monument. Truman reveals that a million American troops would land in southern Japan on September 1 and another million near Tokyo ten days later. "The minimum estimate of our losses is a half million men," he declares. "This is the most difficult decision I have ever made." Then, hardly missing a beat, as if deciding what to order for lunch, he announces, "Take your bomb to the Marianas—and use it."

Already the script was veering from the facts in an apparent attempt to justify the use of the bomb. In fact, the first landing in Japan was not scheduled until November 1 and no credible military estimate placed American casualties in that operation close to half a million, with Japan's supplies and forces growing ever more depleted (if they were still fighting at all).

When the bombing of Hiroshima arrived in his scenario, Wead wrote a side note in the margin: "It is as yet undecided how much of this bombing we will show from the viewpoint of those in the EG [*Enola Gay*], and how much we will show, if any, from the viewpoint of the Japanese." We do find Archbishop Spellman backing the bombing. Then, before the Nagasaki mission, the Americans drop warning leaflets—with some drifting down to their comrades in a Japanese prisoner of war camp. When the Allied officers tour Hiroshima they find a terrible landscape of death (though no bodies are to be shown), but Colonel Nixon is "elated" about the bomb's effectiveness.

Cut to Los Alamos. Scientists there are upset that newspapers are claiming the secret of the bomb can be kept hidden. They are "scared to death." Now, troubled by the twin bombings, young scientist Bill Allen—the new, dull but quintessentially American name for the former Mark Weber—makes up his mind to destroy the lab "and all the knowledge and material it contains." He tinkers with plutonium, but it goes critical and threatens to kill everyone nearby. So he reaches in and receives a deadly dose on one hand. When Jeff Nixon finds him, he explains, "I was going to blow up the place. Then I decided that if a man has helped build something—even if he doesn't believe in it—perhaps his death will make people realize the seriousness of what he helped to do." A doctor predicts he will be dead the next day.

It's likely the new plot twist was inspired by an incident the previous September involving a twenty-four-year-old physicist at Los Alamos named Harry Daghlian. He was exposed to radiation when he dropped a tungsten carbide brick onto the plutonium core during a critical mass experiment at a remote Los Alamos site. Even so, unlike the movie character, it took him over three weeks, not one day, to die—the first fatality from a "criticality" experiment. When the government reported his death to the press the cause was attributed simply to "burns" from an unspecified accident (this would be far from the last nuclear-related official "cover-up").

Following Bill Allen's sad demise in his script, Wead came up with a grand finale: a joint meeting of Congress. All of the main characters, including Groves, express their differing points of view. Several detail the horrors of using the bomb and outline the scientists' fears: There is no advantage in having many bombs, no defense against them. One day bombs will be a thousand times more powerful than the Nagasaki weapon. "Let us lift our faces and assume the moral leadership of the future," one character pleads. "Let us realize the dignity of man." Atomic energy can create a "utopia" for all if used for peaceful purposes, so atomic secrets should be delivered to an international authority.

The closing line: "It is a question of 'grow up or blow up.' This is the Beginning, or the End."

The Wead outline, incoherent as its overall message might be, took pains to suggest that Truman felt he was only carrying out the wishes of his revered predecessor in deciding to use the bomb against Japan. One would never know that a number of close observers, including many scientists (most notably Einstein), felt that it was by no means certain that FDR—with Germany defeated and Japan close to that—would have made the same choice, despite his long support for city bombing.

Roosevelt, of course, would have felt the same burdens that Truman bore: needing to justify the enormous costs connected to the bomb project; wishing to end the war and the killing of young Americans as soon as possible; and the desire to see if such a weapon would work when dropped from a plane over an enemy target (not detonated off a stationery tower, as at Trinity). Still, it remained plausible that Roosevelt would have, at the minimum, waited a few days or weeks to give the Japanese more time to surrender. The *momentum* for use was certainly considerable, but it was not unstoppable.

FDR was, after all, a far more experienced, beloved, and iron-willed leader than Truman, who had just arrived (unwanted) in the White House. Roosevelt was more inclined to—and capable of—standing up to pressure from anyone, even a tank like Groves. He also had exhibited more of a moral compass than Truman displayed. In 1944, as the bomb project approached success, FDR had agreed with British leader Winston Churchill that the weapon "might perhaps, after mature consideration, be employed against the Japanese," hardly insistent language. Four days later, in a discussion with Vannevar Bush, he wondered if the bomb might just be held as a threat instead of actually being used. Others believed that Roosevelt would have been far more open than Truman to modifying the U.S. unconditional surrender demand to allow the Japanese to keep their emperor, forestalling either an invasion *or* the use of the bomb. This was something Secretary of War Stimson and his undersecretary John J. McCloy, among others, had proposed. McCloy, in fact, had advised Truman that "really, we ought to have our heads examined if we don't explore some other method by which we can terminate this war"—that is, via negotiations.

Then there was this: Roosevelt's top adviser on the war was his chairman of the Joint Chiefs, Admiral William D. Leahy. He was skeptical from the start that an atomic bomb could be invented; then decided that it should never be used against large cities. In his postwar memoir, Leahy would declare that "the use of this barbarous weapon at Hiroshima and Nagasaki was of no material assistance in our war against Japan. The Japanese were already defeated and ready to surrender. . . . In being the first to use it, we . . . adopted an ethical standard common to the barbarians of the Dark Ages. I was not taught to make war in that fashion, and wars cannot be won by destroying women and children." When Roosevelt died, Leahy was supplanted by others, such as Secretary of State James F. Byrnes, an aggressive hawk on deploying the bomb, who had Truman's ear in the Oval Office.

Resisting using the bomb against two cities would have taken enormous courage, moral vision, and capacity to step back from unceasing pressure (notably, from General Groves), in what might be called a unique historical situation, with so many American lives on the line. It was far safer, especially in a Hollywood movie aiming to endorse the official narrative, to imagine a sole decision-maker and political heir somehow knowing exactly what FDR would have done, and then doing it.

# 6

# The Rand Report

The new year arrived in Nagasaki with the most bizarre episode yet involving the American occupiers. While movie creators in Hollywood pondered how to dramatize the use of a revolutionary weapon against an enemy, U.S. service members on the ground in Japan were exposed, mentally and physically, to the results.

One month after the bombing, General Thomas Farrell, sent by Leslie Groves to assess conditions in Hiroshima, announced that "no poison gases were released" by the bomb. Vegetation was already growing there. This cleared the way for the first large group of U.S. soldiers to arrive in Nagasaki around September 23, 1945, and in Hiroshima a little later. Marines took Nagasaki, while the U.S. Army entered Hiroshima. Because of the alleged absence of residual radiation, few were urged to take strict precautions. Some bunked down in buildings close to ground zero, even slept on the earth and engaged in cleanup operations, including disposing of bodies, without protective gear. Not everyone wore radiation detection badges. "We walked into Nagasaki unprepared. . . . Really, we were ignorant about what the hell the bomb was," one soldier would recall. Another commented: "Hell, we drank the water, we breathed the air, and we lived in the rubble. We did our duty." The occupying force in Nagasaki grew to more than 27,000 as the Hiroshima regiments topped 40,000. Some stayed for months.

The U.S. Strategic Bombing Survey sent a group of photographers to record the blast effects for posterity while virtually ignoring the human toll and the grim scenes in the hospitals and first aid stations. At the same time, the military seized all images taken by Japanese news photographers in the two cities. The United States also shut down all filming by Japan's leading newsreel company, Nippon Eiga Sha, which had been document-ing the effects—physical, botanical, and medical—for weeks, and took charge of all of the disturbing raw footage the cameramen had already shot.

General Douglas MacArthur's headquarters in Tokyo, mean-while, tightly managed journalists from the United States and other countries who wished to cover the aftermath of the atomic attacks, with access limited and all firsthand reports reviewed by censors. His office also enacted and policed a rigorous press code that restricted any bomb coverage by Japanese media. To this point, therefore, Americans back home had not been allowed to absorb the wide-ranging results of the first two atomic bombs, as photographs and film footage invariably focused on wrecked build-ings and razed landscapes, rarely on injured survivors or those dying horribly from radiation disease. Would Hollywood finally offer a fuller, truer picture?

By all accounts, the Americans stationed in the atomic cities were charmed by their hosts and profoundly affected by what they witnessed. One Nagasaki veteran later testified: "We did not drop those two [bombs] on military installations. We dropped them on women and children. . . . I think that is something this coun-try is going to have to live with for eternity." Mark Hatfield, a young naval officer in 1945 and later a U.S. senator (known for his opposition to the Vietnam war), would reflect on his "searing remembrances of those days" in Hiroshima when a "shock to my conscience registered permanently within me."

Now, on January 1, 1946, back in the States, the Rose Bowl and other college football bowl games were played as usual. To mark the day in Japan, and raise morale (at least for the Americans), two

Marine divisions faced off in the so-called Atom Bowl, played on a killing field in Nagasaki that had been cleared of debris. It had been "carved out of dust and rubble," as one wire service report put it, without mentioning that it was the former site of a high school where hundreds of students perished on August 9. It was dubbed "Atomic Athletic Field No. 2." A commemorative booklet produced for the game included this line: "In the rubble of the atomic bomb, we made a gridiron." Of course, some of that rubble was human in nature.

Both teams had enlisted former college or pro stars serving in the Pacific for their squads. The "Bears" were led by quarterback Angelo Bertelli of Notre Dame, who had won the Heisman Trophy in 1943. The "Tigers" featured Bullet Bill Osmanski of the Chicago Bears, who topped pro football in rushing in 1939 (and then became a Navy dentist). Marines fashioned goalposts and bleachers out of scrap wood that had been blasted by the A-bomb. The weather provided more of a feel of America back home, as the day turned unusually chilly for Nagasaki and snow swirled.

More than two thousand troops turned out to watch. A band played the fight song "On Wisconsin!" The rules were changed from tackle to two-hand touch because of all the irradiated glass shards from the atomic blast remaining on the turf. A referee watched for infractions. Each quarter lasted ten minutes. Press reports the next day claimed Japanese locals observed the game from the shells of blasted-out buildings nearby. The two stars, Bertelli and Osmanski, had agreed to end the game in a tie so that both sides would be happy, but the latter, after leading a second-half comeback, could not resist kicking the extra point that gave his team the win, at 14–13.

Most of the players then fled the radiation-tainted ruins while thousands of their fellow U.S. servicemen—not to mention the surviving citizens of Nagasaki—had to stay behind.

In the first days of the new year, Ayn Rand, in her San Fernando study, completed her sixteen-page "analysis" of what the Hal Wallis movie must cover. It was a paean to Objectivism, her philosophical system. She remained devoted to the idea that the world needed saving from global destruction, and that she and this movie were instruments to do so. Otherwise, she told Wallis, "We will have on our conscience millions of charred bodies—those of our children." Her solution: "a tribute to free enterprise."

To her, the subject of the atomic bomb was inherently political and the main problem was "Statism," the idea that "government must be all-powerful and must control the existence of men." The crucial conflict was between Statism and freedom—between the government and free enterprise. And it was Statism that leads men to war "because that is its nature. It is based on the principle of force, violence and compulsion." (Witness the Germans, Japanese, and Italians in the most recent war.) Therefore the atomic bomb "is safe only in a free society . . . men must be free—or perish."

Yet the global trend, despite the outcome of the war—and now promoted by the Soviets—was still toward Statism, not free enterprise, and that must be reversed. If the Wallis movie improved the argument for Statism, Rand wrote, "we will have blood on our hands," but if they boosted free enterprise they would make "a historic and immortal contribution" to saving mankind. Luckily, she added, the history of the atomic bomb was an eloquent "tribute" to free enterprise. All they had to do was present the issue in such a way that would leave no room for argument "and nobody will dare disagree with us, except the out-and-out fascists and Communists."

Their most important goal, therefore, was to dispute the image of a government- and military-directed Manhattan Project, inspired by FDR, and in debt to his monetary largesse. If the movie bolstered Roosevelt's status as the hero it would be "committing a moral crime by falsifying a historical lesson of tremendous importance." Rather, what must be emphasized was the simple fact that "invention, discovery, science and progress are possible only under a system of free enterprise. . . . If we take the greatest invention of man and do not draw from it the lesson it contains—that only free men could have achieved it—we deserve to have an atomic bomb dropped on our heads." And "if anyone objects to our saying that, he does not deserve the name of a human being."

Yes, the victory of the scientists was a collective one but driven by *volunteer* effort and *individual* discovery. She even quoted Einstein: "I am a horse for a single harness, not cut out for tandem or teamwork." Also to be highlighted, of course, would be the crucial role performed by private industry (e.g., the DuPont Company). In conclusion, she insisted that this picture be nothing less than "an epic of the American spirit."

But what if her fervent views highlighted in this memo did not represent Paramount's approach to the picture? In that case, she instructed Wallis, "I cannot permit myself to take upon my conscience the contribution of a single line to it." But if he did choose to make the picture on her terms, she would "consider it an honor and a privilege to work on the screenplay."

Within the week, Wallis would not only assign the project to her—she would be sitting down with J. Robert Oppenheimer to pick his celebrated brain.

Closing in on his actual target, J. Edgar Hoover had ordered an FBI wiretap on Frank Oppenheimer's home north of Berkeley. At a New Year's Day party at Frank's house the feds overheard two local Communist Party organizers boldly ask his brother Robert to orate about the A-bomb at an upcoming rally. They did this even though he had avoided contact with party members for years. Oppie turned down the offer, but this hardly deterred Hoover from continuing this and other surveillance.

Down in Hollywood, Sam Marx, having secured Leslie Groves as highly paid adviser (with veto power), now set his sights on his number-two target, a man who probably would demand far less, if any, money or control. On January 7, Marx informed Robert Oppenheimer by letter that "we are now working very hard on our atom bomb script," with a first draft due within two weeks. Production would start by March 1. "I hope to please you in any point where the film touches on your life," Marx purred. "In accordance with what you told us in Washington, we are trying to get as close to the truth as we can know or discover it. I think we are succeeding."

Groves, he advised, would be in the L.A. area the following week and MGM had invited him to visit the studio. Would Oppie, living in Pasadena, join them? That would make Louis B. Mayer "exceedingly happy." If not he could stop by with his wife for lunch "any time you feel in need of such relaxation." Oppenheimer did not answer. Perhaps he was busy planning for the visit from Ayn Rand and Hal Wallis, arranged by Paramount. Earlier he had told Marx he didn't want to be distracted from his work by Hollywood chitchat but for some reason agreed to suffer these intruders. Each was certainly more famous than Sam Marx.

Rand had prepared a long list of questions to take with her. Among them were: Was Oppie strongly urged to take his position at Los Alamos or did he volunteer? Who selected the other scientists? How was the work organized—to what extent was it "controlled" and to what extent "free"? What were the crucial turning points? The unexpected discoveries? Which events stood out in his mind? What about the contributions of major industries? Did the scientists really fear German success or were they "contemptuous of the German efforts"? Would he care to mention any troubles or "interference" from the government?

The interview apparently went well. Rand found Oppenheimer to be a fascinating, somewhat tortured figure, and when the session ended she wrote up the highlights for her journal. Among the revelations: Only one scientist turned down Oppenheimer's job offer, despite serious obstacles (the remote location and having to work with the hated Army); two did resign later. Some knew what they were working on at the start, but many others were only told about the bomb a few months later. "They kept it secret without rules—merely by making it a principle to keep it secret," she wrote in her notes. Enrico Fermi contributed enormously and Vannevar Bush was a key figure because he had access to FDR. Overall, "refugee scientists" who fled Hitler were most responsible for the bomb.

Rand insisted on a second interview, and also meeting his wife, which Oppie accepted. While she waited for that, she devised some new questions: Would he describe a "typical day" at Los Alamos? Did he have a bodyguard? Was he controlled in any way by the Army there?

And finally, simply: "Hiroshima."

Oppenheimer's lower-profile Manhattan Project colleague, Dr. Edward Tompkins, now set to serve, at $200-a-week, as chief technical adviser to the MGM film, took leave of his position at Oak Ridge and set off for Culver City for an extended stay. Surely he planned to look up his former high school chem student, Donna Reed. Like her, he had grown up on a farm in Iowa and then fled to California—in his case to Berkeley for his doctorate.

Shortly after his arrival, Tompkins penned a four-page memo for his associates. He admitted that since it had to be "an entertainment type film," and could only cover some of the major aspects of the creation and use of the bomb, there was bound to be "some criticism" of the finished movie. Nevertheless, "everyone working on the picture is very enthusiastic about its prospects and are willing to put forth every effort to make it one of the best productions ever made." The current scenario traced the development of the weapon based on true-life individuals, but it would also portray the "political implications" in the interplay between two made-up characters: a "typical scientist" (with ethical qualms) and a "typical carefree type colonel" (i.e., Groves's assistant, Jeff Nixon).

Tompkins disclosed that "there is some discussion now about having the scientist killed in an accident during the construction of the second bomb. The reason for this would be to increase the drama, and Mr. Marx feels it would do the cause of the scientists a great deal of good by a scene between the colonel and the scientist just before the death of the latter." In a concluding scene, Colonel Nixon, now a convert to arms control, might testify on the dead scientist's behalf before Congress. Tompkins closed by admitting that "we can only act in an advisory capacity." The "final decision as to the content" rested with Marx. He did not know that Leslie Groves held, and planned to exercise, his contractual right of approval.

At the same time, Tompkins wrote a more personal note to Enrico Fermi in Chicago. After reading the Frank Wead treatment, Tompkins had provided "necessary corrections to give as authentic an account as possible." Tompkins had also consulted with the art director to help make the celluloid laboratories appear true to life. "The studio officials hope to make this picture the best of the year," he gushed. He would do his damnedest "to see that it is just that."

Then he got to the true purpose of the letter. Sam Marx had asked him to help secure permissions from key figures, dangling "a substantial donation" to their associations (but with no mention of individual compensation). "Mr. Marx is very anxious to portray you," he added, "because of your early connection with this work and your great contributions to it." He even wanted the ethically troubled young scientist to serve as Fermi's assistant. To flatter Fermi even more, he asked him to send along any advice on the movie. "We hope that through the interplay of characters this picture will be able to get across a message to a segment of the population which cannot be effectively reached in any other manner," Tompkins concluded. "If it does that . . . then it will have served its purpose."

Left unwritten: What exactly *was* that "message"? And was it something on which most of the leading scientists would agree— let alone be endorsed by the often skeptical (at times hostile) military and White House?

Tompkins's optimism about *The Beginning or the End* surely would have been tempered had he been privy to Sam Marx's private view of him, his young associates, and the movie.

In early January, Norman Cousins, the widely admired writer and editor of the popular weekly magazine *Saturday Review of Literature*, had hosted a dinner attended by physicists Leo Szilard and Harold Urey, writer Bob Considine, and MGM's Carter Barron. The latter informed Marx afterward that the dinner had been a big success for the studio. Now, on January 10, Marx wrote Cousins to thank him, adding that during his recent visit east he had found Szilard and Urey mighty impressive. He was currently engaged in overseeing the script with an eye on compressing and fictionalizing some events. But this did not worry him, after meeting Szilard and Urey. "I am no longer concerned lest I offend the sensibilities of the more important scientists," he explained. "I know they will be happy with what we are trying to do." Why? "Their outlook is vast and their understanding is great."

He remained concerned, however, about "the younger and less important scientists who are on the Project." This would certainly include Ed Tompkins. "We are going to be bitterly criticized by them, I know," he complained. "I shall put it down to their youth, inexperience, and, regrettably enough, smaller minds. . . . They are very worried that we will not make a picture that will be a big, long speech for world government. Quite frankly, they are right. We will have no such speech." (This from the man who had just told *The New York Times* that he supported the One World movement.)

Marx claimed that the best way to express the scientists' concerns was to highlight the dangers to the public of an out-of-control experiment or chain reaction.

Fortunately, in Marx's view, the "more important scientists . . . do not seem to have the same misgivings of the lesser group." Why Marx felt this way, given the views of Szilard in particular, was a bit of a mystery. After all, it was Szilard who, a little more than a month before the attack on Hiroshima, wrote that petition to President Truman calling the new weapon "a means for the ruth-less annihilation of cities" and asking the president "to rule that the United States shall not, in the present phase of the war, resort to the use of atomic bombs." After the attacks he told his wife that he considered using the bomb against Japan "one of the greatest blunders of history."

Now Szilard was among those who favored some form of world government to help control the atom. Still, Sam Marx worried less about the venerable Szilard than those in the younger group. "Shall we let them stew along and see the results," he asked Cousins in his letter, "or should we start trying to educate them? The latter seems to be a long, tedious job, but I will face it if you think it wise."

In the meantime, Marx had plenty else to do, including (accord-ing to a United Press dispatch) finding a way to inject some "sex" into this rather technical story. "Everybody knows you have to have sex in there somewhere," the article asserted. "And that's what's worrying the MGM bigwigs." The writer quoted Marx claiming there were "many angles" possible for a "boy-meets-girl story," or two, which they ought to be able to add without distracting from this atomic bomb business. Donna Reed had pointed to General Groves's secretary as a fine candidate for an affair. The studio was just waiting for Bob Considine, the article concluded, "to figure out a formula for mixing uranium and plutonium with stardust and moonlight."

# 7

# Nobody Can Harness Man

Ayn Rand's second interview with Robert Oppenheimer yield-
ed twice as many notes for her journal and for her movie
script. In a kind of overview she wrote simply: "Tormented by
something he can't solve." Still, Oppie recalled for her formal parties at Los Alamos that he likened to "Englishmen in the Congo."
Also: "Scientists like music. Long walks, skiing, horses." Yes, since
she asked, a sentry did stand outside his house all night at Los Alamos, and after 1943 a full-time guard was assigned to him. As for
his typical day: "Talking with individuals about their problems;
trying to give them a feeling of confidence; correcting them while
making them think they did it themselves."

Perhaps to her chagrin, since she claimed scientists took no
orders at Los Alamos, Rand heard Oppie call Groves his "boss"—
true, his "only boss," but still. Nevertheless he affirmed that
scientists were given their choice of projects and were "*free* to solve
problems." Rand pushed him on this point, and later quoted the
exchange verbatim: "I asked him whether the scientists worked
under orders. He looked at me in the way the best characters [from
a novel] would have, and said in a morally indignant tone: 'No one
ever gave an order at Los Alamos.'"

And what of the use of the bomb against Japan? From Rand's notes:

> *Hiroshima—Sunday at Los Alamos . . . took children to go
> swimming.*

> *Next morning he got phone call at lab—everything all*
> *right.*
> *On Tuesday night—a colloquium—800 scientists—worried*
> *that the next one might not work.*

As for that second bomb, her notes only mention it as a fleeting memory: *"Waiting for news of Nagasaki."*

When Rand sat down with Oppenheimer's wife, Kitty, she got a different impression of the response to Hiroshima. Kitty recalled throwing an "evening dress" party for the scientists and their mates after the Trinity test three weeks earlier: "Mood was one of relief." But after Hiroshima "they did not feel like celebrating."

Rand came away from the encounters so impressed with Kitty's husband she would soon use him as the model for the character of Stadler, a troubled scientist involved in "Project X" in the novel she was sketching (later titled *Atlas Shrugged*), even borrowing Robert as his first name. This character was, she would later explain, a "type that Oppenheimer projected—that enormous intelligence, somewhat bitter, but very much the gentleman and scholar, and slightly other-worldly. Even his office was what I described for Stadler—that almost ostentatious simplicity."

While Oppenheimer was usually close at hand in Pasadena, Rand had to make sure to meet Groves during his brief visit to Los Angeles. Groves had signed his MGM deal two weeks earlier but it did not forbid him from informally talking to (that is, guiding) other filmmakers. This also left open for him another option for payments in case the MGM project collapsed.

From him, Rand learned that Groves felt he risked "disgrace" in taking the Manhattan Project directorship. He thought at first it was "fantastic and doomed to failure"—she recorded in her notes—and later only gave it a 60 percent chance of success. But his team pulled it off partly because he had to make crucial decisions often against the advice of his scientific advisers. Groves acted as "salesman" in approaching the key industries, and none refused him. What he wished to see emphasized in her script was "teamwork and American management" (not exactly music to her ears) and that no other country in the world could have accomplished it (that was more like it).

A week later she spoke with a Dr. Kaynes who worked with Richard Feynman, a bit of a "screwball," he said, in the computing group at Los Alamos. In the lab, Kaynes related, Feynman would bang on tom-tom drums—"the more noise, the harder he was thinking." Feynman, despite the high security, often traveled to Albuquerque to see his wife, Arline, who was dying of tuberculosis. Rand also interviewed General Nichols, Groves's top aide.

After completing the interviews, Rand assembled what she called *Philosophic Notes*. She hailed scientists as the leading examples of free inquiry who will never work "under compulsion. . . . Brute force is nothing—thought and principles everything." The atomic bomb, ostensibly a first-strike terror machine, is actually a weapon of "defense . . . of a free country." She was now thinking of how her beliefs and interviews would be expressed in scenes and dialogue on the pages of a script. One character, for example, might say, "Just as a tiny, invisible atom holds forces that determine the shape of matter—so you, each man, by the ideas you hold, determine the shape of world events." Another scene should contrast the Nazi ideal—"a horde of armed brutes"—with a scientist at a blackboard, perhaps James Chadwick of England. "All human activities," the scientist might say, "are like a chain reaction—somebody has to be the first neutron." Then he would look to the sky and declare, "God *did* give us a means for right to win over might"—minds that "cannot work under compulsion."

After all of the preliminaries, Frank Wead, the legendary flying ace, finally completed his first pass at a full script for *The Beginning or the End.* It would, in the main, closely follow earlier texts, and Wead's comments about them, but with some key additions. Within days he added numerous handwritten (in pencil or blue ink) notes to it. After opening in Berlin with Lise Meitner and Otto Hahn, the screenplay briskly traced all of the key scientific discoveries straight through to Fermi and his chain reaction in Chicago. After that crucial test, Wead provided this exchange between Colonel Jeff Nixon and ethical scientist Bill Allen:

**BILL:** Well, most of us don't really want to make the bomb.

**JEFF:** Just get us the bomb and we'll find a place to drop it. And get it before Hitler or the Japs.

**BILL (thinking out loud):** I wonder if we should.

The odd sketch of Oppenheimer picking up a turtle in the desert after Trinity made it into the screenplay. Now, when Oppie takes the creature out of his pocket, he pats it and puts it down, saying, "Scurry away little one—lead a free life while you may."

Truman's decision to use the bomb after briefly looking out at the Washington Monument remained untouched. But Wead cut a scene with two Japanese priests in Hiroshima, before the bombing, congratulating each other for wisely moving there from Tokyo where it had grown so unsafe. Jeff Nixon now appears on board the *Enola Gay.* Witnessing the bombing, Jeff's face appears stricken, "his mind a turmoil of conflicting thought."

In one of the new scenes, to bolster the rationale for the morally troubling Nagasaki attack, Wead pictured General Farrell briefing the bomber crews on Tinian: "Gentlemen—I realize many of you regret the necessity of this second mission. Our radio and leaflet appeals to the Japs have brought no response. We have no alternative but to go ahead with it." Another fresh scene found American

POWs in Kokura, the principal target for the second bomb, as the (fictional) U.S. warning leaflets come fluttering down. A brutal Japanese officer informs them, "No matter what happens—Japan will never surrender!" The POWs expect the worst when they hear American bombers overhead, then are relieved when they pass. "It's a miracle!" one shouts. They are saved. Nagasaki: not so lucky.

With these additions the script was now bolstering all three of the moral arguments on which the rationale for dropping the bomb rested: this was the only way to end the war quickly and it saved up to a million American lives; the two cities were legitimate military targets; civilians were warned ahead of time.

As in Wead's original outline the script climaxed with the joint session of Congress, but after Groves speaks the scientist who offers a rebuttal is now identified as Oppenheimer. "We scientists feel the names of Hiroshima and Nagasaki may lie heavy on our consciences," Oppie reveals, but instead of citing the deaths of Japanese civilians he claims that "saving half a million lives in this war won't mean much if we lose many times that number in the next one." An international authority should have sole control of atomic weapons, for there is no way for America to maintain a monopoly; suspicion, even paranoia, will reign if several nations attempt to develop their own A-bombs.

A tacked-on final scene, set a few months later, explored a reunion of key scientists at a D.C. banquet honoring them. One voluble character reveals his farfetched dream of building "a rocket to the moon—no problem with that!"

MGM kept this first rough script tightly under wraps. It did not, for example, send it to chief consultant Groves, but its on-site technical adviser, Edward Tompkins, had a field day circling factual errors on technical aspects, especially surrounding the Fermi chain-reaction scene. These corrections probably did not bother

Sam Marx—even that one entire scene dubbed "absurd"—but he had to be concerned when he read: "Page 42 . . . and throughout script: Oppenheimer must be portrayed in a different way if he is to O.K. the script. As he stated to me Saturday, Jan. 19, he agreed with Groves on only one thing: the importance of getting an atomic bomb perfected before the Germans. On all other issues they disagreed: the reasons for wanting the bomb, the best methods for getting it, compartmentalization of information etc. Oppenheimer will not allow himself to be represented as a 'friend of the Army' which he certainly was not."

The script often showed Groves, not Oppie, giving orders, especially at Trinity. In the real world of 1946, meanwhile, the military-scientist rift was only growing. Paul Henshaw, one of the activist leaders at Oak Ridge, had told Tompkins just a few days earlier that concerning the Army "we simply stand as being fundamentally disagreed on practically every major point" regarding the existence of the atomic bomb.

Still, all in all, Tompkins, sitting in his temporary office on the massive studio lot at Culver City, felt that the script pictured the scientists and their demands in a generally positive light. The movie might actually do more good than harm. He was the scientists' eyes and ears at MGM, so when he communicated to them his moderate, if still tentative, approval, many of his colleagues expressed relief. They heeded his call to send along "human interest" anecdotes and "amusing incidents" to broaden the portrayals, along with additional technical material. Some activist leaders, however, still insisted that writer Frank Wead visit them at Oak Ridge, Chicago, and other sites (and MGM was at least paying lip service to this unusual request).

Obtaining the permissions from key figures to be portrayed would remain a challenge. Einstein, for example, was reputed to be "very cagey about sticking his neck out on such matters," one association leader warned—and he had already refused to meet Sam Marx in Princeton back in the autumn. Now the spokesman for activists based in New York wrote Einstein, "I know you will not want to lend your name to a picture which misrepresents the military and political implications of the bomb. I hope you will see fit to make the use of your name conditional on your personal approval of the script." Leo Szilard, in a visit to Einstein, expressed skepticism about any involvement with the studio.

Since Fermi appeared here and there throughout the script, his okay, along with Oppenheimer's, was paramount. Marx asked the scientists to also approach Lise Meitner. The studio still envisioned her as a heroine of the story. Well, good luck with that. Meitner rejected the entire notion of a Hollywood depiction, just as she had refused to work at Los Alamos, vowing, "I will have nothing to do with a bomb." After Hiroshima, Meitner said that she was "sorry that the bomb had to be invented."

J.J. Nickson, the activist leader in Chicago, informed Tompkins that he had discussed the permissions issue with some of the scientists, and in his view, "most of the men will be only too willing to cooperate if they are convinced the presentation will be an accurate one." Nickson had spoken to magazine editor Norman Cousins, who had hosted that recent dinner for MGM with scientists Szilard and Urey. Cousins warned that Marx was a poor bet to represent the scientists' views because he was mainly concerned with box office.

Some of the activists, meanwhile, were pushing to hire a Hollywood agent, such as the famed Leland Heyward, to wrangle more money and other concessions from MGM. *Newsweek* had just reported that General Groves "was asking" for $10,000 from MGM for his cooperation (they didn't know he'd already received it). Hal Wallis, on the other hand, had offered the pilots of the planes that dropped the two bombs over Japan a paltry $100 each to be impersonated, the magazine revealed. "Incensed at the low figure as compared with MGM's munificence," the item related, "they jacked up their prices substantially."

MGM's long-promised check for $5,000 to FAS—now housed in larger, less chaotic quarters in a two-story brick building on "L" Street in Northwest D.C.—was being passed along to various groups of scientists like a hot potato. Marx had always framed it as a "donation" but with the understanding it would apply to their overall cooperation and help in gaining those pesky permissions. Because it was an informal gift, there was no contract that spelled out anything. Some scientists wanted to take it at face value as a mere donation; the associations needed the money. Others believed doing so would signal approval of the MGM movie (which the studio could exploit in publicity and to gain permissions) along with their continuing assistance even as doubts about the project rose. The head of the association in New York charged that the $5,000 figure "was off by a figure of ten." Another activist feared they were viewed by MGM as the Federation of Atomic *Suckers.*

With her research and boundless rumination completed, Ayn Rand was ready to outline the Wallis movie in her usual detail—sixteen full pages where a four-page summary might have sufficed. Any resemblance to the MGM script was largely accidental.

She imagined it opening with a shot of an immense night sky full of stars. A single man stands on a hill, a tiny speck in the landscape. He returns home to find his wife in bed. She had given birth earlier that day (apparently thanks to a midwife?) and expresses high hopes for her son, yet her husband speaks bitterly of being a "helpless worm" in the universe—what was the sense of doing anything? He picks up a newspaper, it is 1919, and sees that a British scientist, Sir Ernest Rutherford, has succeeded in smashing an atom of nitrogen. He mocks the event—who cares about scientists? Only men of action count.

Ten years later he advises his son that "there is no such thing as objective truth." The highly intelligent boy's name is, for now, "John X" to suggest he is a universal youth. His father is not happy that the kid just wants to study for school. Behind the scenes, however, E.O. Lawrence is creating his cyclotron and Gilbert Labine has been finding uranium ore in Canada. Soon we see Chadwick discovering the neutron and Urey identifying heavy water. Einstein writes his famous letter to FDR, and bomb research begins. Inspired by these men, John X, now fifteen, tells his father he wants to become a scientist. Dad responds by seizing all of his books—and throwing them in the fireplace! Two years later, John X attends college anyway. The United States enters the war and John X joins the army in military intelligence and speeds to Europe. The Manhattan Project begins as Hitler's bomb program sputters.

Wounded in battle, John X is sent home, where he is assigned to serve as a bodyguard for a famous physicist. He has only contempt for this idea (thanks to indoctrination by his father), but that night meets the rather interesting Dr. Oppenheimer, who sparks in John X a "regeneration and return to spiritual values, as he sees them exemplified in the work at Los Alamos." John X watches as Oppenheimer recruits other scientists. On a lighter note there is the "incident" of a scientist's son asking for an atomic bomb for Christmas.

Now we're in 1945. FDR dies. Trinity is a success. On Tinian, Capt. Parsons arms the bomb—no radiation accidents, nor a scientist's sabotage, in *this* scenario. On August 6: "The bombing of Hiroshima." (That's the extent of her description.) Next day, the gathering of eight hundred at Los Alamos: "Terrific applause when Oppenheimer enters and makes his report." That night, Oppie and John X walk the hills of Los Alamos. What they've accomplished was no accident, the physicist instructs—"only free men in voluntary cooperation could have done it . . . the mind is man's only real weapon, and his mind will always win against brute force." The treatment continues: "The boy is looking at the stars—just as his father did 26 years ago. But his face is shining with pride, courage, self-confidence. Now man does not look like a worm in the face of the immensity of the universe—his figure looks heroic, that of a conqueror."

The boy's last line: "Man can harness the universe—but nobody can harness man."

# 8

# Ticking Clocks
# and Time Capsules

One can only guess what Hal Wallis might have thought on receiving the Ayn Rand treatment, although her earlier philosophizing on this matter ought to have warned him. Clearly his immediate reaction was not one of excitement nor satisfaction, for within days, perhaps hours, he had activated a backup scribe, Robert Smith, to offer an alternative.

Smith and Rand had already collaborated, after a fashion, on a movie the previous year, *You Came Along*, a romantic comedy revolving around a heroic flying ace (Robert Cummings) who happens to be terminally ill. Smith wrote the story and his first Hollywood screenplay before she put her brand on it. Rand called it "a very cute story—not profound, but clever and appealing . . . I kept whatever was good in the original script and wrote the rest. . . . I saved it." Reviews were decidedly mixed. Now, rehired by Wallis for his atomic bomb project, Smith submitted a sample sketch for one scene. The setting: three men in a bare living room in New Mexico—a General Grover (obviously Groves), a Dr. Bernheimer (Oppenheimer), and an Arthur Saxon—the night before the Trinity test.

"I confess I'm beginning to have misgivings," Bernheimer exclaims. "Everything has been calculated . . ."

"Except its effect on the human race," Saxon interjects.

"Exactly. . . . I'd stop it if I could," Bernheimer announces. "I'd stop it now."

General Grover: "No one can stop it."

"No one could have stopped it ever," decides Saxon. "Unless we smashed the first test tube." He then turns on the radio and—too predictable—it's Richard Wagner's *Götterdämmerung*.

"It's the right mood," Bernheimer mutters, adding that he doesn't think "human ethics" had "kept pace with science." Then they get a call to hustle to the Trinity site. . . .

With that sent to Wallis, Smith took elements of Rand's approach, which had been forwarded to him, and assembled an outline with a long list of scenes accompanied by one-paragraph descriptions of each. He opened, as Rand had, with a man and a woman who has just given birth. But instead of the father's doom and gloom we have mom's cheery optimism—Randism without the evil straw man: "I'm glad our son was born in America . . . born to freedom. He can do anything now because he was born free. . . ." None of the characters in that preface, *contra* Rand, ever reappears.

Then Smith introduced his main follow-through: a ticking clock, growing in ominous noise level, sometimes just on the soundtrack, other times in view. FDR okays a bomb project: the clock ticks louder. After the Trinity test, Truman is told that an invasion of Japan will cost a half million lives. "His mind is made up"—the United States will warn Japan, "but one way or another, we'll bring those half million Americans back home alive." *Tick-tock-tick-TOCK*. After the atomic attacks, scientists discuss the need to avoid war so that "atomic power will open up a new and brilliant vista of better life for all," with men of goodwill working together. This is a new race against the clock. The movie would end with a close-up of that clock, now ticking very loudly, engraved with the warning, *IT IS LATER THAN YOU THINK*.

Not content with just ordering Smith to warm up in the bull-pen, Wallis also asked the well-known writer Leo Rosten if he would take a crack at it. The Poland-born Rosten, best known as a humorist for his popular *The Education of Hyman Kaplan* articles and book, had a degree in political science from the University of Chicago and had worked in the Office of War Information. He had recently authored his first screenplay for a Hedy Lamarr picture, *The Conspirators*, over at Warner Bros.

Apparently not aware of these alternate approaches, and with Wallis not calling her off, Rand went to work on fully executing her scenario.

Whatever the cause, Edward Tompkins was now growing increasingly concerned about the MGM project. The question of permissions weighed heavily on him. The studio continued to seek them, giving the scientists temporary sway, but Sam Marx could throw up his hands at any moment and make the picture purely from the military's perspective—or substitute comically fictionalized scientists for any who dragged their feet in signing contracts.

This warning emerged explicitly in his latest discussions with MGM brass. Sam Marx told him he would never provide complete scripts to any of those portrayed, just relevant portions, to avoid endless criticism of the overall story. He vowed to start shooting soon, given the "race" with Hal Wallis. If that happened, he would probably take the "fictionalized scientists" route. Marx preferred engaging Oppenheimer, Einstein, and Fermi, but his patience was growing thin. He had also ruled out a Wead or Considine tour of the atomic sites, again citing the need to beat Wallis.

But Tompkins, the catalyst for the whole project with his letter to Donna Reed, expressed wider frustration in a soul-baring letter to J.J. Nickson, the leader of the Chicago scientists. "I'm doing everything here I can to influence the nature of the picture and have run into some considerable difficulties," he disclosed. "In fact, I've nearly had my bags packed several times already." The scientists' position had become a "poor one," partly because (unlike Groves) they had no rights of approval. Denying permission to portray key characters might only lead to a worse outcome. If the studio plunged ahead without them it would likely lead to "a bad picture showing the scientist in a bad light" while ignoring their appeals for nuclear sanity.

Well, what if the scientists pestered the studio so effectively MGM would cancel the movie entirely? Tompkins quipped: "If you feel that no picture should ever have been made in the first place just recall how many people in this country feel the same way about the atomic bomb." Yet he clung to hope for a positive outcome. Working with the studio to maintain a measure of good will would require a lot of faith and patience, but a better result might emerge. "As you may see," he concluded, "the whole picture is very confused. I have gotten many gray hairs (literally) since I arrived. Right now I think that all we can do is just wait it out and hope for the best."

A director for *The Beginning or the End* had now been hired, and once again Sam Marx had been overruled. Studio exec James K. McGuinness had selected his friend Norman Taurog, a colleague on his right-wing Motion Picture Alliance for the Preservation of American Ideals. Marx respected Taurog but felt there were a dozen preferable options right at MGM, including highly regarded Victor Fleming, Mervyn Leroy—who had directed Bob Considine's *Thirty Seconds over Tokyo*—and Jack Conway.

True, at the age of thirty-two, Taurog had won an Academy Award for best director in 1931 for the lighthearted *Skippy*. He later nabbed another Oscar nomination for *Boys Town*, but his movies after that tended toward musicals and films with youthful leads such as Judy Garland and Mickey Rooney. The short, stocky Taurog looked "like a minor character from one of his own films . . . round-faced, blue-jowled with a bee-stung lip, a wisp of hair and large, inquisitive eyes," as one biographer described him, adding that he could have played a "querulous minor gangster." (He would later direct more Elvis Presley movies than anyone else.)

Bob Considine, meanwhile, continued to propose revisions for the script. He created a scene with evil Japanese leaders vowing to carry on despite the atomic bomb. Yet he also elaborated on the tour of post-bomb Hiroshima by General Farrell and a Japanese radiation expert. "Conditions are shocking," Considine sketched. "Black flies swarm over or cover the dirty, black-burned wounded. . . . A baby with a face burned black nurses from a mother. . . . The death of the city lays heavily on the scene." When General Farrell learns that nine thousand died at "Jap" military headquarters he exclaims, "Good!" He grows quiet, however, when informed that 80 percent of the city's firemen perished along with most doctors and nurses.

Other characters on that tour form their own thoughts—and we see on the screen what's going on inside their minds. One American wonders what would have happened if the "Japs" had an A-bomb to drop on Pearl Harbor. Another imagines the same weapon being used in the future against New York City and Washington, D.C. One wishes the atom had never been split, while another decides this will surely be a force for good. There is some emotional complexity here, for the time being.

In addition to tweaks and inserts provided by Considine, the MGM script now had a fanciful (some might say silly) prologue. Sam Marx felt the movie needed an audience-friendly intro instead of opening in some gloomy laboratory in Nazi Germany. Hal Wallis had recently hired two writers, Norman Krasna and Glen Tryon, to take a crack at this prelude for his *Top Secret*. Krasna had a long list of notable screenplay credits, including *Mr. and Mrs. Smith* for Alfred Hitchcock and *Fury* for Fritz Lang (and he would later write *White Christmas*). Tryon was a former actor. Wallis had rejected their intro, but Marx happily embraced it.

The movie would now open with "a newsreel clip" narrated by a typical *Metrotone* or *March of Time* announcer. Principal characters in the bomb project have gathered for the burial of a silvery time capsule, not to be opened for possibly five thousand years, at a remote site that would likely survive a nuclear attack, perhaps in New Mexico or inside Pikes Peak. Placed inside the capsule would be a movie projector, instructions, and a print of the movie "you are about to see"—that is, *The Beginning or the End*.

Then, after a dissolve, a confident man would stride into a room. This could be Groves, Oppenheimer, Einstein, or even Archbishop Spellman. ("The star of the picture, of course, is the likelihood," the writers observed dryly.) The man smiles and says "How do you do?" to the citizens of 6946, who have somehow figured out how to load and project the print of the MGM movie and, of course, understand twentieth-century English. Why had this time capsule been created? Physicists of his day had just developed a way to commit global suicide, the man explains. They feared this would lead, "inadvertently or deliberately," to an act that would wipe out nearly everything on earth. So here for the viewers—inheritors of a world recovering from a nuclear war or still faced with that potent threat—was the story of how that new weapon was developed, on these fragile reels of 1946 celluloid.

Krasna and Tryon also supplied an epilogue: a prayer for the future accompanied by images of Archbishop Spellman "and the biggest choir you ever did see." Marx wisely junked this but immediately adopted most of the prologue. He did change the schedule for unearthing the time capsule from an absurd five thousand years to a mere five hundred years later. He also moved the location to deep in the imposing redwoods of California. Now a Bible would also go in the capsule. (He knew his audience.) It would also be revealed that a certain president named Truman had supplied the title for the movie. The character addressing the future citizens,

Marx decided, would be filmed standing in front of the iconic white Thalberg Building on the MGM lot. The intro would close with the warning: "A message to future generations! Ours will be no lost race. . . . We knew the beginning. Only you of tomorrow—if there is a tomorrow—can know the end!"

As for casting the MGM epic: While Spencer Tracy, Clark Gable, and Van Johnson had been mentioned earlier, now there was indecision. Perhaps lesser names should be employed, given the film's quasi-documentary tone. The only actors hired so far were Agnes Moorhead, who would play Lise Meitner (if she ever gave permission to be portrayed); and the legendary Lionel Barrymore, picked to impersonate FDR. Barrymore had been confined to a wheelchair for years, so that fit, but he was a very active Republican who opposed Roosevelt in 1944, which surely did not.

# 9

# The End of the Beginning

Hopes for international control of the atom had reached a high point with the appointment by the State Department of a blue-chip committee, chaired by Undersecretary Dean Acheson, with a five-member board led by David E. Lilienthal and J. Robert Oppenheimer. Their task? Produce a major proposal for the first meeting of the United Nations' Atomic Energy Commission in June. The panel soon completed a report labeled "a place to begin." It called for a U.N. body to control all of the earth's fissionable uranium deposits, while exercising the authority to license, construct, monitor, and inspect all global nuclear facilities. This was greeted with enthusiasm by most of the American scientists and by the press, with Leslie Groves the only consultant who protested. A positive response from the Soviets remained to be seen.

With that in doubt, and fulfilling its promise that nothing—including the complaints of scientists—would halt progress in perfecting weaponry, the Pentagon announced the first postwar nuclear tests in the Pacific. They would be carried out under the overall title Operation Crossroads. The Army had wanted General Groves to take charge of the bomb tests, but this would basically be a Navy operation.

Worried that funding for shipbuilding would be reduced if their fleet was viewed as vulnerable to an atomic attack, the Navy wanted to show that only a direct hit could take out an armored battleship or carrier. Scientists were already warning that these calculations ignored the massive radioactive contamination sure to befall any ships near the target (if they didn't immediately sink to the bottom), not to mention the danger to thousands of sailors observing a blast at close range or engaged in the inevitable decontamination and salvaging efforts. So, as with *The Beginning or the End*, it was the military versus the scientists. And once again the scientists seemed to be losing.

The United States had already forced the 167 inhabitants of the Bikini Atoll, made up of some twenty-three tiny islands in Micronesia, to "temporarily" relocate so that America could test weapons for "the good of mankind and to end all world wars." The first test was planned for late spring or early summer 1946. It called for a weapon exceeding twenty-one kilotons in force (the Hiroshima blast was fifteen kilotons) to be dropped over dozens of unoccupied ships in the Bikini lagoon. The second test would be set off in the same area under water, beneath another ghost fleet, by remote control. This might prove to be a turning point for American domination in the atomic era, as the United States presently possessed only nine atomic weapons in its arsenal. Hence the desperate desire for acceleration.

The Bikini islanders learned of their involuntary evacuation when Navy Commodore Ben Wyatt, military governor of the Marshall Islands, arrived to remind them of Biblical passages—the natives had long welcomed Protestant missionaries—comparing them to "the children of Israel whom the Lord saved from their enemy and led into the Promised Land." The Bikinians were none too pleased with this notion, but their leader, King Juda, finally agreed to the relocation, announcing, "We will go, believing that everything is in the hands of God." (Wyatt staged a reenactment for a newsreel, but it required seven takes because King Juda failed to act enthusiastic enough.) The vast majority of the Bikini families were bound for Rongerik, 125 miles to the east—about one-sixth the size of their current home—as their temporary refuge.

In reality, Wyatt and other U.S. officials knew that the islanders would likely never be allowed to return to what was certain to be a heavily contaminated former paradise. *Time* quoted a U.S. officer as boasting that easing out the Bikinians was "one hell of a good sales job." The magazine writer added: "Progress chuckled over a victory."

The U.S. Navy helped the Bikinians disassemble their meeting house and church while the residents packed supplies and personal belongings, then transported them to Rongerik in landing craft. *Time* observed that they took few possessions with them beyond their Bibles, hymnals, and furniture brought by missionaries, along with "latent syphilis left by Yankee whalers of the pre-atomic age." No one lived on Rongerik, which was nice, but the reason for that was not: it had few supplies of food and fresh water. The Navy knew of the challenges the Bikinians would face there, but still left them with only a few weeks' worth of water and food. *Time* predicted that to convince them not to return home after the tests the Navy might have to fly King Juda over Bikini to show him what a tragic wasteland it had become.

The young writer Roger Angell explored all this in a short story for the *New Yorker* titled "Some Pigs in Sailor Suits." Two businessmen and a blowhard colonel are merrily drinking highballs in a club. The colonel hails the bombing of Japanese cities, which proved the perfect targets because of their flammable wooden housing. Morale has never been higher in the military, he boasts. The narrator, George Swan, grows concerned that his friend is a bit too enamored with what he calls atomic "stuff." The natives evacuating Bikini don't seem too thrilled, he points out.

"Oh, hell, you mean the gooks," the colonel responds. "Well, I wouldn't worry about them." When Swan challenges him with reports that pigs and goats will be used as stunt doubles—stand-ins for people on board ships at the tests—the colonel points out that this is ideal, for goats are thick-bodied like humans and pigs have similar skin. Some of the pigs will even get to dress up in flash-proof jackets, "like Navy gunners," he laughs.

Edward Tompkins, truly a fish out of water, had wavered from hope to despair while toiling at the enormous movie studio for weeks. Donna Reed's words of warning back in November—that the studio would likely rewrite the initial scenario from top to bottom—must have haunted him at times. Then came the most disturbing news to date. Tompkins learned that Frank Wead, under orders from the studio, was in the process of changing the names of many of the leading characters in anticipation of MGM never gaining their "life rights." Oppenheimer, decidedly Jewish, had become an ultra-WASPish "Whittier." Niels Bohr was now "Wetzel." Fermi would be called "Ramsey" but, for some reason, still spoke with an Italian accent.

How had this happened? It started with a blowout between Marx and Tompkins in late January. Tompkins had just visited Oppenheimer to brief him on the emerging script and gauge his reaction, not so much on the technical details (which had been upgraded) but on the overall viewpoint of the film and its feeling for the daily life of the scientists. Tompkins came away from it sensing there was no chance in hell Oppenheimer would okay the current script. Oppie also declared that the $5,000 "gift" from MGM was too small and that the scientists could garner much more of a payout, and influence, if they stuck together.

So Tompkins began to formulate a plan: get all of the leading scientists to voice support for the movie but hold off legal approval until they saw a final script. This would encourage Marx to use their real names and personalities when shooting began, and then if the scientists later determined that the script was bad—and threatened to withhold permissions—they would have the studio over a barrel. With so much footage shot and publicity launched, MGM would have to make key revisions demanded by the scientists, who would also be in position to obtain a much larger "donation." All that was needed for this to succeed, in Tompkins's mind, was unity and secrecy.

A few days later, Tompkins went to Marx's office to inform him there was no way MGM would get Oppie's name on a dotted line any time soon. With that, "Marx hit the ceiling and landed all over me," Tompkins would relate to a colleague a few days later. Marx accused him of a major breach—showing Oppenheimer the script—which Tompkins denied. Then Marx said, well, he'd talked to Oppie himself not long ago and found him "most cooperative," so if that had changed he would blame Tompkins for "queering" the deal.

Tompkins replied that, in any case, he knew Fermi would not give his okay, which made Marx even madder. "Are you trying to cooperate with us or trying to get us to not make a picture?" Marx asked, belligerently. He accused Tompkins of being "less than useless" and a double-crosser. With that, Tompkins walked out. At that moment he realized that he was dealing with "a bunch of potential bastards." Sure enough, Marx started freezing him out of meetings, and when the producer did see Tompkins he criticized everything he said. Finally, Tompkins told him to "go to hell" and threatened to quit the project. A slightly humorous exchange followed.

Marx: "That's fine with me. I will get Szilard, who is a real gentleman."

Tompkins: "I wish you would, and if you do you will soon know what real trouble is!"

Marx finally calmed down and asked him to stay. Tompkins said he'd give it another week. Still isolated at the studio, he went over Marx's head and met with his boss, James K. McGuinness. This went nowhere, as McGuinness accused Tompkins of being a "nervous Nelly" in his fears about the movie. Over lunch, McGuinness told him, "in a fatherly way," according to Tompkins, "that I worried too much and was alarmed only because I didn't understand the picture business."

Tompkins might have worried even more if he'd known that members of the MGM creative team were recording his hectoring phone calls and then playing the tapes for studio execs to show how unhinged the scientists had become. By that time, however, Marx (still in a huff) had already ordered Wead to finalize changing the scientists' names in the script—even, for god's sake, Oppenheimer to Whittier—and carry on without having to listen to the activists ever again. He'd had enough. And he still had Leslie Groves up his sleeve.

So, beyond the decidedly odd "buried time capsule" prologue, what was the overall thrust of the heavily revised Wead script? In the main it followed the earlier versions fairly closely but with many key additions and subtractions, in pencil or red ink, not to mention all of those mandated name changes for Oppenheimer, Fermi and others. Lise Meitner was now out completely, so no role for Agnes Moorhead. This version marked a kind of turning point, as many of the inserts clearly justified the development or use of the bomb while deletions softened the original script's empathy with the scientists and bomb survivors.

After the prologue, it continued to painstakingly follow the development of the bomb. The bloated Groves was still "good-looking" and just "a bit stocky." He had now been given a new quip at Trinity when someone casually wonders what observers should do if a radioactive cloud drifted their way: "I don't know about you—but I intend to run!" Secretary of War Stimson says (as he did in previous drafts) that many scientists felt "we ought to tell Japan we have the bomb and ask them to surrender" or perhaps detonate one in a remote spot as a warning shot. But now Groves forcefully replies: "I'm afraid the scientists don't know their Japs. They don't surrender." And Truman, after citing the desire to use the bomb and save lives, adds, rather crudely, "I think more of those half million American boys than I do of all our enemies."

Now when we see Hiroshima before the bombing it is dominated (as it was *not* in real life) by an enormous army complex, planes, and tanks. A general claims the Japanese will greet any American invasion with "suicide planes, suicide boats, troops, women." Overhead, flak fired by anti-aircraft guns greets the now-imperiled *Enola Gay*—a complete fabrication, but added, no doubt, to make the flight seem riskier, more courageous. No longer, after the bombing, do crew members look down at the ruins with a look of shock on their faces, although that landscape is still (as the script had observed earlier) "startlingly arresting."

Ethical scientist Matt Cochran—the new, slightly less dull, name for the former "Bill Allen"—no longer ponders blowing up the Los Alamos lab. Instead he gets his fatal radiation dose while he arms the Nagasaki bomb, and his quick action and self-sacrifice saves forty thousand lives on Tinian. "I couldn't very well let this whole place go up like Hiroshima," he declares. "Maybe this is what I get for helping build the thing when I didn't really believe in it." Before the Nagasaki mission, General Farrell says American planes have dropped so many warning leaflets "the Japs are up to their elbows in them." (The Army after Hiroshima did print tons of leaflets warning of atomic attacks, which would be dropped over Nagasaki—on *August 10*, one day late.)

The scene of POWs in Kokura now featured a "Jap" officer promising, "Soon *we* will drop atom bombs on San Francisco and New York!" Brief images of Nagasaki "should be symbolic of the Japanese industrial war machine," such as a torpedo plant, to further justify the attack. The walking tour of Hiroshima, including graphic images of death and Allied military officers expressing humane attitudes, was crossed out completely, never to return.

Also excised was the final scene in Congress where Oppenheimer once carried the day. Its replacement: Colonel Nixon delivers a letter that the now-heroic Matt Cochran wrote to his wife as he lay dying from that dose of radiation. She asks Nixon to read it aloud, and he does: "By this time the news from Hiroshima will tell you why I went to the Pacific. . . . Believe me I've had my share of doubts," but this letter now reveals the true "voice of my conscience. . . . God knew when to show us this great secret. He did not show us a new and efficient way to destroy ourselves" (though he had not spared Matt). Instead, "atomic energy is the hand he has extended to all of us." It will cure disease, power our homes. "We have not found a way to return to the Dark Ages. We have found a path so bright . . . ."

As Nixon continues to read, a succession of familiar faces appears in the sky behind him: FDR, Churchill, Truman, even Stalin. Matt hails these "men upon whom the future of atomic energy depends," as well as those who made the bomb—we now see Groves, Fermi, Bohr, and Oppenheimer. Then anonymous men, women, and children appear in the clouds, the script relates, "the faces of humanity, uplifted, pleading, full of hope. . . . The screen fills with them. As the music reaches a climax the face of Matt appears, symbolic of all that is best in science and hope for the future."

# 10

## Enter General Groves

**B**eyond whatever new points it was promoting in its revised script, MGM intended to make Oscar-worthy the dramatic Trinity test in the New Mexico desert. This empowered their fabled special effects team to concoct an unprecedented explosion—in advance of even more spectacular displays for Hiroshima and Nagasaki. But in doing this they would have to ignore some of the troubling aspects of the test that Americans still knew little or nothing about. General Groves, for one thing, uttered lines quite different from his joke in the current script about outrunning a radioactive cloud.

In completing their work on building the bomb, Manhattan Project scientists knew it would produce deadly radiation but weren't sure exactly how much of it. Military planners were mainly concerned about the B-29 bomber pilots over Japan catching a dose, but scientists warned of dangers to those living downwind from the Trinity site at Alamogordo (not to mention Japanese civilians). Nevertheless, Groves ruled that local New Mexico residents should not be evacuated, and instead be kept completely in the dark—unless they were awake in the middle of the night and spotted a glow in the distant sky brighter than any sun. Nothing was to interfere with the test. When two physicians on Oppenheimer's staff proposed an evacuation, Groves replied, "What are you, Hearst propagandists?" That line was not likely to make the MGM script, especially since Hearst's Bob Considine was still tinkering with it.

Sure enough, soon after the Trinity shot went off before dawn on July 16, 1945, scientists monitored alarming evidence. Radiation was quickly settling to earth in a band thirty miles wide by one hundred miles long. A paralyzed mule was discovered twenty-five miles from ground zero. Still, it could have been worse; the cloud had drifted over lightly populated areas. "We were just damn lucky," the head of radiological safety for the test later affirmed.

The local press knew nothing about any of this. When the shock wave hit the trenches in the desert, Groves's first words were: "We must keep the whole thing quiet." (This would set the tone for all that followed in the broader nuclear sphere, for years, from national policy right down to the MGM movie.) Naturally, journalists were curious about reports of a mighty blast, so Groves released a statement announcing that an ammunition dump had exploded.

In the weeks that followed, ranchers discovered dozens of cattle that displayed odd burns or were losing hair. Oppenheimer ordered post-test health reports on humans held in the strictest secrecy. Even as scientists, and the White House, celebrated their success, the first radioactive cloud was drifting over America, depositing fallout along its eastward path. When the first reports on Trinity were published after the Hiroshima bombing they made no mention of this at all. Americans found out when word came not from the government but from the president of the Eastman Kodak Company in Rochester, New York, three months later. He wondered why some of his film was fogging—and rightly suspected radioactivity as the cause.

On February 15, Ayn Rand wrote to Esther Stone, the wife of one of her cousins, "I am working now on an unusual assignment—the screenplay for a picture about the Atom Bomb. It is the most difficult job I have ever attempted. And it keeps me chained to my desk as usual." She had completed fifty-five pages, or nearly half of the normal length, by the time she wrote to Stone.

The script followed almost precisely her lengthy treatment, with stiff dialogue and action added. John X now had a real name, John Nash, but his father remained an anti-science cynic ("weak and bitter") who tosses his son's books in the fire. Progress on splitting the atom develops slowly via the usual historical characters. Meanwhile, misguided Americans wish for other types of progress: a "radical" announces that "the property of the rich should be taken over—by force"; a businessman asserts that "workers should be attached to their jobs—by force"; an "old maid" feels "everybody should be compelled to feed the children of the poor—by force."

Yet even at its considerable length, Rand's script still barely reached 1939. We see a map of Europe with a Nazi flag stuck in Paris. A young assistant to physicist Otto Hahn runs down a dark Berlin street. Two Gestapo agents arrest him. He breaks away and runs back toward the house when they fire on him. Fatally wounded, he has time to slip a note to a young girl who emerges from the house, and whispers, "Get this out." The note says, *"Tell Dr. Einstein in America that the Nazis are working on atomic research."* Moving on, ever so slowly, Roosevelt approves the top-secret American bomb project. Groves earns his appointment but reacts "with indignation," pointing out that failure would ruin his reputation forever. (This was straight from her interview with him.) Meanwhile, Oppenheimer meets young John Nash—who in this iteration is no longer a mere bodyguard but a young scientist. Thanks to the inherent limits of Statism, and American spies, the German bomb project falters, then collapses.

And that's as far as she got. Wallis was racing Sam Marx, and Rand had called this movie potentially one of the most important creations in the history of humankind, yet for someone chained to a desk she wasn't exactly making rapid progress. In fact, she appeared to be weeks from finishing. Robert Smith, meanwhile, was completing for Wallis his alternative ending with the warning that it is "later than you think!" It might have been addressed not to the world but to Wallis himself in regard to beating his rival to an A-bomb epic.

While Hollywood scriptwriters of various stripes took pains to avoid portraying what happened to Japanese civilians at the far end of our bomb, *Time* magazine presented what it called the first detailed "eyewitness" account from Hiroshima. Of course, thousands of Japanese could have been interviewed about this months before, but this testimony came from a source no doubt more credible and appealing to Americans: Rev. John A. Siemes, S.J., a thirty-nine-year-old German-born priest and professor of modern philosophy at Tokyo's Catholic University.

On August 6, 1945, he was living just outside Hiroshima, at the Novitiate of the Society of Jesus. Siemes, lightly injured in the atomic blast that damaged the Novitiate, had first written his account for a Jesuit magazine.

> Perhaps a half-hour after the explosion, a procession of people begins to stream up the valley from the city. The crowd thickens continuously. A few come up the road to our house. We give them first aid and bring them into the chapel, which we have in the meantime cleaned and cleared of wreckage, and put them to rest on the straw mats. . . . A few display horrible wounds of the extremities and back. The small quantity of fat which we possessed during this time of war was soon used up in the care of the burns . . . our bandages and drugs are soon gone. We must be content with cleansing the wounds. More and more of the injured come to us.

Eventually the priests made their way to the heart of the city, where they found some of their battered colleagues and witnessed one hellish scene after another as the metropolis burned to the ground. On their return to the mission, all that's left was horror.

> On the Misasa Bridge, we meet Father Tappe and Father Luhmer, who have come to meet us from Nagatsuke. They had dug a family out of the ruins of their collapsed house some fifty meters off the road. The father of the family was already dead. They had dragged out two girls and placed them by the side of the road. Their mother was still trapped under some beams. . . . The rest of us turn back to fetch the Father Superior. Most of the ruins have now burned down. The darkness kindly hides the many forms that lie on the ground. Only occasionally in our quick progress do we hear calls for help.

As bonfires from survivors' burning bodies clouded the landscape, Siemes's report concluded on this note: "It seems logical to me that he who supports total war in principle cannot complain of war against civilians. The crux of the matter is whether total war in its present form is justifiable, even when it serves a just purpose. Does it not have material and spiritual evil as its consequences which far exceed whatever good that might result? When will our moralists give us a clear answer to this question?" Copies of the article—which was titled "A Report and a Question"—would soon turn up in files at both the White House and at MGM.

Rapidly losing any bargaining position, and in a desperate attempt to salvage something from this fiasco, Ed Tompkins drafted a three-page, single-spaced memo to Sam Marx, fully disclosing his keen "disappointment" with the lack of cooperation he'd found at the studio. He admitted that he knew little about the motion picture business but pointed out that Marx knew little about scientists.

Then he listed steps Marx *should* have taken that would have guaranteed more trust and approval from the suspicious-by-nature eggheads. He also lamented the choice of Wead, who had no conception of the scientists "as men." This was why he had warned Marx that the top scientists would not approve the script, a gesture that "aroused not your gratitude but your suspicion and distrust." Now this might force the scientists to hook up with Hal Wallis or search for another alternative. But if, on the other hand, MGM remained flexible, FAS might still "round up" those much-desired permissions before it was too late.

As he was about to send the memo, Marx invited him to meet in his office, where Tompkins delivered his message verbally. Marx said, fine, we don't want to deal with FAS any longer. "FAS needs us more than we need FAS," Marx intoned. He offered to let Tompkins stay on at the studio strictly as technical adviser, with no say in other aspects of the script. Tompkins accepted, to at least monitor the situation.

The next night he met with the writer Leo Rosten, at the suggestion of Margaret Mead and Gregory Bateson, at his sumptuous Beverly Hills home. Tompkins discovered that they saw "eye to eye" on all of the principals in this drama: McGuinness was smart but reactionary; Marx "stupid"; Wead a "good writer of Army-Navy stuff, no good for this picture." Rosten warned that MGM faced no legal problems in turning famous scientists into fictional characters. He added that it was a shame the scientists hadn't pitched *him* on their movie idea earlier, as he could have secured for them a payment of from $100,000 to $250,000 from another studio and probably set it up with his friend Frank Capra (a liberal compared to the MGM crowd). Tompkins asked Rosten to approach Hal Wallis with the idea of the scientists throwing in their lot with him.

The following day, Rosten reported that Wallis showed no interest in that idea. Rosten also discouraged seeking a third option. So Tompkins, the movie project's sparkplug, had finally surrendered. "There is no use trying to dig up a dead dog," he assured one friend. He would stay on at MGM just a bit longer. "A lot of stuff is going in over my objection," Tompkins complained, "but I hope the overall effect is not too bad."

As February drew to a close, a month that began with some naïve optimism about MGM's opus, the activist scientists scrambled to save even a small measure of influence over it. Tompkins finally fled Culver City in disgust and returned to Oak Ridge. To take his place as on-site technical adviser, MGM chose Groves's nominee, H.T. Wensel, a physicist and former information director at Oak Ridge. The Groves takeover of the movie project was now complete.

FAS named J.J. Nickson as their new chief conduit to MGM, working from Chicago, not on the MGM lot. A few days later Nickson wrote a memo strictly for his own files summarizing the current state of affairs. "The script is bad," he declared. The studio was not really interested in working with the scientists. Perhaps, he mused, he should visit MGM with the outspoken Szilard.

While the scientists foundered, their nemesis, Leslie Groves, finally got his hands on a script. His aide, Colonel W.A. Consodine—a former newspaperman in Newark, New Jersey, presently his eyes and ears on the MGM lot—also received a copy, and was first to respond on March 4 with a lengthy list of corrections. Consodine had his own agenda. Back in June 1945 he had been asked to weigh in on an early draft of Truman's planned announcement of the Hiroshima bombing and the $2 billion project that made it possible. "There is too little mention of the part played by the Army," he had advised. "I believe that industry has been given proper attention and that the scientists have been given absolutely too much attention." Consodine went on to handle public relations work for Groves and the release of official statements following the atomic attacks.

A sampling of his critique of the MGM script:

—Take out reference to South Africa possessing quantities of uranium, for security reasons.

—A hot-blooded scientist described only as "The Mad Pole" would too easily be identified by scientists as based on Dr. George Kistiakowsky—and might well provoke a lawsuit since he is made to look "somewhat ridiculous."

—Leslie Groves was never called "Les." His nickname is "Dick." And Groves's office was in the War Department Building not at the Pentagon. Plus: while he was rarely "formal," Groves never called women by their first names, always greeting "the girls" in the office with Miss or Mrs. So-and-So.

—There were a few whoppers in the scene where Groves and Stimson inform Truman about the existence of the A-bomb. Stimson would never walk to the White House from his Washington office at his advanced age, and Groves did not accompany him that day due to secrecy concerns. Groves never called Truman "Sir" but rather "Mr. President" throughout that meeting.

—Cut references in that same scene to the bomb project being the nation's "top secret," since it "gives a boost to the title of the Paramount film."

—Script has Stimson observing that "many" scientists had signed the Szilard letter asking Truman to hold off using the bomb. That should be changed to "some" or—even better—"a few."

—As he awaits word on the success of the Hiroshima mission, Groves rips off his necktie. "As a matter of fact,"
Consodine revealed, "he also rolled up his sleeves at the
same time. Never had I seen Groves take off his tie or roll
up his sleeves until that evening in his office."

————

Another man who could, if he wished, wreak havoc on *The Beginning or the End* by withholding his approval also received the script.
This was Joseph Breen, a prominent Catholic layman and longtime
czar (since taking over for originator Will Hays) of the Production
Code operation at the studio-backed Motion Picture Association
of America. The MPAA, housed on Hollywood Boulevard, had
since 1930 set the rather old-fashioned rules—which were accepted by the timid studios—for what was to be permitted in movies
in terms of sexual language and seductions, provocative or coarse
language, and, on occasion, political sentiments as well. If a movie
was denied full MPAA approval it risked getting banned in various
states and localities across the nation.

The code covered two separate areas of concern. The first section enumerated a set of general principles prohibiting any movie
from "lowering the moral standards of those who see it," especially
for those—such as women, children, and lower-class viewers—
with "susceptible" minds. Pictures must uphold the "correct standards of life" (whatever they were) and never promote the violation
of any law. The second section listed specific proclivities that could
not be depicted, such as any kind of sexual perversion, which covered everything from homosexuality to racial miscegenation. Sex
outside or before marriage could be hinted at only if portrayed in
a rather negative way and—certainly—not to arouse passion anywhere in a movie theater.

The effects of enforcement were wide-ranging. Any whiff of

sexual activity—most famously in *Casablanca*—must remain subtle in the extreme. It prevented for three years the distribution of Howard Hughes's *The Outlaw* not so much for its content but for its billboards and posters, which focused on actress Jane Russell's breasts seemingly attempting to bust out of her tight shirt. Political censorship was rare, but the threat was always there.

Now, after Breen's minions read the script for *The Beginning or the End*, the chief himself sent the results directly to Louis B. Mayer. While Breen was "happy to report" that the basic story fit the standards of the code, they had identified seven problems. One line of dialogue that was totally "unacceptable" quoted a blue-collar worker at one of the top-secret bomb sites saying to a colleague: "I got it confidential—we're making the front ends of horses. We ship 'em to Washington to hook on to the *other* end." Another that had to be axed: a character, informed about radiation hazards, jokes, "Is it true if you fool around with that stuff you don't like girls anymore?" Two exclamations of "Holy mother!" had to go. Also that mention of "latrines." Reference to a "Mexican" settlement in New Mexico near the Trinity site might be viewed as "derogatory" and "offensive" to Mexicans. Also don't portray those folks as "superstitious."

Breen closed with his customary warning that his final judgment would await a review of the final script. The following day he sent over another required cut, from some bantering between Jeff Nixon and his girlfriend, an "objectionable joke" apparently too risqué for Breen's taste. This was it:

**JEFF:** To think that you can cook too.

**GIRLFRIEND:** What does that "too" mean?

**JEFF:** In addition to . . . typing.

———

By that time, Groves had messengered to MGM's man in Washington, Carter Barron, his own numerous, handwritten comments and corrections, based on his reading of the 135-page script. Most dealt with technical or minor details; others indicated that the script had seriously departed from historical chronology or injected characters into events where they never appeared. "Bohr, Parsons, and Wyatt were not there," he wrote concerning one scene. "Neither was I."

Several times he asked for changes in light of what he considered the "hostile" view of the Army still rampant (to his eyes) in the national press. He even rewrote the dialogue in the scene where he was assigned to lead the bomb project. Among the other issues he flagged:

— The bomb itself must be portrayed only in "a hazy way" without a shape or proper size shown.
— At Trinity some of the witnesses did *not* lie on the ground, where the script placed them. Also they didn't wear special goggles but looked through smoked glass.
— Change Kokura to Nagasaki as the alternate target for the first bombing. The use of Kokura, he wrote mysteriously, "would lead to endless questioning and unnecessary trouble for me." (Most likely Groves's concern was tied to his personal approval of Kokura despite being reminded that it housed an Allied POW camp.)
— Delete any reference to the height that first bomb exploded. This was a "must."
— The timing of the blast wave over Hiroshima was all wrong. "The flash of light should precede the rocking of the plane by an appreciable time—in fact it was about a minute."

—The scenes showing Groves and others fretting and pacing as they awaited word on Hiroshima "couldn't be more fictional if you tried." It was far "more dramatic than what really went on."

—Delete reference to plutonium being ten times more powerful in a weapon than uranium. This would "cause too much difficulty." As for the death of Matt Cochran overnight from radiation exposure: "most remarkable scientifically."

MGM's Barron responded by thanking him, as W.A. Consodine discussed each item with Sam Marx and others. Consodine then sent a lengthy play-by-play to the general. His cover letter set the stage: "The first thought here seems to be that there must be a realization of two broad principles. The first principle is that MGM will spend about two millions of dollars on the completed picture. Being a commercial enterprise and not a non-profit educational institution such as Harvard, they are interested in getting a profit on their investment. Therefore, the picture must be made salable. The second principle is that it is necessary to fictionalize for dramatic purposes. That makes it necessary to add to facts and sometimes to telescope several incidents into one scene." Consodine, however, was happy to assure Groves that most of his complaints surely would be accepted, while adding in other cases that "the change you suggest can be made although the wording may not be exactly as you suggest." Perhaps most important: "Any implication tending to make the Army look foolish will be eliminated."

Groves had also charged that the British were given too much credit for development of the bomb. Consodine informed him of a purely commercial calculation: The movie would be shown to millions throughout the British Empire "and their shillings represent a considerable portion of the profits of MGM on the picture. It, therefore, becomes necessary to give the British a credit they do not deserve." Then there was Groves's complaint that his office had been falsely placed in the Pentagon (where some of the other characters were based) instead of at the War Department. The studio, Consodine explained, didn't believe "that an American movie audience can be jumped around from building to building without having to think." He also asked Groves to accept MGM sticking him in a key episode at Trinity where he did not actually appear "since you are the commanding general and it would look sort of funny not to have you in one of the most dramatic scenes." The immodest Groves surely wouldn't object to that.

In closing, Consodine advised, "Hollywood is very interesting." The studios had a habit of "rewriting everything ten or twelve times. However, they only work about an hour a day out here."

# 11

## "Top Secret" Is Out

Hal Wallis had been first to pursue an epic movie on the creation and use of the atomic bomb, and happily pushed forward when MGM made a race out of it. Nervous from the start about the point of view Ayn Rand would impose on the script, and then disappointed if not appalled by her submissions, he enlisted Robert Smith and even tried to hire Leo Rosten. Now, in mid-March 1946, he was ready to quit the contest, even though it would hand a humiliating public relations victory to Paramount's rival MGM.

Of course, this being the movie business, Wallis was paid off handsomely by L.B. Mayer for his troubles. MGM would cover all of his expenses on the abandoned project plus award him a share of any profits on its own movie. (Some in the industry wondered if counting on profits from this particular picture rather than taking a straight fee would prove to be wise.) Al Cohn, the inspiration for the project the previous autumn, got a nice cut as well. Wallis visited MGM to meet with its creative team, where he brashly critiqued their script, which they must have really loved. Paramount sent over, as part of the deal, all of the work Wallis had secured so far on his film, including every sketch and partial screenplay completed by Ayn Rand.

*Variety* broke the news, calling the handover at this advanced date "unprecedented," while noting that this cooperation mirrored the United States getting its allies engaged in the Manhattan

Project. *The New York Times* carried its report under the headline "Hollywood Atom Race Ends," noting that instead of a "contest" MGM now had "a clear field." Wallis had simply concluded that "duplication would not make for satisfactory box office results." Some of the scientists, however, heard there was another reason: Wallis learned that MGM was having trouble wrangling permissions for portrayals, knew he faced the same issue, didn't have the heart or courage to face that, and decided to cash in his chips. In any event, gossip columnist Louella Parsons declared she was "happy to say our industry is adult enough not to war with itself."

MGM now was set to start shooting in six weeks and would probably borrow some of the scenes in the Wallis script, the *Times* reported. Camera crews for the studio were already shooting B-roll footage at far-flung Manhattan Project sites. Its special effects team was building a "miniature Hiroshima" and experimenting with process photography to "provide a cinematic effect of cataclysmic horror and destruction," according to the article. Sam Marx promised that it would be "more terrifying than anything ever before recorded on the screen—even greater than the earthquake scenes in *San Francisco*."

When Ayn Rand got the word on the MGM-Wallis deal, she took it badly. There was all that wasted time and work, and now strangers at MGM would review her far-from-polished script. She seemed especially angry about the way she found out about it—in a visit (she had no phone) from a Wallis aide, not even from "the Boss" himself. Rand would likely be assigned to another film, but she was anxious to get started on her next novel (which would become *Atlas Shrugged*). A few days later, on March 19, she wrote a lengthy letter addressed, "Dear Boss." It was in the form of a ten-point ultimatum outlining the conditions under which she would continue to toil for Wallis. She labeled it "not a legal agreement, but a moral one." She demanded personal conferences with him (not staffers) to discuss stories and revisions; no weekly deadlines; a heads-up on any major changes in her work; and a chance to perform a last-minute final polish on any script. And after the shocking news of the past week: "Whenever you have something important to tell me (like last Saturday)—please tell me yourself, not through a third person."

At least one other player expressed some rancor in the aftermath of the MGM-Wallis deal. Al Cohn took issue with a column by gossip queen Hedda Hopper that omitted his role in setting up the Wallis project. He wrote to inform her that his "first impulse" was to call her editors and demand that she be fired. Then he calmed down and decided that he didn't want to send her to a "bread line" with "other unfortunates" and besides, "we old-timers must stick together." So he just wanted to ensure she didn't make the same mistake again. The whole idea of the atom bomb picture "originated with me," he insisted, then outlined the fateful lunch with Oppenheimer, Lawrence, and Magnuson the previous year.

He also revealed what he viewed as another reason for the collapse of that project: "the unsympathetic attitude of Paramount" when it seemed that Wallis's other commitments might delay production.

One of the most significant critiques of the atomic bombings arrived in March with the report from a distinguished panel of theologians (including Reinhold Niebuhr), philosophers, and church historians assembled by the leading Protestant organization, the Federal Council of Churches. The panel was divided on whether the use of atomic weapons could *ever* be justified but left no room for confusion on what had already transpired: "We would begin with an act of contrition. As American Christians, we are deeply penitent for the irresponsible use already made of the atomic bomb. We are

agreed that, whatever one's judgment of the ethics of war in principle, the surprise bombings of Hiroshima and Nagasaki are morally
indefensible." Why? It involved "the indiscriminate slaughter of
non-combatants" in a notably "ghastly form." The first bomb was
dropped without warning and the second before Tokyo had any
reasonable chance to respond to the first. Japan was in a "hopeless"
condition already. "We have sinned grievously against the laws of
God and the people of Japan," the commission concluded. The
bombing of other Japanese cities had taken a massive death toll,
but this was something new.

Shortly after this, the influential monsignor at Catholic University, Fulton J. Sheen, called the use of the atomic bomb
against Hiroshima contrary to moral law, adding that it invited
"retaliation" in some future form. The bomb had erased the necessary distinction, even in war, "between civilians and the military."
Sheen denounced the argument that the use of such an immoral
weapon could be justified to "save lives" in war, going so far as to
compare this to what Hitler claimed after bombing cities in the
Netherlands. "Once the primary consideration is the winning of
a war" by any method, he concluded, "then all men are reduced to
vermin and all appeals to justice are voided."

No matter the impact of the scientists' warnings and the religious and moral protests, nothing would stop the United States
from beginning what was envisioned as a long series of nuclear
testing in the Pacific. In addition, while many Americans retained
at least some measure of appreciation for the Soviet Union as
crucial allies against the Nazis, that was swiftly eroding. A key
moment, though not universally recognized at the time, came
when Winston Churchill on a visit to Missouri delivered a speech
depicting a new "Iron Curtain"—an expression rarely used before
this. "From Stettin in the Baltic to Trieste in the Adriatic, an Iron
Curtain has descended across the Continent," Churchill asserted.

"Behind that line lie all the capitals of the ancient states of Central and Eastern Europe."

Just days earlier, George Kennan, deputy chief of the U.S. mission in Moscow, had sent a lengthy missive to Secretary of State James Byrnes outlining a get-tough, or "containment," policy toward the Soviets in Europe, which would prove to have enormous influence. Kennan believed that a new, powerful federation of Western European states, tightly aligned with the United States, needed to be organized to counter the Soviets and their hold on Eastern Europe.

As the competing Wallis opus collapsed, Frank Wead completed work on a third version of the MGM script, which accommodated many of the corrections sought by Groves and W.A. Consodine. Oppenheimer was still "Whittier," but Fermi had a new name, more Italian than "Ramsey," to at least fit his accent: "Lucci." When Matt Cochran questions atomic research becoming a munitions project, Lucci now asks him: "Which end of the bomb do *you* want to be on?" As his colleagues celebrate the successful chain reaction, Matt mutters, "May God forgive us." In the same scene three scientists announce they are quitting on principle, but this is softened by the fact that they are pacifist Quakers, so what would one expect? Also: this exit was pure fiction.

More critical was an addition reflecting the growing effort to justify the use of the bomb against Japan (as criticism of that action grew in the real world). When Groves informs Truman that the bomb should be ready by August 1945, the new president tells him that the Germans may not last that long in the war. Groves replies, "Japan will," and adds: "And they may meet our ships and troops with atomic weapons." In fact, no one in the military leadership believed this, as they knew Japan's nuclear bomb program had faltered badly. Nevertheless, Groves would insist in the new script, after citing the number of Americans expected to perish in any invasion, "If the Japs do have atomic bombs it'll be much higher."

Another revealing change: What was once merely "thin flak" greeting the U.S. planes approaching their target in Hiroshima (already a fabrication) had become heavy flak—and joined by the worrying appearance of eight mythical Japanese fighter planes tracking them. The Americans must be seen as amazingly brave, not as airborne assassins.

Now the closing scene where Jeff delivers Matt's deathbed, pro-nuclear, letter to his wife is set at . . . the Lincoln Memorial, the country's iconic symbol of decency. And in a parenthetical note on the script, Frank Wead asked Sam Marx if adding a ghostly image of the deceased Matt sitting next to his wife and speaking the final words of his letter directly to her would be a nice touch. At least he wasn't suggesting having Abe Lincoln say them.

Portraying, or even acknowledging, the Nagasaki tragedy posed a special problem for the filmmakers. Many Americans, and some commentators, who thoroughly supported use of the bomb against Hiroshima, wrestled with the moral issues raised by the second bombing.

Whenever the attacks on Japan were mentioned, it was likely that one word, *Hiroshima*, would be used as shorthand for the two separate catastrophes. This meant that Nagasaki quickly sank almost into oblivion. Yes, the death toll caused by the off-target bomb was less than two-thirds of the numbers in Hiroshima; on the other hand, that still meant at least 80,000 dead (overwhelmingly women and children), and the justifications for using the second bomb were also much weaker. "Dropping the bomb on Hiroshima was a mistake," Samuel I. Allison, one of Szilard's colleagues at the Met Lab in Chicago, had declared. "Dropping the bomb on Nagasaki was an atrocity."

A lovely city dotted with palms largely built on terraces surrounding a deep harbor—the San Francisco of Japan—Nagasaki had a rich, bloody history as the country's gateway to the west. The Portuguese and Dutch settled here in the 1500s. St. Francis Xavier established the first Catholic churches in the region in 1549. Urakami, a suburb of Nagasaki, became the Catholic center. Thomas Glover, an early English trader, supplied the rifles that helped defeat the Tokugawa shogunate in the nineteenth century. In the Puccini opera, Madame Butterfly, standing on the veranda of Glover's home overlooking the harbor, sings, "One fine day, we'll see a thread of smoke arising." If she could have looked north from the Glover mansion on August 9, 1945, she would have seen, two miles in the distance, a thread of smoke—with an ominous mushroom cap.

By 1945, Nagasaki had become an important site for Mitsubishi's industrial war effort, but the blockade of Japan was hindering production. Few Japanese soldiers were stationed here—far less than in Hiroshima—and only about 250 of them would perish in the atomic bombing. It was still the Christian center in Japan, with more than 10,000 Catholics among its 250,000 residents. Most of them lived in the Urakami district, the poor part of town, where a magnificent cathedral seating six thousand had been built. At 11:02 a.m. on August 9, the plutonium bomb known as "Fat Man" hit with the force of twenty-two kilotons, far beyond the uranium bomb's blast in Hiroshima. It was detonated almost directly over Urakami, more than a mile off target. The massive cathedral there was nearly leveled, killing dozens of worshippers awaiting confession. Concrete roads melted. While Urakami suffered, the rest of the city caught a break. The bomb's blast boomed up the valley but didn't reach the congested harbor or scale the high ridge to the Nakashima valley.

If the bomb had exploded as planned, directly over the center of the city, the death toll in Nagasaki would have made Hiroshima, in at least one important sense, the Second City. Nothing would have escaped, perhaps not even the most untroubled conscience half a world away.

One had to wonder about the overwhelming impulse to almost immediately use a second bomb even more powerful than the first. Criticism of the attack on Nagasaki centered on why Truman did not step in after the success of the first to allow Japan a few more days to contemplate surrender before targeting another city for extinction. In addition, the United States knew that its ally, the Soviet Union, would join the war within days, as previously agreed, and that the entrance of Japan's most hated enemy as much as the Hiroshima bomb would likely speed the surrender. (Indeed, Truman had written in his diary at Potsdam, after he secured Stalin's promise to attack Japan in August, that this meant "Fini Japs" even without use of the A-bomb.) If that happened, however, it might lead to a wider Soviet claim on former Japanese conquests in Asia. So there was much to gain by getting the war over before the Russians advanced. In that sense, the Nagasaki bomb was not the last shot of World War II but the first blow of the Cold War.

Whether Stalin was the main audience or not, there was no presidential directive specifically related to dropping the second bomb. The atomic weapons in the U.S. arsenal, according to the official July 2 order, were to be used "as soon as made ready," and the second bomb was operational within three days of Hiroshima. Nagasaki was thus the first and only victim of automated atomic warfare. That's one reason Telford Taylor, chief prosecutor at the Nuremberg trials, would later assert that while the "rights and wrong of Hiroshima are debatable" he had "never heard a plausible justification of Nagasaki." The tragedy might have been prevented if Truman and his aides had kept closer watch on the atomic assembly line. They simply did not care or, to be charitable, did not take care. There was little compelling evidence that the second bomb boosted the already-surging Japanese desire to surrender after Hiroshima and the Russians entering the war.

In any case, after Nagasaki, Truman quickly ordered that no further bombs be used without his express permission—one bomb, one city, and eighty thousand or so civilian deaths too late. When they learned of the Hiroshima attack, the scientists at Los Alamos generally expressed satisfaction that their work had paid off. But many of them took Nagasaki quite badly. Some would later use the words "sick" or "nausea" to describe their reaction.

Still, would any of this complexity—or anything at all attached to Nagasaki—make it as far as the final script for the Hollywood reckoning?

By early April, work on special atomic effects on the MGM lot was well under way. The conjurer in charge, A. Arnold "Buddy" Gillespie, who had worked cinematic miracles for *The Wizard of Oz* and *Thirty Seconds over Tokyo*, had already submitted two records of money expended. One for $26,518 covered "preliminary experiments in duplicating explosions" via two methods: "power and gas explosions in the air" and "liquid explosions in distilled water." Trying another method, $5,209 was spent for setting up shots for "explosion and plume . . . Hiroshima" in a glass tank.

Now it was finally time to fully cast the movie. For whatever reason, stars of the magnitude of Clark Gable and Spencer Tracy were no longer in the picture. Scientists had heard that Tracy, originally pegged for the Groves part, had insisted on playing the ethical scientist instead, but this may have been pure rumor (and he was too old for the role anyway). In any event, the studio bosses were now, to Sam Marx's chagrin, only considering so-called secondary actors and actresses.

Why? The studio should have been riding high on this project after the Wallis desertion. Perhaps they feared that special effects costs would climb out of control, leaving less for a high-priced cast. Or maybe they firmly believed that a glamorous star would capsize, or seem tasteless, in a docu-drama that focused on a weapon that had killed tens of thousands of civilians. Gable had the moustache and "frankly, I don't give a damn" bearing to portray Groves, but probably radiated too much charisma. Or the studio was simply finding it hard to cast certain key roles when they still didn't know if they would be true-life portrayals or, in the end, mainly fictional—Oppenheimer or "Whittier"?

In any event, they had chosen Brian Donlevy to embody the character increasingly likely to lead the ensemble. He looked nothing like General Groves—far thinner, more handsome, and with darker hair—but that had hardly stopped Hollywood before. (In fact, they ran this hire past Groves himself and, no surprise, he approved.) Well, Donlevy, at least, did have the requisite moustache. A twenty-year veteran of the screen, he usually toiled in lead roles in B-movies, but had also landed supporting parts with famous directors in *The Great McGinty*, *Union Pacific*, *Jesse James*, *The Miracle of Morgan's Creek*, and *Destry Rides Again*. He often played unsavory characters, causing some of the scientists to take private delight when they learned he'd won the role of Groves—perfect typecasting, they believed. For what it was worth, he had supported Dewey for president over Roosevelt in 1944.

Donlevy had earned an Oscar nomination for *Beau Geste*, a 1939 film, but it was hard to say where he ranked as a box office attraction in 1946. The same could be said for an actor chosen for a role that did not require permission from an actual person. The cocky fictional Groves aide Colonel Jeff Nixon would be played by Robert Walker, a matinee idol type, although not of the first rank.

A rebellious teen, which informed his later roles, Walker had turned to acting to channel some of that aggression. He married another up-and-comer, Jennifer Jones, and both were signed to MGM by the fabled David O. Selznick, with whom she began an affair. (Walker was devastated and turned to the bottle.) He earned supporting roles in the war dramas *Bataan* and *Thirty Seconds over Tokyo* and with Greer Garson in *Madame Curie*. Then his film with Judy Garland, *The Clock*, failed to live up to box office expectations, despite a groundswell of sympathy for Walker among reporters and movie fans because of his very public marital scandal. When he accepted the *Beginning or the End* role he was still only twenty-seven years old.

A third key role was more problematic. At the moment, Robert Oppenheimer had given little indication that he would ever sign away his life rights to MGM, although Sam Marx remained optimistic. So he was still "Whittier" in the script, but this could change in a flash if the scientist gave any nod of approval.

Given this uncertainty, the studio went with an actor who looked and sounded little like Oppie. This was Hume Cronyn, who was far shorter and thicker than the tall, rail-thin physicist, and with longer and lighter hair; he was slightly jug-eared, to boot. He was also Canadian and far from Jewish. His father was a member of the Canadian parliament, his mother an heiress to the Labatt brewing fortune. After emerging on the Broadway stage he secured his first film role in 1943, and the following year appeared in the Hitchcock classic *Lifeboat*. He nabbed an Academy Award supporting actor nomination for another Hitchcock film, *Shadow of a Doubt*, in which he appeared with his wife, Jessica Tandy. Then he joined Tandy again in *The Green Years*—playing her *father* this time.

Cronyn surely had the acting chops and intelligence (if not the gaunt profile) for the *Beginning or the End* role, be it Whittier or Oppenheimer, but he was hardly a major star. Sam Marx much preferred that Cronyn portray the genuine article, and now set out to make that happen.

# 12

## Dinner with the Oppenheimers

Back in January, Sam Marx had invited Robert Oppenheimer to meet him at the studio (as General Groves would do), and even bring his wife. It was a short jaunt from his new home in Pasadena, although he was often still in Berkeley. Oppie had never seized that opportunity, even as various scientists with knowledge of MGM's thinking were warning of the dangers ahead for *The Beginning or the End* and the wisdom of holding off any approval at least until he read the script.

Now he would have that chance. On April 18, Marx sent him a copy of the screenplay with the hope he would at least "glance through it" before they met three days hence in Berkeley. That Saturday he left the Palace Hotel in San Francisco bearing gifts for Kitty Oppenheimer: an Easter lily and three pairs of nylon stockings, which her husband had hinted she would very much enjoy. Marx hoped this would be all he would ever have to pay for Oppenheimer's signature on a release. (Later he would ask holdout scientists if they would accept what Oppie asked for signing, and when they said yes, he would announce their prize: "Nylons.")

Marx soon arrived at Oppenheimer's rambling one-story villa, built in 1925 with a red-tiled roof high up on Eagle Hill Road with an expansive view of three canyons, the bay, and sunsets over the Golden Gate. The Oppenheimers had purchased it in 1941. It had whitewashed walls and a living room with a huge stone fireplace, a beamed ceiling, redwood flooring, and bookcases lining the walls.

Through French doors one could stroll into an attractive garden. Guest quarters were found over the garage.

During dinner, Oppenheimer spoke frankly about the script, in his usual manner. In a letter to J.J. Nickson he would recount much of this discussion. It likely went something like this:

Oppenheimer: "Some of the themes in the movie are sound, but most of the supposedly real characters like Bohr and Fermi and myself are stiff and idiotic. When Fermi hears of fission he says *my what a thrill* and my most characteristic phrase is *gentlemen, gentlemen, let us be calm.*"

Marx: "I understand."

Oppenheimer: "Most of the trouble rests in ignorance and bad writing, rather than in anything malign."

Marx: "That may be true, but look at these newly signed agreements by Fermi and others."

Oppenheimer: "Well, what kind of agreement can you and I make? For example, how about hiring as technical adviser my former aide and Los Alamos historian David Hawkins? Also, I want to be portrayed as a friend of that ethical scientist, what's his name, Matt Cochran."

Marx: "Okay on all that. In addition, we will correct all of the factual errors you mentioned and take seriously all of your other gripes and proposed additions."

Oppenheimer: "If all that is done, and you show me the next version of the script, I will likely sign a release. But I don't want a fee—just send any proceeds to FAS or set up science fellowships for students."

Marx: "Let's shake on it."

Oppenheimer would tell Nickson that he found his visitor from Hollywood "sympathetic." Marx seemed "honestly eager to get the script improved," but even after the revisions, Oppie predicted, "It won't be very good." At least in the current story, he added, the scientists seemed to be treated as "ordinary decent guys, that they worried like hell about the bomb, that it presents a major issue of good and evil to the people of the world." He concluded: "I hope I did right. I think the movie is a lot better for my intercession, but it is not a beautiful movie, or a wise and deep one. I think it did not lie in my power to make it so."

Oppenheimer seemed uncommonly insecure, however. "Let me hear from you," he asked Nickson, "particularly if you think I did wrong or want me to try again." He had other things to worry about as well. The FBI had started tapping the phone in his Berkeley home and recording the conversations, and shadowing him on his many travels to the East. In obtaining approval for the phone tap, J. Edgar Hoover had cited the need to determine "the extent of his contact with Soviet agents, and for the additional purpose of identifying other espionage agents."

When Sam Marx returned to Hollywood he immediately began revising the script. Perhaps most critically, in a burst of confidence, he ordered that "Whittier" be disappeared, replaced by the real Oppenheimer. And while the studio had decided on Hume Cronyn to play him, that might change. Marx doubted they could find a better actor, but they could certainly secure a more impressive movie "name." Kitty Oppenheimer had voiced some opinions on that over dinner, and Marx had asked if she wanted "to volunteer more ideas."

Fawning over his new friend, Marx assured him in a letter that he had just spent two full days "rewriting" the script (a savvy exaggeration), and had impressed on writer Wead and director Taurog "that the character of J. Robert Oppenheimer must be an extremely pleasant one with a love of mankind, humility and a pretty fair knack of cooking." Also he passed along to them Oppie's view that in the script the fictitious characters came to life but "the living characters failed to breathe." Most critically—and sure to provoke blowback from certain military figures—Marx also revealed: "We have changed all the lines at the New Mexico test so that General Groves is merely a guest and you give all the orders." And in Matt Cochran's movie-ending letter to his wife from the great beyond "we have added your thought and hope that men will learn to live together."

Marx, however, could not resist chiding the physicist for his tardy involvement in the production. Their meeting in Berkeley "occurred too late," he asserted. Marx was "pretty limp when it was all over. . . . We could all have been spared some indignation if we had consulted earlier." He put the blame partly on Oppenheimer, noting that he knew the previous December that a script was being prepared but had asked Marx to not bother him. "Unfortunately," Sam admitted, "I could have gotten to the truth if I had bothered you more." If that had happened, "your nerves and mine and Mrs. Oppenheimer's might have been spared something if we had held a meeting at an earlier date."

He closed: "Everyone now is most enthused about the changes I brought back from Berkeley. We are as eager for the truth as you are. . . . I would rather see you pleased with this picture than anyone else who has been concerned with the making of the atom bomb." Marx may well have been sincere about that, but it never hurt anyone to appeal to Oppie's vanity. Still, he knew it was Groves he'd have to "please" in the end.

One reason (though perhaps not the main one) MGM continued to bow to military control of its movie narrative was that it needed the Army's cooperation, and hardware, in shooting key on-location sequences away from the Culver City lot. How extensive that might be was captured in a four-page, single-spaced memo of requests from the studio submitted on April 18, covering numerous scenes.

First off, they had selected as the stand-in for Tinian the Army's auxiliary airfield at Muroc Dry Lake in California, where very little was then transpiring. The commander there already had approved its use. For the filming, scheduled to start in mid-May and run for a full week, the studio would require:

— Three fully operational B-29s, along with military crew, for the simulated flight to Hiroshima, plus four of those bombers to be parked at the airstrip to suggest wartime footing (they were already at Muroc and could be towed into place when needed). The mission to Hiroshima from the Marianas over the Pacific could be filmed off the Southern California coast.
— An operational C-54 transport to be shown carrying the bomber crews to the base, plus three C-47s in the background.
— Another B-29 to be used by the studio for its own camera operators.
— Miscellaneous vehicles: seven jeeps, a fire truck, two gasoline trucks, two staff cars, two ambulances, six bomb carriages, plus personnel to operate them, just to give the impression of "a busy tactical airfield."

The memo also covered requests for the Trinity test site scenes, to be filmed at the studio and in the desert near Muroc. An ordnance officer at Camp Cooke in California had offered to provide two tanks ("no longer needed" there) and ship them to the studio, where shop personnel would alter their appearance to match the vehicles at Trinity. Finally, for shooting at the studio, they needed "complete flying clothing for forty actors and extras representing B-29 crewmen," including parachutes. MGM also required a complete fuselage of another B-29, perhaps one already sent to "salvage," for the critical interior shots of the *Enola Gay*. The studio offered to pay for this and retain it permanently (it might come in handy for movie productions still to come). They would need this as soon as possible, as the technicians required a few weeks to ready it for filming.

Approval for all this came within days from the War Department. Their only caveat was that an Army security officer be present for all the shooting at Muroc and that nothing "classified" could be filmed (with certain aircraft instrument panels a concern). Lieutenant Colonel Gordon Swarthout, chief of the military's Pictorial Branch, emphasized that signing off on this request and clearing security during the filming "does not imply War Department endorsement of factual accuracy or opinion."

While Hollywood pushed forward its cinematic treatment, the subject appeared too unsettled and complex for American novelists. There were no reports of any prominent fiction writer even attempting to take a crack at it. What happened to Hiroshima and Nagasaki may have been impossible to imagine, let alone render. One recalls Whitman's comment on the Civil War: "The real war will never get in the books."

A writer best known for his nonfiction did take up the challenge, but even he had to do it in a shorter, satirical form. James Agee, only thirty-five years old but already fearing he was a has-been, had raised questions about the creation and use of the bomb in the pages of his main outlet, *Time* magazine, where he made his name as a film critic and all-purpose scribe. (His book with photographer Walker Evans, *Let Us Now Praise Famous Men*, had flopped.) As an American, Agee felt personally implicated in the killing of thousands of civilians. He considered development of the bomb "the worst thing that's ever happened—so far" and Hiroshima "the only thing much worth writing or thinking about."

His response in fiction was a bizarre fantasy called "Dedication Day." He labeled it a kind of "rough sketch" for a motion picture (he had long wanted to break into movies), but first he submitted it as a short story to *Politics* magazine, edited by a prominent critic of the decision to drop the bomb, Dwight Macdonald.

It depicted a postwar celebration of the bomb featuring a great arch, made of fused uranium, designed by Frank Lloyd Wright. President Truman and General Groves attend, and the ceremony is broadcast via the first national television hookup. But during this event a bugler, assigned to blow "Reveille," instead plays "Taps." It seems that one of the scientists who worked on the bomb has gone "a little queer in the head." He insists on joining a group of badly injured survivors of "the experiments of Hiroshima and Nagasaki" who had been "forgiven" by the Americans. They were now enlisted in a must-work project connected to the memorial. Attendees could view the scientist in agony, tearing at his hair as he toiled alongside the survivors and mockingly flashed the "V" for "victory" sign to the tourists. Later, out of sight, the scientist commits suicide, with a note pinned to his coat calling this an ethical "sacrifice." This, of course, somewhat marred the "dignity, charm and decorum" of the celebratory event.

The scientist is then buried with full honors at the Trinity test site, where speakers warn that this is what happens to those who make "the grievous error of exaggerated scrupulousness." Clergymen and philosophers embark on a campaign of "controlled ridicule." Along the way to this conclusion, Agee skewered every facet of American life: government, business, advertising, religion, science, psychiatry, modern art, and public opinion. Any attempt to atone for Hiroshima will be viewed as evidence of madness, he warned.

Agee hardly stopped there, however. He remained obsessed with the subject, making plans to write a nonfiction book on the effects of the bomb. He even aimed to collaborate with Charles Chaplin— Agee was one of the few U.S. critics to champion his current film,

*Monsieur Verdoux*—on a movie project titled *The Tramp's New World*. It would inject the star's most famous character into a post–nuclear holocaust era. He wanted the Little Tramp to roam the world asking scientists to abandon their "genius with gadgetry" and all of their lethal projects, to no avail, leaving him in the end utterly alone. Agee must have felt much akin to Chaplin in this scenario.

While esteemed poets and writers grappled to find a way to explore this subject, pop songwriters faced fewer obstacles, as humor (black or silly) could more easily be employed. Slim Gaillard concocted an "Atomic Cocktail": "That's the drink that you don't pour/When you take one sip you won't need anymore." The well-known Golden Gate Quartet gospel group recorded "Atom and Evil," claiming, "If you don't break up that romance soon/We'll all fall down and go boom, boom, boom!"

A few days after meeting the Oppenheimers, Sam Marx lived up to part of his bargain by offering young David Hawkins the consulting position at MGM. Hawkins, while working toward his PhD in philosophy, had become friends with Oppenheimer in the late 1930s at Berkeley, where the pair enjoyed discussing, among other things, Hindu philosophy. Like many others there, he joined the Communist Party. Oppie nevertheless recruited his fellow polymath for Los Alamos, where he would serve as his aide and military-civilian go-between. Hawkins helped pick Alamogordo as the site for the Trinity test and wrote the official (classified) history of the Manhattan Project. He also worked with Edward Teller's "Super" group probing the possibilities for developing a hydrogen bomb. Hawkins harbored mixed views about Hiroshima but hated that the bomb was used again three days later. That fall he joined the Federation of Atomic Scientists.

Now Hawkins asked Oppenheimer if he should accept the temporary position in Hollywood. Would this be "useful"? Oppie advised through an aide, yes, but he should please know that the script "is not bad generally but that 'real' characters are stilted, lifeless" and "without purpose or insight." Soon Hawkins with his wife Frances (who had taught nursery school at Los Alamos) and infant daughter would head west, where they moved into an MGM guesthouse in Beverly Hills. There they watched in amusement one night when slot machines were unloaded from a truck and carted off for a movie director's fancy party on the property. It was a long way from Los Alamos in more ways than one.

The FBI knew about his new role because of its phone tap on Oppenheimer, and now started watching Hawkins and his wife, citing his Communist Party past. They listened in when he'd chat about the MGM movie with Kitty Oppenheimer; on one occasion Hawkins claimed the film was "going along pretty well."

Despite his musings about hiring a big-name actor to play Oppenheimer, Sam Marx decided to stick with Hume Cronyn, who had been studying newsreel footage of his subject and other material for many days. Cronyn, writing from his home on North Rockingham Avenue in the Brentwood section of Los Angeles, told Oppie that he wished to meet him but, given the physicist's busy schedule, this missive probably would have to suffice.

In his two-page letter, Cronyn proved to be brutally honest about his task and the movie itself. He recognized that Oppie must be apprehensive about being portrayed, and possibly "misrepresented," on the screen, and in truth, "I have little talent for either mimicry or impersonation." In addition, "I am hardly your double." Even more challenging, "to be blunt about it, the roles of the various scientists appearing in the story are not good acting parts." No matter how well he and others perform they are "bound to disappoint you and the others similarly involved." Cronyn would do his best, however, to offer a credible "impression" of Oppenheimer's finest qualities. Larding it on a bit thick, he added, "I gather that simplicity, warmth and complete lack of affectation are essential to your character."

But, oh, that script! Cronyn was pleased that Oppie had made so many suggestions about it, which "cannot help but be an improvement." He had been "wondering how in God's name" he was going to keep saying "gentlemen, gentlemen" and some of the other original Oppenheimer lines. "I could go on and talk about the script at some length," he wrote, "but perhaps it would be better if I didn't!" In fact, he added, it might be best if he attached a postscript to this letter along the lines of "The sentiments expressed herein are those of the writer alone and are not to be construed as the opinion of his employers." Cronyn closed by promising to contact David Hawkins for more insight on Oppenheimer's manner and personality. Knowing the physicist was busy, the actor expected no reply to the letter. He just meant to say that in playing this role "I will endeavor to do everything possible to give an honest impression of your character to the public and no offense to you."

Two weeks later, near the end of a lengthy phone conversation—taped as usual by the FBI—Kitty Oppenheimer informed her husband, who was in the east, that he had received a letter from a "Hugh Cronin" (as the name was recorded in the transcript), "explaining why he would like to be you." Oppie asked: "Bill Cronin?" Kitty: "Hugh Cronin—that bloke that belongs to MGM."

"Well, I'll tell you what I did on this," Oppenheimer replied. "This very ugly creature, [Colonel W.A.] Consodine, called me and said that Marx had said it was all right and would I sign the release, and I said sure. I got the release and I signed it with a paragraph written in saying that all of this is subject to my receipt of a statement from Mr. Sam Marx that he believes the changes that have been made are satisfactory." Possibly to reassure his wife, he pointed out that their friend David Hawkins was still at the studio.

Kitty: "Oh."

Robert: "Well, I didn't think there was anything else to do. I don't want anything from them and if I can work on his conscience, that is the best angle I have. It just isn't worth anything otherwise, darling."

At this juncture, the call faded in and out. "The FBI must have just hung up," Robert quipped. The transcript recorded Kitty's response as: *Giggles*. Then Robert concluded: "The only thing we can do there is to try to persuade them to do a decent job."

After returning home and reading the Cronyn letter (to which he did not, indeed, reply), Oppenheimer informed J.J. Nickson that the note was "long and very polite." Proving that the actor was no household name, Oppie—like the FBI—misspelled his name as "Cronin."

Donna Reed with former teacher Dr. Edward Tompkins on a visit
to MGM, with crucial letter he sent to her a few months earlier.
*Bettmann/Getty Images*

First movie to include reference
to atomic bomb after Hiroshima.
*Michael Barson Archives*

Leslie Groves with J. Robert Oppenheimer at Los Alamos, August 1945. *Marie Hansen/LIFE Picture Collection via Getty Images*

Producer Sam Marx and director Norman Taurog brush up on some atomic research. *Photofest*

Ayn Rand in New York, 1940s. *Photofest*

Posed publicity shot of unidentified actress checked by MGM cop entering sound stage for movie. *Photofest*

MGM publicity shot from the set with "Censored" hiding "bomb" prop. *Photofest*

Full-page ad for the March of Time's "Atomic Power" film short, August 1946, with Einstein and Szilard at upper left. *Michael Barson Archives*

Truman explains decision, from re-take ordered by the White House. *Author's collection*

From the trailer for *The Beginning or the End. Author's collection*

Cover of movie magazine with story inside by Bob Considine. *Author's collection*

"We've got a job on our hands... the biggest job in the world!"

THE BEGINNING
OR THE END
BRIAN DONLEVY · ROBERT WALKER

"Give her this! I've written her a lot of things that were in my heart...
and that I never told her!"

THE BEGINNING
OR THE END
BRIAN DONLEVY · ROBERT WALKER

Two "lobby cards" (originals were colorized) to be posted at theaters for
release of *The Beginning or the End*: top with Brian Denehy and Audrey
Totter; bottom, an irradiated Tom Drake gives Robert Walker "farewell
letter" for his wife. *Michael Barson Archives*

Publicity photo featuring Tom Drake and Beverly Tyler. *Photofest*

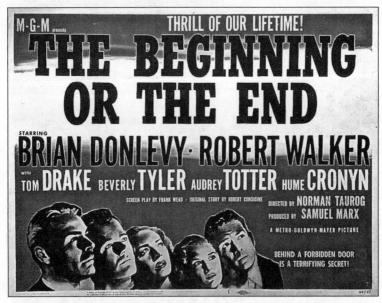

Poster for film. *Michael Barson Archive*

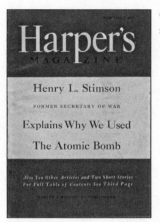

Cover for issue boosting the influential article by Henry L. Stimson, February 1947. *Author's collection*

Ads prepared for newspapers and magazines. *Michael Barson Archives*

# 13

## Those Japanese A-Bombs

Robert Oppenheimer and Leslie Groves weren't the only critical figures in the atomic bomb regime to finally receive an MGM script this month. They had only helped create the new weapon; President Truman had ordered its use, twice, against Japanese cities. The three men, therefore, shared responsibility for what had happened, and what might happen next, in the "atomic age." Only one of them appeared to harbor any regrets about his role.

Truman, in fact, seemed more distant from the bomb than remorseful. At a Cabinet meeting he admitted he did not know how many atomic weapons were in the U.S. arsenal and did not really care to know, earning a lecture from his secretary of commerce, Henry Wallace. He also revealed to Wallace that he was worried that atomic energy would one day reduce the number of hours in an average workweek, causing laborers to "get into mischief." By now, Truman's rising popularity following the Japanese surrender had faded in the face of crippling labor strikes and threats of same, particularly involving the railroads. Common wisecracks around D.C. and in the press asserted "To err is Truman" and "I'm just mild about Harry." Some wags asked, "What would *Truman* do if he were alive?" Many in the old New Deal coalition found him too moderate, while the conservative wing of his party considered him too liberal.

Now, in any case, what would Truman think of the MGM script?

Apparently it seemed fine with him, as his press secretary, Charles Ross, voiced only three fairly minor areas of concern to MGM's Carter Barron (and, yes, he claimed, Truman himself did read the script). Ross ordered removed any reference to the president supplying the title of the film. The actor playing Truman must be filmed only from the rear. Also the White House wanted excised any reference to Truman, as senator, rising to fame leading the committee investigating military waste, including the mysterious massive spending on some kind of secret operation (not yet revealed as the Manhattan Project). While the scene depicting Truman turned away at the Hanford gates seemed harmless, the president probably feared it made him look like a silly snoop who might have exposed and thereby derailed the bomb project. So that had to go.

MGM's Barron quickly leaped to the task, and a few days later wrote a formal letter to Ross to "confirm my agreement on behalf" of MGM to execute those deletions. Yes, "the President will be depicted only from the rear or from the side in such a way as not to show his countenance in any way." Barron closed by expressing gratitude "for your speedy attention to our problem." (It was an odd way to refer to the studio's own script.) Ross replied the same day, explaining that if these promises were kept the White House would have "no objection" to MGM moving forward in making their picture, although the president would never offer any kind of public endorsement. One wonders what the White House would have done if MGM had not caved.

Soon after, an MGM press release announced that the studio had secured approvals to be impersonated from Truman, Groves, Oppenheimer, Fermi, *Enola Gay* pilot Paul Tibbets, and others. "Never has a single motion picture presented such an array of prominent living personalities," the release boasted. The Oppenheimer claim had to be based on his verbal, and qualified written, commitment to Marx. One other, even more famous scientist to keep an eye on was Albert Einstein, who had just received the screenplay.

So what remained in the current script that was now being circulated to a few key players? Changes were still being made week to week, for better and worse. Frank Wead's original manuscript was again filled with messy pencil edits, major cuts and hand-scrawled inserts. Groves's secretary—Jeff Nixon's love interest—was no longer Nancy but Jean (befitting the real gal, Jean O'Leary, who was an attractive widow in her mid-thirties). A note in one version of the script helpfully advised that in pronouncing Oppenheimer's name please know that it's *OPP* as in *TOP*.

With Marx now confident about Oppie's eventual consent he ordered that the character who appears in the prologue must be changed from a generic actor posing in front of the Thalberg Building to Hume Cronyn commanding a physics laboratory. Cronyn would address the audience of 2446, "I believed, as did every man, that my age was the most enlightened in all history," a sentiment now thrown into question by the new weapon he helped create. He was described in the screenplay as "a scientist of dignity and poise."

Among the smaller changes:

—Fermi now responds to Matt Cochran's moral concerns after the three Quaker scientists quit the bomb project by instructing, "Sometimes it takes greater principles to stay than to go."
—Now it's Matt, not Oppie, who picks up the turtle at Trinity and lets it scurry away.
—Instead of American POWs it is a "ragged" Japanese boy who picks up one of the (fantasy) U.S. leaflets warning

of the atomic attack. For some reason he tastes it, either
to see if it's real or to suggest starvation levels in Japan?
—And in the closing scene, Wead makes real his threat to
not merely place Matt's face up in the heavenly clouds
speaking to his wife but eventually show his ghost sitting
right next to her on the steps of the Lincoln Memorial.

Elsewhere, the script accelerated its desire to portray the atomic
attack in a heroic way—and as one absolutely necessary to save
America from meeting the same fate. FDR now claims that his
psychological warfare experts told him that the "Japs will fight
right down to the women and children." When the purely fictional
Japanese fighter planes approach the *Enola Gay* near Hiroshima
they are so close (in the movie) that the brave Americans need
to return fire. The accident that dooms Matt Cochran's life now
occurs before Hiroshima, not in the run-up to Nagasaki—which
enabled the script to *totally eliminate any depiction* of the morally
questionable second bomb.

Nagasaki, as usual: overlooked, already forgotten.

Even more revealing was the addition of two new warnings
about the Japanese obtaining atomic weapons to greet a U.S. invasion. One of them had Roosevelt musing, "Our latest intelligence
worried me . . . the Japs may have atomic weapons before we do."
Groves, as before, claims that the half million U.S. death toll in
an invasion will climb horribly if the Japanese greet the Allies
with atomic bombs. When a U.S. military adviser warns, "The
Germans have sent many atomic experts and materials to Japan
by submarine," all of those in the room "are shocked" (a sentiment
that would have been shared by any serious historian). The adviser
continues, "We're slapping down every sub that shows its nose, but
some are bound to get through!"

This desperate rewriting of the script, and history, culminated in the wildest scene yet, adding an element of unintentional black humor.

The setting: a cove near Tokyo very late in the war. Japanese sailors and scientists gaze over the water with binoculars . . . and spot a submarine surfacing. A Nazi officer with his aides soon comes ashore. He is accompanied by Dr. Schmidt, Germany's leading atomic scientist. Professor Okani greets him, then tells his colleagues that Schmidt has brought uranium "and everything else we will need." The Japanese have "factories, men and materials" ready for Schmidt to use to make his bomb.

Schmidt says the only reason Hitler didn't get the A-bomb first was because the German labs could not be protected from Allied bombs, but here on Japan "it will be different." A Nazi officer booms: "Yes! We are not defeated. We can sink the enemy fleet, wipe out their men and bases and begin to fight our way back to Axis victory." He adds: "*Heil* Hitler!" The Japanese respond, "*Banzai* Nippon!"

And then the kicker. "We have prepared a fine laboratory for you," Okani tells the Germans, "at our new army headquarters in . . . Hiroshima."

With public criticism of the creation and use of the first bombs still rather muted, it was little wonder certain scientists embraced work on new and bigger weapons, even one that might not be merely nuclear but "thermonuclear." Edward Teller, who had spearheaded work at Los Alamos on what was known as "the Super," continued his efforts after leaving New Mexico and returning to the University of Chicago as a professor.

The previous year Teller had privately expressed qualms about using the atomic bomb against Japan but, after consulting Oppenheimer, refused to sign Leo Szilard's now-famous petition. He wrote to Szilard at that time that progress on building even more apocalyptic weapons could not be halted: "I do not feel that there is any chance to outlaw any one weapon. If we have a slim chance of survival, it lies in the possibility to get rid of wars. The more decisive a weapon is the more surely it will be used in any real conflict."

Now, from April 18 to 20, Teller took part in a secret conference at Los Alamos to review all work on the Super, from fuel to design. The lab had disseminated its first major technical review, written by Teller and others, titled *"Prima facie* Proof of the Feasibility of the Super."* Alas, participants at the confab concluded that Teller was unduly optimistic about creating a hydrogen bomb. The use of deuterium as fuel was problematical due to the quantities needed and various workability issues. The addition of tritium would be immensely expensive and might not even help. Nevertheless, Teller would claim in his own report that a hydrogen bomb was still feasible, even "likely," and called for further development.

Also present at the conference: Los Alamos physicist, implosion expert, and Soviet spy Klaus Fuchs, who would closely study all of the internal reports on the Super and prepare his own dossier—for Moscow.

Leaving Los Alamos for good that month, however, was the machinist David Greenglass, a young Communist Party member approached to spy for the USSR in 1944. Greenglass had passed nuclear secrets to the Soviets via courier Harry Gold and a Soviet official in New York City. Now Greenglass had returned to his native Manhattan, where he planned to open a machine shop on East 2nd Street with the man who had married his sister Ethel—a fellow Communist named Julius Rosenberg.

Less than a year after Harry Daghlian died after being exposed to radiation, Los Alamos witnessed a second fatal accident during a criticality experiment gone wrong. This involved the brilliant Canadian native Louis Slotin, age thirty-five, who had helped arm the Hiroshima bomb and then the core slated to be used in the first Bikini blast, which he had planned to witness. Enrico Fermi had warned Slotin months earlier that if he continued his risky criticality experiments—known as "tickling the tiger's tail"—he would be dead within a year. Unlike in the solo Daghlian accident, this time eight Los Alamos personnel were exposed to the radiation, with Slotin getting far the worst of it.

As Slotin lingered near death for days, the government avoided citing radiation as the culprit in any public statements—just as it had done after the Daghlian tragedy. Then his friend, the physicist Philip Morrison (who had witnessed even worse in Hiroshima), insisted on an honest reckoning. In *The Beginning or the End*, Matt Cochran would miraculously die within a day. Slotin would experience nine days of suffering; the others exposed would survive. When his passing was announced, Slotin was commonly referred to as "the first peacetime victim" of radiation from the bomb project.

To balance the horrors of what nuclear accidents might mean for the future, officials played up the "hero" angle—how Slotin had saved the others by sacrificing himself, reaching in and separating components to halt the runaway atoms. General Groves had written a note to him before he died hailing his "heroic actions" and dispatched a military plane to bring his parents to his bedside. The *Time* headline called him "Hero of Los Alamos" but admitted that radiation releases "may become a familiar factor in the atomic age."

By now, MGM was completing its casting of other major characters in *The Beginning or the End*, beyond Groves, Oppenheimer, and the fictional Jeff Nixon. Donna Reed, who had played such an important part in launching the movie, was not available, however. *They Were Expendable* had just premiered in D.C., her visit there marked by General Groves giving her a special present: a small box of pale green sand fused by the Trinity test blast (she would retain it for decades). Now *It's a Wonderful Life* was filming at RKO in Culver City and in Encino on sets for the mythical town of Bedford Falls. Much fake snow fell. A swimming pool scene was filmed at Beverly Hills High.

Shooting the film had been delayed as director Frank Capra slowly eased out famed writing partners Albert Hackett and Frances Goodrich in favor of Jo Swerling, who had already revised scenes behind their backs. Dorothy Parker, who had co-written *A Star Is Born*, had been on the outs in Hollywood due to her left-wing politics, for calling studio executives "cretins," and shouting out the window of her MGM office, "Get me out of here, I am as sane as any of you!" Now she had been brought in to polish the script. The original ending, with Jimmy Stewart falling to his knees and reciting the Lord's Prayer, had been axed entirely. Donna Reed, meanwhile, would earn her first *Life* cover but with a demanding director (Capra had always questioned whether she was right for the role), and so many veteran male co-stars, she felt "terrified" most of the time, she later related.

With Reed out of the MGM picture, the tendency to tap the studio's "B-team" of contract players continued.

Tackling the role of the ethical (if mythical) young scientist Matt Cochran would be Tom Drake. A Brooklyn native in his late twenties who was discovered by MGM on Broadway, his most prominent role so far was playing the boy-next-door to Judy Garland in *Meet Me in St. Louis*. More recently he had appeared in *The Courage of Lassie*. Both his looks and manner were rather bland. Playing his wife would be the bubbly, little-known Beverly Tyler. The far more interesting Audrey Totter would portray Jeff Nixon's girlfriend. She had just filmed *The Postman Always Rings Twice* with Lana Turner, and seemed to be crafting an image of a sassy, tough girl, on the way to becoming a *film noir* fixture over the coming decade.

Impersonating Einstein would be Ludwig Stossel, who after fleeing Nazi Germany had established a career as a character actor, appearing in such films as *Casablanca* and in *King's Row* with Ronald Reagan. (Years later he became a TV fixture as "that little old winemaker me" in Italian Swiss Colony commercials.) Taking the role of *Enola Gay* pilot Paul Tibbets would be Barry Nelson, a youngish actor with little ticket-selling appeal.

Another character actor, Roman "Bud" Bohnen, was set to play President Truman. There was nothing weak about his acting credits, which included *Of Mice and Men*, *The Best Years of Our Lives*, and *Song of Bernadette*. His political ties, however, might concern some in the White House if they came to know about them. Bohnen had been a leading member of the left-wing Group Theatre, along with colleagues such as Elia Kazan, Clifford Odets, and Lee J. Cobb. He starred in several Odets plays, including *Waiting for Lefty*, *Awake and Sing!*, and *Golden Boy*. When the Group Theatre disbanded, Bohnen had co-founded the Actors' Laboratory Theatre in Hollywood, which put on performances for servicemen but also presented social issue plays from a leftist point of view. He had joined the Communist Party himself.

An MGM press release announced Bohnen's hiring under the heading "Janitor Becomes U.S. President . . . in Movie," a reference to his current role in an L.A. production of *Awake and Sing!* When he inhabited Truman, the release claimed, he would only need to shave his moustache, get his hair grayed, and don wire-rim glasses, as his "features, height and weight" were "almost identical with the president." Not so his politics, however, just as Red-baiting began appearing in the media.

Politics certainly did play a role in what became the studio's most controversial casting, described by a famous Hearst reporter as "the oddest political squabble to ever hit this or any other drama mecca." Eleanor Roosevelt was still very much in the public eye as chairperson of the new U.N. Commission on Human Rights and for her syndicated newspaper column, "My Day." When she learned via a Hollywood producer that the studio planned to cast Lionel Barrymore as her late husband she was not pleased. The fact that Barrymore was confined to a wheelchair did not impress her because she recalled that the actor had made several disparaging remarks about FDR (he was particularly incensed about Roosevelt promoting the graduated income tax). He campaigned for Thomas Dewey against Roosevelt in 1944. As chairman of Hollywood for Dewey, he helped organize the biggest Republican rally in memory, with 93,000 filling the Los Angeles Coliseum for an extravaganza produced by right-wing director Cecil B. DeMille. Earlier that day the honored guests attended a luncheon staged by David O. Selznick with the chance to shake hands with Barrymore, Ginger Rogers, and Gary Cooper, among other stars. It was well known in Hollywood that Barrymore "hated Roosevelt," as Lauren Bacall once put it.

Back in the 1930s, when Franklin Roosevelt was asked if Barrymore was the country's greatest actor, he reportedly joked, "*I* am the greatest actor in America."

Now Eleanor, through her son James, who lived in Los Angeles and had once worked for producer Sam Goldwyn, informed Marx and McGuinness that the Roosevelt family would "prefer" another actor in that role. MGM set up a screening for James and two other family members so they could view scenes already shot featuring Barrymore. At least one of the three remained opposed, but James Roosevelt believed that if Barrymore wrote a conciliatory letter to his mother that she would relent.

Barrymore agreed. He assured the former First Lady that, while his politics indeed did not match FDR's, he had never "defamed" him, while admitting, "I'm inclined toward salty language." The letter was deemed so important it was delivered personally to

Eleanor in New York by Loew's Inc. chief, Nicholas Schenk, the ultimate power over MGM. This still did not move her. James informed MGM that the family was not asking them to remove Barrymore—but "we'd be happier if you did." Barrymore was close to Mayer, his fellow Republican, but MGM fired him anyway.

How did this colorful, behind-the-scenes drama emerge in the press? It arrived in a lengthy, syndicated Hearst column written by none other than Bob Considine. Given his key role within the movie project, one presumes it was a fairly accurate account. Considine noted that Barrymore had now accepted the role of small-town banker in *It's a Wonderful Life*, joking that this was quite a demotion from playing the president of the United States. MGM, meanwhile, announced, after briefly considering Raymond Massey, that the fully abled (and pro-Democrat) actor Godfrey Tearle would play FDR.

The current script, like the previous version, was labeled "final" when it was dutifully sent to Joe Breen at the MPAA for his blessing. His office was still at the center of controversy over its long refusal to provide a clean bill of health for Howard Hughes's *The Outlaw*, centering on Jane Russell's bust line. The *New Republic* had recently covered this in a humorous item. "A while ago Hollywood interest was centered on atomic films," it began. "Fission was in fashion. But now interest has shifted to the anatomic." Questions concerning the Hughes film remained: "How graphic can a movie advertisement be without being pornographic? Who among the lady stars wears falsies? Is one of these stars just indulging in a publicity gag in attacking a news magazine because it said she wore them? These questions agitate Hollywood."

*The Beginning or the End*, now under firm military control, promised a smoother ride with the Production Code office. In response to the latest script, Breen calmly replied that three of the violations he had cited in his previous report had not yet been corrected. And he flagged a new passage: "We presume that there will be no excessive brutality or gruesomeness in the action indicated in scene 30, in which the Pole is trampled upon."

General Groves had also received from MGM the latest "final" script for the movie. His issues with it had shrunk, in number and severity, since the previous round after so many changes inspired by his critique and the one from W.A. Consodine. Still, his new six-page list was extensive and varied enough to prompt him to create a letter grading system for each citation. "*A*" meant that something was false but he did not really object to it being used. "*B*" referred to a rewrite he generously provided but if they still foolishly preferred their version, that was okay. "*C*" signaled a falsehood that was truly objectionable that he *really* wanted changed or cut, while "*D*" flagged something not necessarily false but still highly questionable. An asterisk meant "must be changed without question."

Earning a modest "A" from Groves: His hair was black, not brown. Another "A" was placing himself, Conant, and Bush at the Trinity site way too early—and, he noted, "We were not covered with lotion and we didn't wear goggles." He continued to flag the often "moronic" statements by Colonel Jeff Nixon, and helpfully provided new dialogue. A scene from 1942, laughably out of sequence, earned an urgent "C" as it "tends to support a thesis which certain mudslingers are trying to inculcate into the minds of the American people, namely, that the Army was handed a completed project and that all it had to do was to spend some money." And he still insisted that all references to Kokura (with its American POW camp problem) as a target be removed—this earned the harshest *must-cut* asterisk.

Then there was the personal. Groves advised that "all attempts to make me demonstrate emotion, such as getting mad or excited or pacing the floor . . . is entirely untrue to life. . . . I never paced in my life even when I was waiting for [the birth of] my children." And what about being depicted as something of a chocolate hound? Displaying a sense of humor for a change, he declared that he could not imagine "where Mr. Marx or Mr. Taurog would have learned that I infrequently eat a chocolate or two." Still, he wanted at least one of the two references to that habit eliminated.

But his most critical notation, which must have surprised Sam Marx and Frank Wead—who had been trending in exactly the opposite direction—came when he flagged the recently inserted statement attributed to him, that the Japanese might meet our invading soldiers with "atomic weapons." He suggested substituting for that "suicide planes." As he rightly explained, "we always knew that Japan could not produce an atomic bomb." This was an admirable call for accuracy and restraint. More revealing, however, was that Groves *did not insist on this* with a letter grade of "C" or "D" or an asterisk. He would prefer that they make that significant change, he found it "desirable," but "would not object if you find it essential to dramatization."

The following day, Groves sent MGM's Barron a note describing the new script as, overall, fair and well done. Barron assured Groves that most of the changes he requested would indeed be executed. But the preposterous scene in the cove, with the German physicist bringing atomic secrets to Japan, earmarked for that lab in Hiroshima? That was still in.

# 14

# Dr. Einstein, I Presume?

While turning aside requests from MGM to sign a release, Albert Einstein's efforts to control the military uses of splitting the atom only grew. From Princeton he sent a telegram far and wide seeking $200,000 in funds for his new Emergency Committee of Atomic Scientists. It would contain one of the most oft-quoted sentences of the century: "The unleashed power of the atom has changed everything save our modes of thinking, and thus we drift toward unparalleled catastrophe."

Einstein confessed that he and other scientists "who released this immense power have an overwhelming responsibility in this world life-and-death struggle to harness the atom for the benefit of mankind and not for humanity's destruction. Bethe, Condon, Szilard, Urey, and the Federation of American Scientists join me in this appeal, and beg you to support our efforts to bring realization to America that mankind's destiny is being decided today—now—at this moment. . . . Urgently request you send immediate check to me as chairman. . . . We ask your help at this fateful moment as a sign that we scientists do not stand alone.

In an interview a few days later for *The New York Times Magazine*, Einstein said:

> Today the atomic bomb has altered profoundly the
> nature of the world as we know it, and the human race
> consequently finds itself in a new habitat to which it

must adapt its thinking. . . . Before the raid on Hiroshima, the leading physicists urged the War Department
not to use the bomb against defenseless women and
children. The war could have been won without it. The
decision was made in consideration of possible future
loss of American lives—and now we have to consider
the possible loss in future atomic bombings of *millions
of lives*. The American decision may have been a fatal
error, for men accustom themselves to thinking that
a weapon which was used once can be used again. . . .
To the village square we must carry the facts of atomic
energy. From there must come America's voice.

*Time* magazine would soon feature an illustration of Einstein on
its cover—next to an elongated mushroom cloud. But hopes around
international control of the atom had plunged with Truman's
appointment of Wall Street financier Bernard Baruch to "translate"
the recent proposals by Acheson, Lilienthal, and Oppenheimer in
exchange for White House backing. Oppenheimer told a friend
they had "lost." He despised Baruch and considered him a fool.

The FBI, which had maintained for years a thick file on Einstein
and his ties to left-leaning groups, now stepped up its monitor-
ing. Back in January, agents had proposed tapping the phones of
Einstein and his secretary but the bureau declined, fearing a backlash if this was revealed. Nevertheless, agents tracked his mail and
phone numbers of those who called him. Agents monitored his
writings, speeches, broadcasts and his role with political or science groups, sometimes via informants who attended meetings.
FBI director J. Edgar Hoover was known to have called Einstein
an "extreme radical."

So on May 27, for example, an agent reported that the San
Francisco office had been tipped off—by a Manhattan Project

engineer at Berkeley, no less—that he and others had received by mail Einstein's solicitation for funds for his Emergency Committee. That office suggested that agents in the FBI's Newark bureau (closer to Einstein's home in Princeton) launch "an investigation" of that group to determine if it was "Communist infiltrated and dominated." Another report asserted that Einstein "has been used by various Communist Front organizations."

Still, MGM tried desperately to get Einstein's signature on the dotted line. Turning back the latest attempt, Einstein wrote to Louis B. Mayer himself. "Although I am not much of a moviegoer," he admitted, "I do know from the tenor of earlier films that have come out of your studio that you will understand my reasons. I find that the whole film is written too much from the point of view of the Army and the Army leader of the project, whose influence was not always in the direction which one would desire from the point of view of humanity."

Mayer, surely miffed but too intimidated to reply in his own words to the world's most famous genius, instead asked former writer James K. McGuinness to draft a reply he could sign. President Truman, the letter asserted, "was most anxious to have the picture made" and had personally read and approved the script. This apparently was supposed to impress the scientist who had just labeled the Hiroshima decision unwise and warned about the direction of Truman's current nuclear policies. "As American citizens we are bound to respect the viewpoint of our government," Mayer advised.

Then there was this: "It must be realized that dramatic truth is just as compelling a requirement to us as veritable truth is to a scientist." Trying to assure Einstein that his moral views might be included, Mayer informed him that MGM had cast Tom Drake as the fictional ethical scientist. "We selected among our young male players the one who best typifies earnestness and a spiritual quality," Mayer gushed. "You need only recall his performance in *The Green Years*," where Drake portrayed an Irish orphan.

There was a pretty fair chance Albert Einstein had missed that picture.

Unlike his friend Einstein, Leo Szilard was willing to at least meet MGM halfway, going so far as offer to trek out to Culver City and rewrite the sections of the script where he was portrayed. He told Sam Marx that he and Einstein would only sign contracts if the studio donated $100,000 to FAS, which infuriated the producer. Then Leo cut the suggested gift to $5,000, before finally dropping any conditions for signing, beyond approving the script.

Marx surely wondered how Szilard might react if he got a look at the script's increasingly unsubtle championing of the use of the bomb against Japanese cities. After all, in his cover letter with the famous petition trying to halt that decision the previous summer, Szilard had written:

> Many of us are inclined to say that individual Germans share the guilt for the acts which Germany committed during this war because they did not raise their voices in protest against these acts. Their defense that their protest would have been of no avail hardly seems acceptable even though these Germans could not have protests without running risks to life and liberty. We are in a position to raise our voices without incurring any such risks even though we might incur the displeasure of some of those who are at present in charge of controlling the work on "atomic power."

About seventy in Chicago and at Oak Ridge would sign the petition. Edward Teller planned to circulate it at Los Alamos but was

talked out of it by the morally ambivalent Oppenheimer, who considered it "meddling."

Groves, who hated Szilard's bumptious nature and believed the
petition undercut other scientists and jeopardized secrecy, tried
that summer to gather evidence that he was a security risk to get
him off the bomb project. He also made sure the petition never
got to Truman's desk (and after the war had it classified "secret"
so Szilard could not release it to the press). As Szilard spoke out
against the May-Johnson bill and developing new weapons, the FBI
followed his movements closely, inspiring the physicist to make a
game out of jumping in and out of cabs to shake surveillance. An
Army colonel at the War Department asked J. Edgar Hoover to
open a full probe of Szilard, as "he has constantly associated with
known 'liberals' . . . and has been outspoken in his support of the
internationalization of the atomic energy program."

One of the many reports from agents in his FBI file for 1946
admitted that he was "well aware that he has been watched closely
inasmuch as the post office inadvertently advised SZILARD and
FERMI that General GROVES had ordered all their mail to be
opened." Groves blasted Szilard at length in off-the-record remarks
to a *Time* magazine reporter, concluding, "I don't like certain Jews,
and I don't like certain well-known characteristics of theirs, but
I'm not prejudiced."

Unlike Szilard, another physicist who worked on the bomb in
Chicago, Eugene Rabinowitz—later a founder of the *Bulletin of
the Atomic Scientists*—had considered revealing the existence of
the new weapon to a well-placed journalist *before* its use against
Japan. He reasoned (as he wrote to a friend) that "if a crime like
the bombing of Hiroshima and Nagasaki were to be carried out
in the name of the American people, these people would have at
least known" in advance, even if they still ended up approving of
it. In this way they would at least have "the opportunity to accept

the responsibility for mass murder on an unprecedented scale—of which they now stand guilty before history without having known anything about it beforehand."

Now, Leo Szilard, in the midst of his usual varied and frenetic activity—including drafting a plan to organize a National Science Foundation—boarded a train for Los Angeles. When he arrived, Sam Marx showed him some of the footage already shot for the movie. It took Szilard only three days at the studio to rewrite scenes that pictured his crucial meeting with Einstein in Princeton and his early lab work with the bomb project. Then he returned to New York to lobby at the U.N. for international control of atomic energy, now imperiled by the intervention of Truman's man, Bernard Baruch.

Marx wrote Einstein again, informing him that his friend Szilard "was, to some extent, impressed that we are doing a sincere job and one that will reflect only credit on science." But the wheedling was still not working. Einstein, who just wanted to be left alone, quickly informed Marx that he had already told his boss, L.B. Mayer, "no," and he stood by that. At least for a while.

Then Szilard told Einstein he had decided to sign his release after MGM assured him his script rewrites would be honored and sent him the relevant pages. "Have received new script from MGM," he wired, "and am writing that I have no objection to use of my name in it. Understand that Sam Marx has mailed to you." Einstein, no doubt weary of the whole matter and willing to follow Szilard's lead, scribbled on the back of the telegram a return message, "Agree with use of my name on the basis of new script."

Far from Hollywood a new American visitor arrived in real-life Hiroshima (or what remained of it). This was the correspondent and novelist John Hersey, who at the age of thirty-one had already won a Pulitzer Prize for his 1945 novel *A Bell for Adano*. Weeks before, he had proposed writing something about Hiroshima in a chat with his *New Yorker* editor, William Shawn. Hersey, who was born in China to Protestant missionaries and covered the Pacific war for Henry Luce and Time-Life, imagined an article documenting the power of the new bomb and the destruction it caused to a city. Ultimately he decided he'd prefer writing about what happened not to buildings but to humans. He just needed to find a form to tell the story.

Shawn was enthusiastic and urged him not to rush since, nine months after the epochal events, "No one has even touched this" subject, the editor advised. This was, sadly, true.

On the way to the Far East that spring, Hersey had read Thornton Wilder's novel *The Bridge of San Luis Rey*, which explored an eighteenth-century disaster in Peru through the eyes of a handful of victims. Hersey sensed this might be the best way to personalize the far more vast and deadly Hiroshima story. Arriving in Hiroshima in May, he interviewed several dozen survivors, before settling on six who told powerful stories but were not exactly representative of the city as a whole: two doctors, one Catholic priest and one Methodist minister, and two working women. (It might also be said that they were not typical because these six had *survived*.) Their movements in the shattered city occasionally crossed, one of the novelistic requirements the author had set.

Conducting interviews and research with a translator at his side, Hersey was "terrified all the time," he later explained. The Rev. Kiyoshi Tanimoto, one of his six subjects, who had been educated at Emory College in Georgia and spoke and wrote English well, scribbled his memories out on paper for Hersey. It included his prayer for the wretched he had abandoned on the day of the bomb so he might save others: "God help and take them out of the fire." Among other scenes of horror, he recalled removing five dead bodies from a boat so he could row across a river and fill it with the merely wounded, "all the day long."

Hersey had seen the devastation of war many times before, most recently in Italy, China, and Tokyo, but Hiroshima was different: these ruins had been created by one weapon in one moment—extermination in an instant—a truly terrifying notion. If Hersey felt that nine months later, how must the people who were there at the time have experienced it? So he set out to struggle to understand.

Unlike the cases of Einstein and Szilard, gaining approval from Vannevar Bush, who headed the federal Office of Scientific Research and Development in Washington, was hardly a top priority for MGM. Still, the studio had needled him about this for some time. Bush had founded the company now known as Raytheon, then served as vice president of the Massachusetts Institute of Technology and as president of the Carnegie Institution. As an engineer and inventor, he was a pioneer in the field of analog computers, digital circuitry and the "memex" (an early system of hypertext). MGM wanted to picture him engaging with FDR early on and then placing him on the ground at the Trinity test.

Now Bush deflected another such request after being sent a script. He was willing to accept fact-challenged details as necessary for dramatization but found the scene showing him delivering Einstein's crucial letter to FDR in 1939 totally false—for one thing, he did not do that. When Sam Marx got wind of this he wrote Bush to assure him that the movie "is being made with the fullest resources" of MGM "and can only be considered a high tribute to all of the men and women who were involved with" the Manhattan Project. "Only actors of the very highest type will be used"—something of a white lie—"and there will be no effort spared to present this film in a most dignified and high minded way."

As further inducement, he enclosed two photos of the actor slated to portray him, one Samuel S. Hinds, although he advised Bush to imagine him wearing wire-rim glasses and "without the moustache." Hinds, he reported, "has a fine, rich voice and has always portrayed men of dignity." (His most prominent role: Dr. Kildare's father in a series of films.) In addition, the script had been revised to show Bush chatting amiably with FDR about the prospects for creating an atomic bomb long after the Einstein letter had been delivered.

The studio had also inserted a line Oppenheimer claimed Bush said to him after the Trinity test: "Well, Robert, a great many men not yet born will be grateful to you for this day." (The script also included Oppie's true-life response to Bush: "I hope they'll have reason to be grateful.") Marx gushed that his movie would give credit to all engaged in the bomb project, "of which we consider you a foremost figure."

Bush quickly thanked Marx for the note and asked him to convey his best wishes to actor Hinds, his "impersonator. . . . He is a fine appearing man—much better than the original." But Bush stood his ground against approval, at least until he saw the revised script. MGM's response? They immediately changed Bush's name in the script.

It was little wonder that Bush soon informed Truman's press secretary Charles Ross that he remained "puzzled" by the whole MGM matter. The White House faced a much rougher crisis, however. A series of labor strikes, and rising consumer prices, had angered millions and sent Truman's approval rating, which stood at 82 percent after Hiroshima, into a steep decline toward 50 percent. With a national strike looming in May, Truman seized control of the railroads, but two key unions struck anyway, immobilizing passengers along with 24,000 freight trains.

Truman personally drafted an incendiary message to Congress that called for mobs comprised of war veterans to enact frontier justice on union leaders. "Every single one of the strikers and their demagogue leaders have been living in luxury," he alleged. "Now I want you who are my comrades in arms . . . to come with me and eliminate the [John] Lewises, the Whitneys, the Johnstons, the Communist [Harry] Bridges"—all notorious union chiefs—"and the Russian Senators and Representatives. . . . Let's put transportation and production back to work, hang a few traitors and make our own country safe for democracy. . . . Come on boys, let's do the job."

Naturally his staff objected. They knew that Truman was prone to dashing off deeply felt but best-left-unsent memos, such as the recent one where he fantasized, "Get plenty of Atomic Bombs on hand—drop one on Stalin, put the United Nations to work and eventually set up a free world." Now he was forced to soften the "hang the traitors" directive but the memo still called for all railroad strikers to be drafted into the U.S. Army. The House of Representatives even passed a bill with that directive by a vote of 306 to 13, although it was tabled in the Senate. Critics asked if this was America or Russia. In an address to the nation the president compared the labor crisis to the Japanese attack on Pearl Harbor. Soon the bitter rail and coal strikes were settled, but the president's standing with the public remained wobbly.

This potential *Beginning or the End* headache might linger much longer, however. In his letter to Truman aide Ross, Bush revealed that he kept seeing drafts of the script that remained "decidedly inaccurate" and telescoped history radically. It seemed to him "to be pretty important that a film which will fix a pattern of history in the minds of the American people"—well-chosen words—"ought to be just as accurate as possible." Even so, he had been told that a large number of scientists and military figures had signed releases and that the White House "has approved the script. I should value a word from you as to just how the matter does stand."

Ross replied the next day, saying that he understood Bush's unwillingness to sign. While he knew that some condensing of history was often required in such dramas, "in this case the tele-scoping has gone too far." Ross revealed that the White House "neither approves nor disapproves the film and certainly does not want to seem to be persuading anybody to sign such a release. . . . This is a matter in which each individual concerned must exercise his own judgment."

Bush, in any case, now fired off a note to General Groves, who, according to Ross, had approved the script. What did the general really think of it, and what could be done about the falsehoods?

When Groves replied he attempted to place his role in shap-ing the film in a minor key: he was only acting to "protect secu-rity" and allow no "discredit" on the military and others engaged in the project, "including naturally myself." He further claimed that since he understood that some of the scientists would also be reviewing the script "I did not go into the historical correctness of scientific credit." Of course, he had already done just that. "I would much prefer to see the picture historically correct," Groves concluded, "but I hesitate to get involved in any more battles than I can help, after all I am in a number now that I have not asked for. My own view is that we should concentrate on the correction of the historical errors of real moment and let the minor ones go." This from the man who had just asked MGM to hide from the world his passion for chocolate.

# 15

# A Possible "Prophylactic"

Shortly after the attack on Hiroshima, several Hollywood studios awkwardly inserted references to the earth-shaking event in nearly completed B-movies. Now it was about to turn up by design in at least one classy production, directed by William Wyler, who had already won five Academy Awards. Two years earlier he had made the widely hailed documentary *Memphis Belle* about a legendary Europe-based U.S. bomber and its crew. Now he was shooting *The Best Years of Our Lives*, a searing drama about war veterans returning, with considerable difficulty, to postwar America.

Early in the movie one of the vets, who had toiled in occupied Hiroshima, proudly shows his teenage son a samurai sword he had picked up in Japan. Unimpressed, the boy asks if he saw any Hiroshima survivors suffering from the effects of radiation? When the answer is no, the youth appears perplexed. He reports that his teachers were talking a lot about the dangers posed by the invention and use of the bomb. The father sarcastically replies that maybe he should have stayed home instead of going off to war—then, like his son, he'd know what was really going on.

By early summer, filming for *The Beginning or the End* was also well under way, mainly on giant sound stages at Metro. The Culver City complex covered 185 acres with six separate movie lots where a dozen or more films might be shot at about the same time, connected by a rail line. As many as six thousand people worked there.

It even had its own police force of nearly fifty. Although work on the atomic bomb movie was said to be "top secret"—both in execution and content—the studio did not shy away from inviting entertainment reporters to visit Culver City for the usual on-the-set previews, while distributing publicity stills to their editors and others.

The first major piece appeared in the *Los Angeles Times*, topped by a photo of several of the film's co-stars in the Fermi chain reaction scene, plus profile shots of brunette Beverly Tyler and fair-haired Audrey Totter (with bare shoulders and offering a come-hither glance). The writer Philip K. Scheur opened the article by pointing to the publicity hook for his visit to the set, noting that his pass for the day was printed with *"Admit—To Restricted Atomic Bomb Production Area—Compliance with security regulations is requested."* The "requested" did seem to undermine the premise, however. With a studio minder guiding him, he found Tom Drake in a Quonset hut on Tinian (in sound stage #15, the largest on the lot) about to receive a dose of radiation while working on a "torpedo-shaped object"—that is, the innards of the first atomic bomb. Wait, wasn't this supposed to be top secret? Technical adviser H.T. Wensel assured Scheuer that he would *not* be allowed to look inside the dummy casing "for security reasons." That was more like it.

Scheuer learned that the highlight of the shoot so far was said to be the Trinity blast. Director Taurog called it "terrifying." Taurog also told the reporter that the movie would not preach "one world" or any other theory but "will make people think and talk—draw their own conclusions." The real message of the film would be expressed in that letter near the end from irradiated Cochran to his wife, and Scheuer was allowed to quote part of it. Citing Donna Reed, "of all people," as inspiration for the film, Scheuer predicted that just a year after she contacted her former teacher, *The Beginning or the End* "should be out and standing your hair straight up."

A female reporter, meanwhile, observed that all that extra security also "gave the studio cops a chance to frisk young lady visitors."

One of the new press photos memorialized a most notable visitation. Robert Oppenheimer had finally motored to Culver City from Pasadena and found his far-from-doppelganger, Hume Cronyn, about to portray him in a scene that followed the Trinity test. The real-life Oppenheimer, dressed in tweed sport coat, khakis, and tie, had watched in silence, but when the director shouted "Cut," he sailed his trademark porkpie hat in the direction of Cronyn, crying, "Hello, Oppie!" The press photos, however, would find him sitting quietly on a bench, smiling, next to Cronyn, both men wielding cigarettes.

After that photo op, Marx ushered Oppenheimer into a projection room to show him rushes revealing preparations for the Trinity blast. Oppie sat quietly until the bomb was being raised to the top of the tower. Suddenly he leaped to his feet and shouted, "Too fast! Too fast!" Perplexed, Marx called Taurog into the room. "Gentlemen," Oppenheimer explained, "you're taking that up as if it could get up there in ten minutes." It actually took days. Taurog replied that if he showed it at any greater length "I'll be working at Republic [a small movie studio] tomorrow!"

Later, Marx treated his visitor to dinner at Romanoff's, the celebrity hotspot in Beverly Hills. Oppenheimer insisted on making his own martini for both of them, which turned out to be nearly all gin and quite explosive—a failed scientific experiment. Then Oppie proudly whipped up his own salad dressing, easily the worst Marx had ever tasted. Owner Mike Romanoff came by the table, sat down, and to Marx's surprise talked knowledgeably about the bomb. Marx also introduced his guest to a newspaper columnist who shook his hand but seemed unimpressed. Later Marx learned that the columnist thought the stranger was the British novelist E. Phillips Oppenheim. And Oppenheim had died earlier

that year. So maybe the physicist was not so famous or recogniz-
able after all.

One wonders if Oppenheimer had finally visited MGM as a bit
of a lark to escape a mounting threat to his elevated Wise Man
status. He had recently invited his old friend Haakon Chevalier
to a cocktail party at his home in Berkeley. He had met Chevalier
when both were supporting the anti-Franco forces in the Span-
ish Civil War. Chevalier also taught at Berkeley, as a professor of
French literature. They had attended parties and meetings where
Communist Party members appeared. In 1943, shortly after Oppie
took charge at Los Alamos, Chevalier rather casually mentioned to
him that he knew someone named George Eltenton who might be
willing to pass U.S. secrets to our then-allies, the Soviets. Oppenheimer ignored this offer.

Now he learned that Chevalier had just been interrogated by
the FBI for ten hours. The subject was Oppenheimer's awareness
of Soviet interest in spying at Los Alamos, and the lies he might
have told about it to the FBI—that he was only one of *three* scientists approached—to protect Chevalier. Hearing this, Oppie's
face darkened, Chevalier observed, and he grew tense and nervous.
Those lies would haunt Oppenheimer for the rest of his life.

Even before the defeat of Germany in the spring of 1945, Secretary
of War Stimson ordered the formation of the U.S. Strategic Bombing Survey (USSBS) to embark on a massive study of the successes
and failures of air power in the European theater. After Japan surrendered in August, USSBS teams headed for that arena, with Paul
Nitze as vice chairman. His top directors came largely from outside the military, and included sociologists and economists such
as John Kenneth Galbraith. Now they had released their lengthy
and quite frank report, running to thousands of pages, which drew
wide press attention.

Overall, the wide-ranging U.S. air effort was found to have helped win the war, but was also judged inefficient, squandering precious American lives and resources. Both Germany and Japan had collapsed for reasons that went well beyond the highly destructive assaults from the skies. The summary report closed with a lengthy assessment of the staggering damage in Hiroshima and Nagasaki, but it was the conclusion to this section that raised eyebrows. It was far from an endorsement of the official (and emerging Hollywood) narrative that only the use of the bomb prevented an American invasion of Japan that would have cost half a million or more lives. "We underestimated the ability of our air attack on Japan's home islands, coupled as it was with blockade and previous military defeats, to achieve unconditional surrender without invasion," the USSBS declared.

> By July 1945, the weight of our air attack had as yet reached only a fraction of its planned proportion, Japan's industrial potential had been fatally reduced, her civilian population had lost its confidence in victory and was approaching the limit of its endurance, and her leaders, convinced of the inevitability of defeat, were preparing to accept surrender. The only remaining problem was the timing and terms of that surrender. . . .
>
> There is little point in attempting precisely to impute Japan's unconditional surrender to any one of the numerous causes which jointly and cumulatively were responsible for Japan's disaster. . . . Nevertheless, it seems clear that, even without the atomic bombing attacks, air supremacy over Japan could have exerted sufficient pressure to bring about unconditional surrender and obviate the need for invasion. Based on a

detailed investigation of all the facts, and supported
by the testimony of the surviving Japanese leaders
involved, it is the Survey's opinion that certainly prior
to 31 December 1945, and in all probability prior to
1 November 1945, Japan would have surrendered even
if the atomic bombs had not been dropped, even if Russia had not entered the war, and even if no invasion had
been planned or contemplated.

The first leg of the U.S. invasion, as it happened, was not scheduled
to take place until November 1. So this top-level official report was
sketching an inconvenient truth—and now the widely embraced
claim (from the White House to Culver City) that only dropping
the bombs saved half a million or more U.S. lives was an argument
that was clearly tottering.

The fact was: Once the bomb passed the Trinity test there was
little chance the U.S. would ever have to invade Japan. All those
depressing scenarios for lives lost were now fading. The only
plausible options in August 1945 that remained were: wait for a
Japanese collapse after Russia entered the war, while speeding the
end by modifying the unconditional surrender demand to allow
the emperor to remain on the throne—*or* use the three atomic
bombs in its arsenal (and then more as they became ready) in the
coming days or weeks.

It was extremely unlikely that Truman would ever order a bloody
invasion in November 1945, and send many thousands of American
boys to their deaths, once he had atomic bombs in his pocket. The
only question was: if and when to use them.

As many of the activist scientists feared, the Acheson-Lilienthal
initiative at the United Nations had come to nothing, doomed
by White House mismanagement via Bernard Baruch. The U.S.

wanted to retain full freedom to expand its nuclear arsenal until international controls took full effect, and even then reserve the right to ignore them. As expected by Oppenheimer and other insiders, this was promptly rejected by the Soviets. Out in the Pacific, meanwhile, the atomic tests scheduled for the Bikini Atoll were fast approaching. Robert Oppenheimer had decided not to play the role of distinguished eyewitness. He had seen more than enough as a "destroyer of worlds" (as he'd put it) at Trinity.

The first Hiroshima-sized bomb at Bikini was to be set off above a fleet of antiquated ships, testing its power at sea, on July 1. This was not without controversy. Few in the media cared what happened to the Bikinian natives, but some worried the blast might ignite the atmosphere, trigger tidal waves, or create a fissure in the earth's crust. Newspapers carried witty accounts of Los Angeles residents planning to enjoy picnics high in the hills on the day of the blast instead of on the beach in case a tsunami rose from the ocean.

Oppenheimer had explained in a message to Truman that he had severe "misgivings" about the tests, which were shared by many other scientists. If the purpose of the test was to judge how vessels might survive—well, no such blast was needed: "If an atomic bomb comes close enough to a ship . . . it will sink it." For just one percent of the projected $100 million cost for the tests "one could obtain more useful information." As for the radiation studies: they, too, could be obtained more accurately and cheaply in a lab. And why a "trivial" test at sea? Everyone knew the purpose of the new weapon (as the world had already been shown by Truman himself) "lies in their use for the bombardment of cities." Most importantly, Oppenheimer questioned "the appropriateness of a purely military test of atomic weapons, at a time when our plans for effectively eliminating them from national armaments are in their earliest beginnings."

Truman was not swayed. He forwarded the letter to Acting Secretary of State Acheson, reminding him that this was the same "crybaby scientist" who claimed he had blood on his hands when they met in the Oval Office the previous October. "I think he has concocted himself an alibi in this letter," Truman decided.

No matter. MGM prepared a breathless, ten-minute short, *Bikini—The Atom Island*. It captured, among other scenes, the entire populace reciting the Lord's Prayer before loading their "pathetic belongings" onto ships for their "holy pilgrimage" to their new home. There King Juda was pleased to discover that unlike in Bikini there seemed to be no flies on Rongerik. A review in *The Cinema* magazine captured the film's inspirational message. It starred the "humble, God-fearing natives" who "relinquished their ancestral homeland" for the good of all mankind. This was an "unparalleled example of unselfish altruism . . . one of the most eloquent sermons ever to be delivered." And why? Christianity was a religion which the natives had long embraced "and whose precepts they obey." No mention was made of the mendacious and absurd U.S. promise that encouraged them to leave—that their radiation-soaked islands would soon be habitable again.

When the day for the bomb blast arrived, a special ship hosted observers from the press, including Bob Considine, who was covering the event for the Hearst chain. One afternoon on board the USS *Appalachian* the ship's loudspeaker squawked that a "valuable manuscript" had been lost. A reporter returning to his stateroom found his roommate, Considine, quite frantic. A few minutes later the missing pages were returned to him by another correspondent who had been enjoying reading the current script of *The Beginning or the End*.

Norman Cousins of the *Saturday Review* had called the event "authorized insanity" but was there to witness it, believing that at least it would remind people of what befell Hiroshima. Many in the media, however, would find the explosion (dubbed "Able") less than impressive, possibly owing to their distance from the blast, at some fourteen miles. One newsman told Cousins that now he figured "the next war's not going to be so bad after all." Cousins couldn't tell if the man was more relieved or disappointed. Only a handful of the eighty-seven ghost ships sank immediately. Even with all that planning and expense, the bomb exploded two miles off target (in that regard it was more Nagasaki than Hiroshima). Palm trees on Bikini were still standing; so were most of the poor goats arrayed on ships to judge the physical and mental effects of such a blast.

Hours later it became known that, actually, as many as two dozen ships suffered severe damage or raging fires. Considine observed: "The whole forward section of the carrier *Independence* was turned into a snarl of twisted metal, and many yards of her flight deck were caved in, as though some giant fist had punched the vessel. . . . Fighter planes aboard the *Independence* were melted into the inferno as flames swept the ship."

Despite belated reporting such as this, Norman Cousins would title his report in the *Saturday Review* "The Standardization of Catastrophe." Too many Bikini observers felt the bomb had been "oversold," that it was "merely" another weapon of war. Its "novelty" had passed. Cousins, like the scientists in previous weeks, reminded his readers that too little attention was focused on radiation effects—and on the fact that bombs many times more powerful would be created in years to come. He proposed that the Navy tow the *Independence* to the United States and anchor it off coastal cities so Americans could see the true results of the test and "let its meaning sink in."

Within four days a Frenchman named Louis Reard dubbed the daring, two-piece bathing suit he had designed: *le bikini*.

Three weeks later, the second nuclear test, "Baker," proved more clearly potent and destructive, which must have reassured civilian and military leaders but stunned the Navy. This time the device was set off underwater. Of the ninety-two "junked" vessels, all but two either sank, were damaged, or suffered heavy contamination. A six-thousand-foot column of radioactive water sprayed observer ships and their crews; some likened it to "a witch's brew." This time, Vice Admiral W.H.P. Blandy, who was in charge of the operation, declared the bomb "a form of poison warfare" after he was unable to inspect many of the ships due to the wildly clicking Geiger counter that accompanied him.

In a sign of things to come, radioactive particles were detected over San Francisco a few days later, and after that over Paris, bringing this "fallout" threat to wide public attention for the first time. Also endangered were the forty thousand U.S. sailors and soldiers who had been crowded cavalierly nearby, or who mounted the ships later to inspect or clean them—with safety guidelines widely ignored—and were exposed to troubling levels of radiation.

For the developers of the bomb who retained concerns about errors and false portrayals in *The Beginning of the End* some sort of salvation was now at hand. A nonfiction film, they learned, was about to be shot—and they would even get to play themselves in it!

The producer would be Time Inc. for its venerable *March of Time* series. These newsreel-like short films, focusing on social issues or current events, had been shown to huge audiences every month since 1935. Managing it as usual would be Richard de Rochement, with trademark narration by the portentous Westbrook Van Voorhis. Recent *March of Time* shorts had titles like "Report on Greece," "Problem Drinkers," "Night Club Boom," and "Palestine Problem." Controversy sometimes erupted over staged scenes. Who could forget "Inside Nazi Germany," filmed partly in New Jersey?

The stars of the bomb project, from Groves to Einstein, first got an inkling of what was up in early July. Oppenheimer received a wire asking if he was able to take part in some sort of re-creation of Trinity (in a fake control shack "as though at Alamogordo"), but plans were vague. Apparently the producers had hoped to film earlier in the year but felt the subject needed a fresh hook. Now they realized it could be timed to the first anniversary of the atomic attacks around August 6.

A *March of Time* script for what was now titled "Atomic Power" was submitted to FAS for their input. (The association was now known as the Federation of *American* Scientists, with the "atomic" part deleted, and claimed three thousand members in seventeen chapters.) Vannevar Bush informed his friend James Conant, the Harvard University president, that both of them would be invited to appear, adding, "If the script turns out to be for a good factual narrative stressing the necessity for action looking toward international collaborative control, the picture can, I think, turn out to be a very useful thing, and it may serve as somewhat of a prophylactic to the other [i.e., MGM] one."

A week later, the two men would sprawl on a sand-covered warehouse floor near Harvard Square to reenact their handshake in the desert celebrating the Trinity blast. Oppenheimer, meanwhile, fiddled with some fake control panel knobs while managing the Trinity countdown. Fermi pretended to prepare his pile for the chain reaction in Chicago. Even Lise Meitner, who shunned all MGM approaches, faced the *March of Time* cameras. Leo Szilard visited Princeton so he could return to that day in 1939 when he encouraged Einstein to write his crucial letter to FDR. The usually animated Szilard looked stiff in his white shirt and tie, while Einstein—slouching in shirtsleeves while smoking a pipe—seemed his natural self. In a second scene, Einstein was recorded speaking just one line, in response to hearing a strong proposal for international controls: "I agree!"

Whither Ayn Rand? When Hal Wallis sold her script for *Top Secret* out from under her to MGM, where it was not so much subsumed as vaporized, she was still scheduled to work at Paramount for several more months under her contract. Her peevish letter to Wallis after the collapse of the atomic bomb epic had not produced whatever it was she wanted from him, so she had stopped making the regular trip from her modernist San Fernando ranch house to the studio. Instead, she devoted herself almost full-time to answering fan mail inspired by the paperback revival of *The Fountainhead*—as well as a nationally syndicated comic strip based on the book—which had popularized her hyper-individualist ideas.

Rand happily referred to her followers as a "cult" though she would later denounce those who used that term. She also started sketching out the plot and characters, such as a John Galt, for a novel she titled *The Strike*. (It would eventually become known as *Atlas Shrugged*, originally the title of just one chapter.) Coincidence or not, she would call part one of the dystopian novel "End" and the second part "Beginning." Work on producing dozens of pages of outlines went far more quickly than it had for *The Fountainhead*. And having interviewed Dr. Oppenheimer, she had a head start in creating the character of brilliant but weak Dr. Stadler and his "Project X."

All the while, she maintained her correspondence with a growing legion of fans. To one young woman she replied, "I am glad that *The Fountainhead* helps you when you feel unhappy, but you should not feel that you are 'a peculiar failure' at the age of 18." To an older woman: "Don't ever apologize for your brains, if you were able to understand and enjoy *The Fountainhead*. As you see, I do not apologize for saying this." To a Mr. Coleman: "In regard to the girl who sent you *The Fountainhead*, I would guess that sex was not the point she wanted you to see in the book; sex is only a minor aspect of a much wider theme." She also found time to offer Royal Typewriter Co. an endorsement of their product, adding, "I have no photograph of myself using my typewriter, but I shall be happy to pose for one if you wish to have one taken." And to Leonard Read, founder of the pro-capitalist Foundation for Economic Education, she roasted George Orwell: "As an advance warning, for God's sake DON'T recommend *Animal Farm*," which "is being whooped up as a lesson against Communism, which it is not. I have read it. It made me sick. It is a book against Stalin, not Communism."

After a few weeks of this, Rand was approached by Wallis with the idea of writing something for Barbara Stanwyck. Rand sent the actress a note, suggesting a lunch to discuss the project in Beverly Hills. The idea was to revive the first script she ever sold, to Universal in 1932 (when she was still working in the wardrobe department at RKO), titled *Red Pawn*, a spy thriller set in the Soviet dictatorship. Stanwyck informed her via telegram that she and her manager had decided that *Red Pawn* was not "the right kind of story" for her at this moment. So, for Rand, it was back to blissful isolation on her ranch and the world of John Galt. "As to my next novel," she informed her literary agent, "I am progressing on it very well and hope to have it finished by Spring of 1947. But don't hold me to the date."

# 16

## John Hersey and the End of "Whoopee"

The eighteen-minute *March of Time* film short "Atomic Power" reached theaters on August 9, the first anniversary of the Nagasaki bombing. Print advertisements for it boasted, "30 Million Minds a Month Focus on the *March of Time*," along with headshots of nine of the film's true-life stars arrayed around an illustration of a mushroom cloud. In the end, the newsreel's producer had managed to get every leading figure on film, even if fleetingly in some cases, all crisply narrated by Westbrook Van Voorhis.

In the faux control room at Trinity, Robert Oppenheimer announced to Isidor I. Rabi as the countdown continued, "The automatic control's started now. Rab, this time the stakes are really high!"

Rabi: "It's going to work all right, Robert, and I'm sure we'll never be sorry for it."

Oppie: "In forty seconds, we'll know!" The countdown continued. The dialogue here, and throughout, could hardly have been more stilted.

Cut to the explosion—from the official U.S. footage of the test—and the awed look of the scientists as they peered through smoked-lens glasses, followed by the Bush-Conant handshake on the sandy desert floor (filmed in that Boston warehouse). Then, after fifteen minutes, just when one might think the film was mere commemoration, it suddenly took on current issues surrounding the twice and future bomb. The scene shifted to the offices of the

FAS and boosted the appeal for funds by the Emergency Committee headed by Dr. Einstein. Then it claimed that the Baruch
Plan, though rejected by the Soviets, had the "overwhelming"
support of the rest of the world. The narrator even asserted that
with global controls the United States would be willing to destroy
its nuclear arsenal and eliminate for all time "the nightmare of
nuclear war."

The National Board of Review hailed it as "a vivid short . . . a
good condensation of masses of material into simple, clear exposi-
tion." *Time* called it the first moving picture to portray the birth
of the atomic era "not as cloak-&-Geiger-counter melodrama
but as deadly serious historical fact." And the characters! "Shy"
Albert Einstein looked more and more like "a sagacious old yak."
Then there was the "quick-eyed" Lise Meitner. The "strongest and
strangest drama," according to *Time*, occurred at the end of the
Trinity test, however. At the actual site, according to some reports,
a few scientists danced a kind of jig to celebrate the success. But
history and humans were "not yet tough enough to endure that
sight," the *Time* report affirmed. Instead what we saw was simply
Conant and Bush stretched out on that fake desert floor, "solemnly
shaking hands."

While the *March of Time* short covered the bomb-makers and
the political aftermath, it (like its MGM counterpart) barely cited
the effects in Japan. It did include a few seconds from Hiroshima
shot by an American crew, including a vivid moment with a U.S.
soldier pointing to the shadow left by a vaporized Japanese citizen
on a concrete bridge. Then it moved on.

It was looking more and more like this might be pretty much all
American audiences would see of footage from the atomic cities.
That black-and-white Japanese newsreel footage capturing graphic
effects on survivors, seized by the U.S. military back in October,
had been returned to the film crew so they could assemble a

160-minute documentary out of it. When completed, it was con-
fiscated again by the Americans, along with all the raw footage
and outtakes, and sent to the Pentagon. Some of the footage was
screened for tactical and medical experts, then labeled top secret,
and buried deep in the military archives, perhaps never to emerge.
The one threat to this plan: members of the Japanese newsreel
team had secretly made one copy of their documentary before the
American seizure and hid it in the ceiling of an editing suite, to
remain there at least until the occupation ended. (None of it would
appear on a screen in the West until a few segments were smuggled
to French director Alain Resnais for use in his classic 1959 film,
*Hiroshima, Mon Amour*.)

An elite U.S. military team, meanwhile, had shot a dozen hours
of film in the atomic cities over the course of several weeks, this
time in blazing color, the only such footage that existed. Included
was extensive coverage of badly injured survivors undergoing treatment in hospitals and clinics. The filmmakers felt certain that the
military would order them to produce an important documentary
for American audiences, revealing the true effects of the bomb as
a warning that it must be handled with care, if at all, in the future.
But once again the footage was shipped to the Pentagon, viewed
by a few experts and officials (who were startled by the human
effects), and stamped *classified*. They ordered that it only be used
for training films for the military and never shown to the public.
The director of the color footage, Lieutenant Daniel McGovern,
would later confide, "I was told by people in the Pentagon, hell no
and damn no, they didn't want those images put out because they
didn't want the general public to know what their weapons had
done, the horror and devastation—at a time when they were planning on more bombs." None of the color footage would emerge for
more than thirty years.

———

While American audiences met the flesh-and-blood figures who had created the bomb in the *March of Time* short, MGM was wrapping up its filming of many of the same men portrayed by actors on its sound stages. Visits to the set by reporters had concluded, so the studio attempted to maintain publicity momentum by distributing staged photos and stills. MGM repeatedly highlighted that "because of the nature of the picture, which will be approved by government officials before its release . . . all usual studio passes were rescinded to the sound stage." Driving this home, one photo showed "studio cop" Walter Cloud, "who remained on duty on set throughout the production, checking passes," according to the caption. Another found saucy actress Audrey Totter studying a barred door which carried a sign, *"TOP SECRET: All Stage Passes Rescinded for Security Measures. The Atom Bomb Picture Is Being Made on This Stage."* One shot simply displayed a studio ID card with: *"Admit Brian Donlevy to Restricted Atomic Bomb Production Area."*

Robert Walker posed in flight gear getting checked out by the lead pilot on the Nagasaki mission, a grinning Charles Sweeney, a paid consultant. (Walker had perhaps the thickest head of hair ever to fit under an officer's military cap in wartime.) Leslie Groves, smiling broadly and in full uniform, chatted with Donna Reed, who looked youthful and gorgeous in a stylish dress and black gloves. But when Groves stood next to Donlevy the grin disappeared; perhaps he was aware of the embarrassingly wide difference in their girth.

Elsewhere, Sweeney studied with director Norman Taurog a strip of film depicting a few seconds of the Hiroshima mission before offering his approval (according to the caption). David Hawkins, Oppenheimer's former aide, met Hume Cronyn. Roman Bohnen reclined on a lawn at the studio, studying a script before tackling his role as President Truman. James K. McGuinness, quite fat and dressed in a bow tie and argyle socks, visited with Taurog and technical adviser H.T. Wensel. Dr. Edward Tompkins was shown renewing his acquaintance with Donna Reed, both wearing dark suits, as she held the very letter, it was claimed, that launched the movie. Reed, this time in a light summer dress, displayed the same letter to Tony Owen, her much older husband.

Owen, although promised a hefty finder's fee for bringing the project to MGM, had played no role in developing the movie, but was exploiting his contacts with the scientists on another major endeavor: a radio series titled *The Atomic Story*, to be hosted by (or starring) Orson Welles. Owen asked FAS to sign a seven-year contract to provide their exclusive cooperation. Tempted by the promise of badly needed funds, the organization nevertheless demurred, wary of the "exclusive" promise, and the project appeared stillborn.

When a new issue of *The New Yorker* arrived at the very end of August, the cover featured a generic picnic scene, with people sunbathing, hiking, riding horses. The first few pages held the usual ads for nylons and women's clothing from Lord & Taylor or Bergdorf Goodman. But there was something unique about this issue: there was no "Talk of the Town," few cartoons, no book reviews. The entire issue was devoted to one feature, sixty-eight pages long (some thirty thousand words), written by war correspondent and novelist John Hersey. His temporary titles for the piece, "Events at Hiroshima" or "Some Experiences at Hiroshima," had fallen away in favor of the simple and powerful: "Hiroshima."

In a note to readers, the editors explained that they had taken this extraordinary step based on the conviction that most people still did not recognize the profoundly different power of this weapon—"the almost total obliteration of a city"—and now "might well take time to consider the terrible implications of its use." Hersey's first sentence set the scene like none other to date: "At exactly fifteen minutes past eight in the morning, on August 6,

1945, Japanese time, at the moment when the atomic bomb flashed above Hiroshima, Miss Toshiko Sasaki, a clerk in the personnel department of the East Asia Tin Works, had just sat down at her place in the plant office and was turning her head to speak to the girl at the next desk." Clearly he was going to go far beyond, in both style and content, the wrenching first-person report from the Jesuit pastor John Siemes earlier in the year.

When Hersey submitted the article as a four-part series, William Shawn, who edited it, proposed running it in one issue for maximum impact. Mission accomplished. The article caused an immediate sensation. All copies sold out on newsstands. The mayor of Princeton, New Jersey, asked every resident to read it. Newspapers requested reprint rights, which Hersey granted if proceeds went to the Red Cross. Plans were announced for narrating the entire story over the ABC radio network on four consecutive evenings. *The New Yorker* was flooded with requests for extra copies—Albert Einstein, for example, wanted one thousand to distribute to members of his Emergency Committee of Atomic Scientists. When Einstein sent out copies he included in his cover note, "I believe Mr. Hersey has given a true picture of the appalling effect on human beings. . . . And this picture has implications for the future of mankind which must deeply concern all responsible men and women."

Columnists and editors, most of whom had expressed strong support for the use of the bomb, nevertheless praised the article, many calling it the strongest reporting of its time. *The New York Times* declared that every American "who has permitted himself to make jokes about atom bombs, or who has come to regard them as just one sensational development that can now be accepted as part of civilization . . . ought to read Mr. Hersey." The editorial reminded readers that the "disasters at Hiroshima and Nagasaki were our handiwork," and that the crucial argument that the bomb reputedly saved more lives than it took might appear unsound after reading Hersey. On top of that, Hersey chronicled the gruesomely unique way so many perished in death-by-radiation, which caused at least 20 percent of the casualties. Writing to *New Yorker* editors, the journalist Janet Flanner compared the article to Matthew Brady's photographs during the Civil War, one of the first "records of how people really looked in war."

Just one of dozens of brief, riveting episodes in the article: "Everything fell, and Miss Sasaki lost consciousness. The ceiling dropped suddenly and the wooden floor above collapsed in splinters and the people there came down and the roof above them gave way; but principally and first of all, the bookcases right behind her swooped forward and the contents threw her down, with her left leg horribly twisted and breaking underneath her. There, in the tin factory, in the first moments of the atomic age, a human being was crushed by books."

Some readers felt this grim account of the first atomic bomb survivors was somewhat diminished by its surroundings—the usual ads for quality booze, Tiffany pins, leg cosmetics, and vacations abroad. A flood of letters to *The New Yorker*, however, revealed that most readers were terribly moved. A college student wrote, "I had never thought of the people in the bombed cities as individuals." Many mentioned that they were now ashamed of what America had done. A young scientist, once proud of his work for the Manhattan Project, revealed that he wept as he read the article and was "filled with shame to recall the whoopee spirit" with which he and others had received the news of the bombing, recalling a "champagne dinner" that night. "We didn't realize" the horror and human effects, he added. "I wonder if we do yet."

One reader not pleased was Henry Luce, Hersey's main employer. *Time* claimed that Hersey "had practically stumbled into" this story and that editor Harold Ross ("a man given to juvenile and profane tantrums") had only printed the article at that length in one issue because he was notably short of good material. The novelist Thomas Mann had an interesting take himself. He hailed the article but declared it should not be translated for the postwar Germans because it is "their only pleasure to enjoy the mistakes and sins committed anywhere else in the world."

Would "Hiroshima" provoke a public rethinking of the wisdom of Truman's decision to use the bomb? To date that debate had centered on what to do with the *next* bombs, not what had been done with the first ones. Atomic scientists who had never before addressed the divisive Hiroshima decision—the *Bulletin of the Atomic Scientists* had just called it "water over the dam"—were now speaking out. Albert Einstein commented that the bomb probably was used primarily to end the Pacific war before Russia got into it.

Not everyone responded positively. "I read Hersey's report," one subscriber wrote *The New Yorker.* "It was marvelous. Now let us drop a handful [of atomic bombs] on Moscow." General Thomas Farrell, currently being portrayed in the MGM movie, was so angry he asked Bernard Baruch to propose another article to the editors at the magazine—about six POWs mistreated by the Japanese and how *they* felt about the bomb. (That American POWs died in the Hiroshima attack would remain a secret for decades.)

Others felt Hersey had not gone far enough. The writer himself admitted to publisher Alfred A. Knopf that he had "been at great pains to keep the tone of guilt about using the bomb at a minimum." *The New York Times,* in a second "minority opinion" editorial, charged that Hersey had merely "given us a picture of war's horrors as the world has long known them, rather than a picture of the unprecedented horrors of atomic warfare." The simple number 100,000—indicating the number killed in one day—conveyed more about the meaning of Hiroshima than any evocative anecdote.

The left-wing critic Dwight Macdonald was more caustic.

Macdonald despised the article's "suave, toned-down, underplayed kind of naturalism," its "moral deficiency" in vision, its "antiseptic" prose. Naturalism, he suggested, was no longer adequate "either esthetically or morally, to cope with the modern horrors." The writer Mary McCarthy mocked *The New Yorker* for declaring a moral "emergency" while surrounding the Hersey article with all those cigarette and perfume ads. While agreeing that the atomic bomb threatened the continuity of life, she unfairly characterized the key survivors in the Hersey article as "busy little Methodists": "What it did was to minimize the atomic bomb by treating it as though it belonged to the familiar order of catastrophes. . . . The existence of any survivors is an irrelevancy, and the interview with the survivors is an insipid falsification of the truth of atom warfare. To have done the atom bomb justice, Mr. Hersey would have had to interview the dead."

But it was *Saturday Review* editor Norman Cousins whose reaction would end up having the most impact. He had already argued that the bomb might have been aimed at the Russians as much as the Japanese. Now in an editorial titled "The Literacy of Survival," he asserted that Americans, despite Hersey's achievement, still did not fully comprehend what they had done. "Have we as a people," he asked, "any sense of responsibility for the crime of Hiroshima and Nagasaki? Have we attempted to press our leaders for an answer concerning their refusal to heed the pleas of the scientists against the use of the bomb without a demonstration?" He concluded by calling for a national "moratorium" on all normal habits and routine, "in order to acquire a basic literacy" on the moral implications of the atomic bombings and the atomic age. If this accomplished little it would at least "enable the American people to recognize a crisis when they see one and are in one."

What this editorial, along with the Hersey article, would accomplish more than anything was to inspire pro-bomb authorities, from James Conant to Henry Stimson, to take redemptive action, involving a quite different major article in another leading magazine, to reinforce the Hiroshima narrative they had promoted from the start.

While this new debate far from Hollywood raged, an influential local conservative, W.R. "Billy" Wilkerson, was getting ready to put forces in motion that would rock the movie colony for more than a decade.

The slick, mustachioed owner, publisher, and editor of *The Hollywood Reporter* since 1930, also managed nightclubs in Los Angeles. The previous year he had bought a large plot on the dusty fringes of Las Vegas to build what would become the groundbreaking Flamingo casino and hotel. The project, however, was soon taken over by mobster Bugsy Siegel after he purchased a two-thirds stake. Now Wilkerson, who had long warned about Communist sympathizers in the Screen Writers Guild ("The Red beachhead"), planned to start naming names in his magazine's popular "Tradeviews" column. Wilkerson knew this would be controversial, and that studio owners might order an advertising boycott of his publication, fearing that some sort of "blacklist" of writers and performers might catch fire. So he went to confession at the popular Blessed Sacrament Church, two blocks from *The Reporter*'s office. "Father, I'm launching a campaign," he began, "and it's gonna cause a lot of hurt. But they [the Communists] are, you know, antipathetic to my faith. They are my natural enemies. And I just need to know what to do."

"Get those bastards, Billy," the priest supposedly replied.

So, as the summer wore on, that's exactly what Wilkerson tried to do. In a column titled "A Vote for Joe Stalin" he listed eleven Hollywood figures as Communists or sympathizers. They included Dalton Trumbo (who had written *Thirty Seconds over Tokyo*, among

other films), Howard Koch (best known for *Casablanca*), and Ring
Lardner, Jr. (*Woman of the Year*). "This is not an issue that concerns
merely a few hundred writers," he charged. "It concerns millions
of readers who must depend upon the free trade of ideas. . . . It
concerns still more millions of children—who can't read yet—but
who were born with the right to hope for a free world." That tally
of eleven names, rumored to have been assembled with intelligence
help from studio legend Howard Hughes, was still missing CP
member Roman Bohnen, who was about to play Truman in a certain high-profile MGM movie. But Wilkerson would be adding to
what became known as "Billy's List" in coming weeks. Hollywood
would never be the same.

Robert Oppenheimer faced his own career-threatening challenge
related to "Red" connections: another interview with the FBI
on the subject of who had approached him back in 1943 with the
notion of possibly transmitting atomic secrets to the Soviets.

Back then, Oppie had told the bureau that an individual he would
not identify had informed him that three Los Alamos scientists
were solicited for such a leak, and the man allegedly offering his
services as a conduit was a scientist named George Eltenton. Later,
pressed on the matter in a Los Alamos security review, he told
General Groves (who promised to keep it a secret, and did) that the
man who approached him about this offer was Haakon Chevalier,
his close friend from Communist Party circles in Berkeley. Nothing had come of it, he told the general, and it might have just been
loose talk anyway. This troubled Groves, but he desperately needed
Oppenheimer at Los Alamos so he overlooked it. By the summer of
1946, however, both Chevalier and Eltenton had been questioned
by the FBI about this sensitive matter.

Now, on September 5, Oppenheimer's time to answer questions
from the G-men arrived. In his Berkeley office he politely admitted

that he had associated socially with Communists but still refused to name any of them. More damaging, he finally admitted that he was the one and only scientist targeted by Eltenton in the "spy" move. He had invented the two other targets to protect his friend Chevalier, who otherwise would have been quickly identified by the bureau as the likely conduit. Oppenheimer tried to shrug off his earlier lie to the FBI as merely a "complicated, cock-and-bull story," told merely to help a friend who, like himself, was certainly loyal to his country. He had, in any case, rejected the Eltenton maneuver rather than succumb to "treason." The FBI, he suggested, need investigate no further. Unfortunately for him, this would hardly be the end of this story.

# 17

# Preview in Pomona

L ouis B. Mayer had viewed the latest cut of *The Beginning or the End* and considered it "a great job" but wished to "add tremendous dramatic value and world impact for the finish"—that is, to "vividly show the destructive force of the bomb on Hiroshima," MGM's Carter Barron informed General Leslie Groves. To accomplish this, Mayer ordered an expansion of the script and new special effects for the Hiroshima sequence, necessitating retakes and a delay in the film's premiere.

With this, Sam Marx summoned the veteran scribe, John Lee Mahin, who had worked over the Wead script months earlier, to return to the project and draft a new treatment quite different from the one inside the *Enola Gay* already filmed. Mahin could hardly have been more different than Frank Wead: Harvard educated; a former newspaperman; friend of Ben Hecht, who he joined in writing the celebrated screenplay for *Scarface*. Hired by MGM, he churned out one movie after another (including *Dr. Jekyll and Mr. Hyde*) with several starring Clark Gable. He even provided some uncredited help to *The Wizard of Oz* and *Gone with the Wind*. His first Oscar nomination arrived for *Captains Courageous*, and he became one of the highest-paid writers in town. He had just written the screenplay for *The Yearling*.

Mahin helped found the Screen Writers Guild in 1933 but soon left to chair the rival, and much more elitist and conservative, Screen Playwrights, a company shop. He bragged that his group "spied" on alleged Communists in the guild and claimed that he told Dalton Trumbo and other screenwriters that they would be blacklisted sooner or later because of their ties to the "Reds." How his views would inform *The Beginning of the End* was hard to guess, although he (like Wead and McGuinness) was not likely to sympathize with the scientists' call for working with the hated Soviets to curb the spread of nuclear weapons.

His scenario would require on-the-ground Hiroshima images if the studio actually dared to show them. Mahin proposed an ambitious sequence relying on flashbacks during the reading of the late Matt Cochran's letter to his wife at the Lincoln Memorial. "When you have read this," Matt intoned in the current script, "the bomb dropped on Hiroshima will have told you why I went to the Pacific." Beyond that he could obviously say nothing more because—thanks to the fatal accident—he missed any chance to board the *Enola Gay* and observe the bombing.

This challenge would seem insurmountable but—this was Hollywood! In the new Mahin concoction the ghostly image of Matt's face would appear faintly behind his pregnant wife, looking at her tear-stained face. "Oh, Anne darling, I *was* there," he now reveals. "I saw it all. I saw everything," at least in his vivid imagination. He knew the power of the bomb well enough to be able to detail for her in his letter (with cinematic images applied) "the indescribable destruction" that he had missed witnessing.

First, a view of Hiroshima before the bomb, residents shopping, the sound of an approaching plane. *Matt: "People . . . our enemies, it's true . . . but human beings just the same, going to work. . . . One plane? What could that do?"* Then a shift to the military camp in the city, where Japan's "mighty army confidently waited the invasion," with anti-aircraft fire in the distance (which did not actually happen but, okay, this was all in Matt's imagination). Women wash clothes in the river, men relax in an outdoor café, workers enter a factory, two painters work on a mural showing a Japanese soldier in a death struggle with an evil Uncle Sam. *Matt: "A new day had begun."* Missing, notably, are any children heading for schools.

Suddenly at a bridge "flesh and air and earth become a cauldron. . . . Where the people have been standing are dark patches on the ground." *Matt: "They had only time to cast their shadows."* At the military camp the same sort of scene and more shadows. And goodbye to the women washing clothes at the river, the people in the café, and the workers as "flame and smoke pour from the inside" of their factory.

An overview of the city reveals the earth dissolving "to a hundred thousand flames, licking the cold white face of final death." Then a return to "Matt's spirit," who advises Anne that for her, their soon-to-be-born child, and their fellow men and women, something like this happening again simply must not be. *Matt: "Here, with this new power, Man has dared to study and operate the loom of God's weaving. . . . We stand now where the early savages stood, when they ceased running away from fire and began to use it well. If those primitive savages learned to use fire, we of an enlightened age can learn to use atomic energy for a more constructive, full and richer life."*

Matt, and the movie, would close:

> God has not shown us a new way to destroy ourselves. Atomic energy is the hand He has extended to lift us from the savagery and ruin of war and to lighten the burden of peace. Now, in the greatest hour of life on earth, Man has found the secret of the power of the universe. What we have unleashed is not the end. With all my love I tell you this: Men will learn to use this knowledge well. They won't fail. For this is the timeless moment that gives mankind the chance to prove

that human beings are made in the image and likeness
of God.

The new sequence certainly supported the evolving, pro-nuclear
theme, but would its focus on innocent Japanese civilians (albeit
absent any children) about to be exterminated stand any chance
of making the final cut? MGM's McGuinness, General Groves,
and the White House would all have to approve the Mahin scenario and allow the studio to proceed. Groves took a quick look
and replied, neutrally, that the proposed sequence at least did not
undermine national security. But did it threaten moral security?

Legendary director Fritz Lang might have been asking the same
question concerning his movie, *Cloak and Dagger*, starring Gary
Cooper as an Oppenheimer-like physicist recruited to spy on the
German and Italian atomic bomb projects. The film was about to
be released via Warner Brothers but Lang was seething over the
producer killing the final reel (after approving the script).

It showed Cooper and others storming a Nazi hideout in the
mountains where they discovered that the Germans had disman-
tled their atomic bomb lab and possibly hauled it off to Argentina
or Spain. The scene ended with explicit warnings about a nuclearized future as Cooper (according to the script) "senses possible
defeat for mankind through misuse of the new scientific era that
lies ahead." He pleads: "God have mercy on us." With the reel
removed, the story would end instead on an optimistic note, focusing on Cooper and his lover, played by Lilli Palmer.

The word from the studio was that the film's advisers had protested that the final scene, as pure fiction, ruined the factual basis
for much of the rest of the movie. Lang believed it was more ideo-
logical, a move to destroy his "plea for peace," believing it would
never have been cut absent "Hiroshima and Nagasaki." Then there
was the fact that three of those who labored on the script—Ring

Lardner Jr., Alvah Bessie, and Albert Maltz—were suspected Communists (and would be arrested the following year in the Hollywood Ten case).

Over at the Production Code office on Hollywood Boulevard, Joe Breen, meanwhile, read the new Mahin scene and pronounced it acceptable. His office also sent over to MGM its first formal "analysis" chart on the entire picture. It listed all of the characters in the movie, and noted if each was prominent or minor, and "sympathetic" or not. It also broke down the cast by race, nationality, profession, and if he or she were a public official or "religious worker." Under the category "liquor" it noted a "toast with wine by scientists upon successful experiment." But overall there was "very little" drinking in the movie. Apparently that was quite admirable.

Then under the heading *Crimes* there was this: "No. of Killings—Many individuals in war." And regarding *Other Violence*: "War."

The odds that the conservative MGM executives and the White House would ultimately approve the new Mahin scene, with its civilians-about-to-be-extinguished aspect, appeared dim in light of the continuing popularity of John Hersey's "Hiroshima" article, now on the verge of publication as the nonfiction book event of the season. Sam Marx assured three Manhattan Project veterans in a letter that whereas the Hersey article was "making many readers feel that the creators of the atomic bomb are the world's greatest war criminals . . . it should be a relief to many scientists that a motion picture of this magnitude is on its way, hailing their achievement as the most magnificent triumph of modern times."

Those close to Truman, nervous about this new challenge to his decision to drop the bomb, had largely remained silent about the Hersey article. They didn't want to stir controversy and draw even more attention to it. So the White House was far from pleased when Leonard Lyons reported in his widely syndicated gossip column:

"A White House visitor asked President Truman: 'Did you read the Hiroshima piece?' He said: 'What was that?' and the visitor told him: 'The John Hersey piece in *The New Yorker*.' Mr. Truman replied: 'I never read *The New Yorker*. Just makes me mad.'"

Perhaps a little perturbed, famed *New Yorker* editor Harold Ross two days later sent Charles Ross at the White House three copies of the issue that contained the Hersey opus (along with a clip of the Lyons item), as he felt the Hiroshima article was "one that should be read by all the influential people in the world that can be got to read it." Would Charles Ross read it himself and perhaps recommend it to the president? "I wouldn't have paid any attention to this," the editor explained, "but I was told by a Washington newspaperman today that he is certain President Truman had not [even] heard of it." That would indeed make him one of the few in government or intellectual circles who had not. Harold Ross added: "I think he ought to know about it."

Charlie Ross replied quickly, claiming that *he* had read the article when it first came out and found it "magnificent." Ross, before becoming Truman's press secretary, had a strong journalistic background. He had won a Pulitzer Prize for his reporting on Depression-era economic issues in 1932 for the *St. Louis Post-Dispatch* and then became editorial page editor of the paper. Now he told the *New Yorker* editor he could not say whether or not Truman had read the piece but, in any event, he doubted that his boss ever said what Lyons had him saying. And surely if he did mutter that a magazine "just makes me mad" he had to be referring to another publication. Now, in any case, he would make sure Truman received a copy of that issue. He asked Harold Ross to keep all this hush-hush.

The editor replied immediately, revealing that a staffer had written a small piece on the Lyons report but now he wavered on publishing it because it might not be "fair" to the president. But he still hoped Truman would read the article. "There is, of course, a feeling of holy zeal about the Hiroshima piece in this office," he explained, "and a hope that the leaders of all countries will read it. This feeling extends considerably beyond the office, as a matter of fact."

On October 22, Charlie Ross informed Harold Ross that he had asked Truman point blank if he ever said *The New Yorker* "just makes me mad" and he denied it. Truman added that he was happy to now have the Hersey piece (indicating that, indeed, he had not yet read it). "I may be able to make a *New Yorker* fan out of him yet," the president's secretary declared. Harold Ross then concluded the unusual exchange by revealing that he had gone ahead and killed that item in the magazine.

The Hersey article and influential Norman Cousins editorial threatened to upset the official narrative promoting the utter necessity of using the bomb against Japanese cities. Behind the scenes, however, it had also produced a backlash that promised to bluntly reassert that narrative, perhaps for all time.

James Conant, who had just appeared on the cover of *Time* magazine, had grown so alarmed by the threat posed by the Hersey and Cousins pieces that he had called his friend Vannevar Bush to complain that the two magazine writers had failed to put the use of the bomb in proper context. Conant then wrote to Harvey Bundy, former assistant to Secretary of War Stimson, and enclosed a clip of the Cousins column. "I am considerably disturbed about this type of comment which has been increasing in recent days," Conant explained. He warned of a potential "distortion of history" that would be passed down by "a small minority" to succeeding generations—likening it to those who claimed America never should have entered World War I—if Hersey and Cousins were not challenged. It was vital that someone with great authority, such as

Stimson, compose a "statement of fact," in the form of a popular article, and soon.

Declaring he was "unrepentant" about serving on the committee that approved using the two bombs against Japan, Conant even outlined the points Stimson should explore: the atomic scientists had "raised no protest" (actually not true); a demonstration shot in a remote area was "not realistic" (debatable); and it was just "Monday morning quarterbacking" to assert that Japan was ready to surrender (in fact, several prominent Truman advisers had raised the issue before the attacks). This latter argument also seemed contrary to what the U.S. Strategic Bombing Survey found. Admiral William "Bull" Halsey had recently declared that Japan was trying to quit but the Americans "had a toy and wanted to try it out."

Stimson readily accepted the writing assignment, however, which he would undertake with his former aide's son, McGeorge Bundy. Soon he regretted it, as he recalled the doubts he had harbored about using the bomb against any civilian target (not just Kyoto) as the decision was being made. He had even spent some sleepless nights over this. If anything, Stimson was among the more "dovish" of Truman's advisers on ending the war without resorting to mass slaughter. He had also been at the center of an incredible, if little-known, episode involving perhaps the only Manhattan Project participant to act as a "whistleblower" in directing his opposition to using the bomb against Japan straight to the president.

This was an engineer for a leading project contractor, the Kellex Corporation, living in New York City, named Oswald C. Brewster. Deeply involved with the separation of uranium isotopes, he supported the race with Germany for the bomb. Then, on May 24, 1945, after Germany's surrender, he risked arrest for security violations (indeed he would later claim he was followed by agents and his phone tapped), by penning a powerful and prescient three-thousand-word letter. Then he carefully transmitted it through Army channels to Truman, Stimson, and Secretary of State Byrnes. Brewster warned that an atomic bomb would easily destroy an entire city and produce a massive number of civilian casualties, spread dangerous radiation, and inspire other countries to race for their own such weapon. Therefore he opposed using it against Japan. While admitting this was an "unpopular and minority view" among his peers—and might be considered by some "treason"—he felt duty-bound, as one of the relatively few Americans who knew about this plan, to take his protest to the top.

Brewster recognized a key factor influencing the decision to drop the bomb: all of Truman's advisers, tightly bound to the project and its success—and especially Groves—had strong personal or career reasons for making sure the new weapon was utilized. He pleaded for Truman to seek "disinterested counsel" from "unbiased" observers. "This thing must not be permitted on earth," the engineer asserted. "We must not be the most hated and feared people on earth, however good our intent must be. . . . I beg of you, sir, not to pass this off because I happen to be an unknown. . . . There surely are men in this country to whom you could turn, asking them to study this problem."

Against all odds, the letter reached Stimson's desk, and he read it. Rather than rejecting the argument and/or its threat to security, he urged General George C. Marshall, the Army chief of staff, to peruse this "remarkable document" and share "the impress of its logic," just as high-level discussions about using the bomb against Japan were reaching a climax. Stimson then delivered the letter directly to Truman himself, not knowing that the president had been sent his own version. There was no indication, however, that Truman read any version of it or discussed it with anyone. And that was the end of that.

Now, more than a year later, with Stimson rather ambivalent about his writing assignment, McGeorge Bundy solicited rough drafts of the article from his father, from Leslie Groves, and from two others. The White House was not directly involved, but Truman surely approved, as he had separately urged Stimson to write just such a defense. Harvey Bundy argued that the main aim for dropping the bomb was simply to save lives. General Groves painted a picture of thoughtful men exercising great care in making a truly wise decision; as usual, he took wide credit for this. He falsely asserted that the target was always meant to be a city, "primarily military."

Stimson and McGeorge Bundy consolidated the arguments and sent a draft to Conant at Harvard for comment. Conant urged that the article stick to the facts and avoid an argumentative tone. He also insisted that they eliminate any mention of the internal discussions (of which Stimson was a part) about modifying Truman's unconditional surrender demand to allow Japan to keep its emperor—which some thought would speed an early, pre-bombing, surrender offer. Conant rightly called this "the problem of the Emperor." And he was so concerned readers might feel that the idea of a demonstration shot seemed fair that he wrote an insert arguing otherwise.

Conant pushed Stimson to get the article published in a major magazine as soon as possible. But Stimson remained conflicted. "I have rarely been connected with a paper about which I have so much doubt at the last minute," he told a friend. He feared that those who knew him and regarded him as "a kindly minded Christian gentleman" would, after reading such an article, "feel I am cold blooded and cruel."

Sam Marx liked the images evoked by the new scenes of Hiroshima citizens under attack written by John Lee Mahin. Even with that segment not completed, MGM wished to test the current cut on a live audience. So it booked an art deco palace, the Fox Theater in downtown Pomona, which could seat over fifteen hundred, for this purpose and it attracted a capacity audience.

Afterward, the man who arranged it would report to MGM that the "outstanding" movie kept the crowd "spellbound for its entire showing." The theater manager agreed that it was "so thought-provoking, so great in scope and so real its presentation that it is deserving of every expressive adjective in the book." The only letdown those two men sensed was in the ending, which seemed weak compared to the tempo of the rest of the production. (Sam Marx and other MGM officials on the scene seemed to agree, the report noted.) Among the patrons' comments scribbled on notecards when they exited:

> —*If this picture does not stir every person in the U.S., something is wrong.*
> —*It was the most wonderful preview I've ever seen. I believe it should remain as it is with nothing cut out.*
> —*Truly a wonderful, exciting movie. The atom bomb blast was really sensational.*
> —*I could see the whole movie again just to hear the bomb go off again.*
> —*An excellent picture very wonderfully played by a fine cast.*

While it was true that the vast majority of the reviewers were quite positive, if often not very specific, the critical comments might have given MGM pause about certain aspects.

> —*A magnificent picture but "over the heads" of three-quarters of us.*
> —*How will the citizens of year 2446 account for the idiotic, neurotic flavor?*
> —*Very good [but Matt] shouldn't have died.*
> —*It's too scientific—too many facts. It would be all right for educational purposes but not for entertainment.*
> —*It was a good picture but too drawn out.*

*—Bomb is fake. Cast at times looks foolish.*

*—It may help our enemies.*

In addition, at least three complained about the drinking scene, and one asserted that FDR's hair was "too white. Darker at the corners would look better."

At this juncture, Sam Marx wrote his first letter to Robert Oppenheimer in months, informing him that the studio was "building up the scenes at Hiroshima" to provide a "new and terrifying climax." Therefore, the movie's premiere would be delayed about eight weeks. "The delay is not pleasant for us, but it seems to be the universal feeling of our studio executives that this picture is so important and has so much to say that time is no longer a consideration. Unhappily, the problem of the bomb is here to stay and nothing is likely to affect this problem in the next few months."

The main reason Marx wrote, however, was to report on the recent test showing in Pomona as an enticement for Oppie and his wife to attend a private screening at MGM—and then endorse the final version. Marx was so thrilled with the Pomona response that he attached several pages of the (mainly positive) comments scribbled by the preview audience. He called these results "very fine." James Roosevelt, the late president's son, had viewed it and exclaimed, according to Marx, that he hoped the picture would be re-released every year "until it was known that every man, woman and child in America had seen it."

Marx acted almost cocky about the quality and audience appeal of his picture. "We are no longer concerned with how the public will receive the showing of this picture," he boasted. "Such showings will be overwhelmingly enthusiastic and exciting." So would Oppie please take a look at MGM's latest triumph? "Men like yourself," he explained, "who have been so cooperative and helpful, constitute my last remaining worry. I think if we can know that you are pleased we can cancel all the orders for aspirin and feel that 'the big headache' is finally over."

As was often the case in recent months, Marx acted overly optimistic. Niels Bohr continued to deny use of his name and image, although he had tentatively agreed to view the movie.

This difficult issue prompted Oppenheimer to call Marx from his Berkeley home, a conversation among the many recorded by the FBI. Bohr, he confirmed, "devoutly hoped" he was not in the MGM movie. Bohr worried about factual inaccuracies that might "offend" his colleagues still in Europe. His decision was sealed when he spoke with Lise Meitner and learned of her refusals. Oppie then helpfully informed Marx where to contact Bohr in Manhasset, New York.

The FBI report to headquarters concluded: "MARX said this was the biggest picture that they had made and that they were going to finish it with the reading of the [Cochran] letter and that he was going to flash back to a tremendous spectacle, the destruction of Hiroshima. MARX stated that he wanted to show people in a visual way what could happen. OPPENHEIMER said he hoped it came out well and that he was sure MARX would find BOHR entirely in sympathy with everything he had in mind."

The latest *Beginning or the End* character to weigh in with a critique was Capt. William "Deke" Parsons. He was portrayed in the movie taking over for the deceased Matt Cochran in arming the Little Boy bomb en route to Hiroshima (a task he had accomplished in real life). Parsons, now at the Navy Department in Washington, had finally read a script and found that it presented the story in "good taste" and with "sufficient accuracy" overall. He enjoyed "the exploits of the mythical Colonel Jeff Nixon," even though the movie falsely showed him aiding Parsons in arming the bomb. But he had a major issue with the Cochran accident scenario, as he told MGM's Carter Barron in a letter.

Parsons recognized that the movie had transferred what he called "the postwar [Slotin] atomic accident at Los Alamos to Tinian." As officer in charge of preparing the Hiroshima bomb for delivery, he had trained scientists and technicians for months and was proud to say that on Tinian there "was not a single accident, slipup or delay of any kind. Such reliability was standard" and "we would have been criminally negligent to do otherwise." So the accident depicted in the movie, while it might have plausibly occurred in a lab or proving ground, "would be plain crazy at an advanced base in the final stages of preparing for battle delivery." He offered a biting comparison: imagine if the movie showed an engineer for the *Enola Gay* "testing her gasoline tanks with a blowtorch and being killed as he put out the resulting fire."

His suggestion: open the film by labeling Matt Cochran and Jeff Nixon as purely fictitious and *specifically* state that the accident on Tinian never happened.

When he heard nothing from MGM's Barron on this matter, Parsons called the studio and learned that, even after the retakes, the Tinian accident remained unchanged and nothing had been added to admit that the accident was pure fantasy. So Parsons took his complaint to the top, to General Groves. "I do not believe that the movie people realize the implication of such an accident," he wrote. "To them it is just another way of making the bomb delivery more dramatic and heightening the tension." If Groves in real life had known about such sloppy bomb-arming procedures he would have "no doubt fired everyone connected with such an impending mess, including me." And because real people are portrayed in the film, and it purports to accurately tell the story of the bomb, it is "very likely to be accepted as historically accurate. . . . I feel that if [left standing] the staging of the atomic accident on Tinian will directly reflect on you, Farrell, Oppenheimer and myself."

# 18

## "A Problem with the President's Scene"

The long-awaited Washington screening for *The Beginning or the End* finally arrived on October 26, held at the Navy Building auditorium. Attendees ranged from famous scientists to the country's most esteemed newspaper columnist, Walter Lippmann, and Truman aides Charles Ross and Matthew Connelly. This came at a low point in the Truman presidency, as his approval rating in polls had fallen to barely half the heady 80 percent mark he enjoyed after the Japanese surrender. Worse, the Democrats faced a possible Republican wave in the upcoming midterm elections.

Hosting for MGM were studio executive James K. McGuinness and D.C. rep Carter Barron, who told the audience the movie might yet be "trimmed" a bit. Already cut: That scene in the cove with the Germans delivering the secrets of the atomic bomb to the Japanese. The Mahin retake with Hiroshima citizens slain had not yet been (and might never be) filmed. Physicist Niels Bohr, whose signature on a contract was still much desired, failed to attend, so now he would be invited to a New York City preview.

And the response? Taking a critical, and potentially far-reaching and dangerous view, was Walter Lippmann. Just a week earlier he had attended a dinner at which various personages expressed fears about the MGM movie, without having seen it. Now, two days after the preview, Lippmann wrote what would turn out to be a highly influential two-page letter to one of the nervous guests at that dinner, Frank Aydelotte, of the Institute for Advanced Study at Princeton. "The film itself bears out your own apprehensions," Lippmann warned. Its basic theme "is not the problem of the atomic bomb in the world, but the success story of the Americans, particularly General Groves, in making the bomb."

This was made worse by the fact that the decisions to deploy the weapon "are melodramatic simplifications and, indeed, falsifications of what actually took place." He was especially incensed by the scene of Truman, with little apparent thought, ordering Groves and Stimson to take the bomb out to the Marianas "and use it" if the first test succeeded, just moments after he learned about the existence of the bomb project. "The scene between General Groves and President Truman is, of course, an outright fabrication and reduces the role of the President to extreme triviality in a great matter," Lippmann complained. "Serious people abroad are bound to say that if that is the way we made that kind of decision we are not to be trusted with such a powerful weapon. As you know, the decision was not made that way, and I consider it a libel not only on President Roosevelt but more particularly on Secretary Stimson who, incidentally appears in it as a doddering old man."

Lippmann was not done. Why was Bohr still in the film when, he'd heard, the scientist had forbidden it? In any case, the impersonation of scientists was "highly objectionable." It did a "great disservice to them and to science," and he expressed surprise that Fermi, Oppenheimer, and Einstein "have permitted it." His conclusion? "The thing should not have been done at all or, if done, it should have been a documentary film with purely educational purpose. But as it is now, it is primarily not a film explaining the atomic bomb, but a film which uses the atomic bomb for a Hollywood film." Could the movie be stopped now? "I don't know that anything can be done about it now, except to raise our voices loudly enough in objection to make people realize that this is not the wholly accepted American view of this matter." Lippmann warned that foreign governments would recognize that the film could not have been made without the assistance of U.S. officials— true enough—"and therefore they will assume it represents the general spirit and attitude of the U.S. Government."

Alarmed by the message from the godlike Lippmann, Aydelotte quickly sent copies of it to a few key people, including Oppenheimer, then in Berkeley. He advised in a cover note to Oppenheimer that "if you and your group were sufficiently insistent something could be done," but he received no reply.

Far from finished, Lippmann dashed off a shorter letter to James Conant. Hitting a lighthearted note, he informed his friend that the actor portraying him looked nothing like him. "If you have no other objections against the film," he advised, "you certainly have a grievance against the fact that, whereas General Groves has been transformed into a dashing, romantic cavalier, you have been de-glamorized in a most unfair way!" But Lippmann wanted to pass along more serious concerns as well, about which he was "very much disturbed." He repeated what he'd told Aydelotte about the harm the movie could do abroad, adding: "The film, of course, is not a documentary film which could be used for education and information; it is a melodrama which has as its central theme a success story—mainly the triumphs of Americans, and particularly General Groves, over the difficulties of making a bomb. . . . When you see the film, I think you are bound to feel that it is a bad example of the vulgarization and commercialization of a great subject by Hollywood."

Then, crucially, Lippmann also voiced his concerns directly to James K. McGuinness, who was then visiting Loew's headquarters in New York.

There was one man in the audience at the screening even more powerful than Lippmann, as he worked in very close proximity to President Truman. This was press secretary Charles Ross. After the screening he wrote to MGM's Carter Barron that he and others "very much enjoyed" the movie and found it "a thrilling picture" with a "beautifully worked out story" and fine acting. He had only one quarrel with it: "something needs to be done about the sequence in which President Truman appears."

As currently assembled, *The Beginning or the End* portrayed an aggressively decisive Truman—normally a good thing from the White House's point of view, given the president's growing reputation for dithering. But clearly, Ross believed, it had ventured too far in the direction of unthinking callousness. A fine line would have to be walked in a retake or the White House would likely no longer approve the movie, and might even try to scuttle it.

In reality, of course, when and how the "decision to drop" was made remained far too complicated to explore in a Hollywood entertainment. It was "not the product of a single mind," author and psychiatrist Robert Jay Lifton would later observe. "Rather, it resulted from a series of choices, of prior decisions, made by individuals and groups involved in a bomb-centered process." Oppenheimer claimed "the decision was implicit in the project." Privately, General Groves downplayed Truman's role, later asserting that the president's "decision was one of noninterference—basically, a decision not to upset the existing plans." He also described the unprepared Truman in that period as "like a little boy on a toboggan."

James K. McGuinness, informed about the new, high-level concerns emanating from two enormous power centers—Walter Lippmann and the White House—wasted no time springing into action. On November 1 he told Lippmann he had already discussed his critique with the top people at Loew's Inc. and at the studio in Culver City. As a result, they would be cutting some of the "personal stories which are trivial in conception and execution and consequently are out of keeping with the serious nature of the picture. This will redress the balance so that, I assure you, there will be no basis for criticism on that score in the finished film." (These cuts would prove to be minor.)

More significantly: the present scene with Truman making his quick decision to use the bomb would be axed completely. "Personally, I was deeply impressed by your feeling that we were showing our country's Chief Executive deciding a monumental matter in what was a much-too-hasty fashion," McGuinness affirmed. In its place: a new scene set in Potsdam in July 1945 that would detail the surrender ultimatum to Japan and Truman explaining to Charles Ross the compelling basis for using the bomb if the enemy did not quit. This would "sum up" Truman's previous conferences on the decision with our military and with Churchill. "For your criticism of the scene you saw and your careful analysis of the dangers inherent in it," McGuinness closed, "I wish to express my own gratitude and that of Loew's."

The same day, McGuinness sent three copies of the hastily written new scene to Ross, who was by then in Kansas City with the president (Truman hailed from nearby Independence, Missouri). It's unclear whether McGuinness or Marx or Mahin, or some combination, wrote the retake. "This seems to incorporate all the matters we talked about," McGuinness asserted, while noting it was only "tentative and I am eager to discuss it with you and to incorporate anything else you deem advisable." Time was now so pressing he even offered to fly to Kansas City to meet with Ross, then catch the luxury *Super Chief* train back to L.A. for the final revisions and retakes.

The package Ross received included an introductory memo by McGuinness describing the setting for the new scene in the president's sitting room at Potsdam. Dramatic lighting would keep Truman mainly in shadow with the camera pointed across the heavy, carved desk to Ross, over the president's shoulder. It would appear to be after dusk, with just a glimmer of light outside and from a desk lamp illuminating the room. Then Ross enters carrying a few sheets of paper.

**TRUMAN:** Sit down, Charlie. The time has come for you to know our nation's top secret—and it must remain just that—top secret. . . . Our country, with the help of scientists from nearly all the United Nations, has developed the most fearful weapon ever forged by man—an atomic bomb.

**ROSS:** Even the word sounds frightening.

**TRUMAN:** It has been tested—and it works. In peace, it will provide such power as will eventually lift most of mankind's burdens. In war—its destructive power is as much greater than any existing explosive as an anti-aircraft searchlight is brighter than a Christmas tree candle.

**ROSS:** If they had it they'd use it on us.

**TRUMAN:** That's a persuasive argument, Charlie—but not a decisive one.

**ROSS:** The whole thing is terrifying. You must have had some sleepless nights over it.

**TRUMAN:** Yes, it has cost me some sleep. I have had to make a tremendous decision. I've consulted about this every day for weeks, now. With the Chiefs of Staff, naval and military; with the Secretaries of State, War and Navy, and Mr. Churchill; with our greatest scientists. The consensus of opinion is that the bomb will shorten the war by approximately a year.

**ROSS:** Who disagreed?

**TRUMAN:** Nobody, actually. Some scientists who worked on the project think we should drop it on an uninhabited area as a warning. But the staff is sure the Japanese militarists would never let their people learn about it.

**ROSS:** I go along with that completely.

**TRUMAN:** The Army has selected certain Japanese cities which are prime military targets—because of war industry, military installations, troop concentrations or fortifications. We will shower them for ten days with leaflets telling the population to leave—telling them what is coming. We hope the warnings will save lives.

**ROSS:** They should—and, if the bomb shortens the war, that should save plenty of American lives, too.

**TRUMAN:** A year less of war will mean life for untold numbers of Russians, of Chinese—of Japanese—and from three hundred thousand to half a million of America's finest youth. That was the decisive consideration in my consent.

**ROSS:** As President of the United States, sir, you could make no other decision.

**TRUMAN:** As President, I could not. So I have instructed the Army to take the bomb to the Marianas and—when they get the green light—to use it.

Along with submitting the script, MGM notified Ross that it had suddenly decided to recast the role of Truman in the retakes. It's not clear if Ross had complained about actor Roman Bohnen or the studio decided on its own—after discovering the actor's left-wing activism. Almost certainly it was Ross. MGM, after all, had distributed publicity photos showing Bohnen at the Actors' Lab, even eating in the café there, which showed they knew about his politics. In any event, the note to Ross revealed that in the recasting "it must be emphasized that the President is a man of upright and military bearing; that he is physically trim, alive and alert, and that his actions are brisk and certain." This seemed odd, since the studio had previously bragged in publicity materials that Bohnen closely resembled Truman in appearance and manner. One more thing: the studio would be adding to Truman's lapel his Bronze Star "discharge button" from World War I.

Chosen for the retakes was another veteran character actor, Art Baker. The white-haired, forty-seven-year-old New York native had just played a detective in Hitchcock's *Spellbound* but perhaps more to the point had narrated for Walt Disney the World War II propaganda documentary, *Victory Through Air Power*.

There would not be any retakes, however, until the White House approved the new script. This would take place in a shifting atmosphere at the White House and elsewhere in Washington. The Republicans had just taken the House in midterm elections for the first time since 1930, and would now enjoy a whopping 246 to 188 margin there. They also seized the Senate. Among those elected were Senator Joseph McCarthy and Representative Richard M. Nixon. The conservative *Chicago Tribune* hailed the results as the greatest triumph for the country since Appomattox and the surrender of the Confederacy.

Within days, Ross returned to MGM a marked-up script for the retake with concise but revealing edits. For example, the already-inflated length of time the bomb would shorten the war increased from "a year" to "at least a year." The peacetime uses of atomic energy, the president must now declare, would lead to "a golden age—such an age of prosperity and well-being as the world has never known." Ross (or his boss, the president) deleted entirely the reference to scientists calling for the bomb to be dropped first on an uninhabited target. Sharing credit for building the bomb with other countries also disappeared. Ross, in the script, was given this new line: "Thank God we've got the bomb and not the Japanese!"

Acting on Truman's behalf, or at his behest, he also cut the lines that followed his telling the president that he "must have spent some sleepless nights over it." Gone entirely was Truman's reply: "Yes, it has cost me some sleep." Now, in this revision, Truman *simply does not reply.* MGM had tried to introduce the humanizing concept of a morally conflicted Truman, which he now expunged. So the sleepless-nights idea is introduced, but Truman will be free to deny it later in life (as he would, more than once).

On November 18, McGuinness thanked Ross for his "courtesy" in editing (some would say "censoring") his studio's script. MGM was readying it for the retakes "and it will be done exactly as it has been revised." There was no quibbling or pushback from the normally abrasive McGuinness. And when MGM's Carter Barron sent the revised script for the retake to General Groves he proudly noted: "This new treatment and dialogue was approved following a conference between Charlie Ross, Matt Connelly, Clark Clifford and the President." So Truman *was* very much a part of the process.

Walter Lippmann, learning about the planned changes, told James Conant that he had to admit that "sufficiently drastic criticism does have its effects upon the producers."

So, finally, Truman's explicit role in making and, nearly as important, describing the decision to use the bomb had been set in cinema stone. It did break new ground, but it omitted a vast number of additional or alternative explanations from Truman himself that might have raised thoughtful questions in the minds of some viewers if they had been included:

—In May 1945, Truman declared in his diary that the bomb
would prove to be America's "master card" in diplomatic
tussles with the Soviets.

—Having just secured, at Potsdam, Stalin's agreement to
enter the war against Japan in mid-August, Truman ex-
alted in his journal not only with "Fini Japs" when that
occurred but "I'll say we'll end the war a year sooner now,
and think of the kids who won't be killed!" This suggested that the bomb, in his estimation, was actually *not*
needed to end the war quickly.

—Allen Dulles, a leading figure in the Office of Strategic
Services (OSS)—and later director of the CIA—reported
to Secretary Stimson in Potsdam on July 20, 1945, that
he had just learned from Tokyo that "they desired to surrender if they could retain the Emperor and the consti-
tution as a basis for maintaining discipline and order in
Japan," he later wrote. Indeed, a Truman diary entry at
Potsdam referred to "the telegram from the Jap Emperor
asking for peace."

—Less than two weeks before the bomb appeared over
Hiroshima, Truman wrote in the diary that "military
objectives and soldiers and sailors are the target and not
women and children," even though the bomb would be
aimed at the very center of large cities dominated at that
time by women and children. Was Truman somehow not
aware of the official targeting plans at that late date, or
had he failed to take the trouble to ask about them—or
was he lying even to himself in his diary entries? And
which was worse?

—After learning of the bomb's utter devastation of a large
city, he grabbed an officer on board the ship *Augusta*
carrying him back to America and boomed, "This is the

greatest thing in history!" A few days later, responding to a letter criticizing his decision to deploy the bomb, he opined, "When you have to deal with a beast you have to treat him like a beast."

———

A third U.S. atomic test in the Pacific had once been planned for January 1947, then canceled due to the lengthy and expensive radiation cleanup required after the second test in July. Despite that taint, a celebration of the completion of the Operation Crossroads tests was held in Washington in November. A controversy that would literally "take the cake" soon ensued, however.

It seems that an aide to the commander of the test series, Vice Admiral W.H.P. Blandy, had the dubious idea of ordering for the occasion a large cake decorated with a billowing mushroom cloud made of angel food puffs. It would be delivered to D.C. by automobile all the way from a bakery in Illinois. At the party a photographer would snap Blandy happily cutting the cake, with his wife (who was wearing a hat that eerily mirrored the mushroom cloud) at his side and another admiral next to her. It was dutifully published in *The Washington Post*, along with images of carefree and expensively dressed women at the party.

Three days later, a prominent local Unitarian minister, Arthur Powell Davies, blasted the cake-cutting image in his Sunday sermon, calling it "an utterly loathsome picture. If I spoke as I feel I would call it obscene. . . . If I had the authority of a priest of the Middle Ages, I would call down the wrath of God upon such an obscenity. . . ." He added:

I only hope to God it is not printed in Russia—to confirm everything the Soviet government is telling the

Russian people about how "American degenerates" are able to treat with levity the most cruel, pitiless, revolting instrument of death ever invented by man. . . . How would it seem in Hiroshima, or Nagasaki, to know that Americans make cakes—of angel food puffs—in the image of that terrible, diabolical thing that brought sudden death to thousands of their friends, and a lingering, loathsome death to thousands of others? It is a crime—a crime against whatever may be left of decency here in America—to do this incredible thing. It is the most corrupt and rotten thing I have seen in eighteen years of living in this land that I love.

He insisted: "The naval officers concerned should apologize to the armed service of which they are a part, and to the American people."

Davies, who was born in England in 1902, was no lightweight. George Bernard Shaw had encouraged him to go into politics, but he had swerved to the church. Coming to America, he ended up preaching in Portland, where he worked as a used car salesman for a week to determine if it was possible to do that while sticking to Christian teachings about honesty. (Basically, no, he would write.) He met Margaret Sanger. Taking charge of the popular All Souls Church in D.C., he expanded his activism in favor of arms control and against racial segregation. His book *The Faith of an Unrepentant Liberal* was published earlier in 1946.

Now national media, including *Time* magazine, took note of his cake attack. No apology from the Navy was forthcoming. The second admiral in the photo, F.J. Lowry, declared that the pastor "probably just doesn't understand the situation." Walter Lippmann, however, felt moved to write Navy Secretary James Forrestal:

The outburst of Reverend A.P. Davies about the atomic bomb cake is, I feel sure, a sign of the times, which I feel should not be ignored. . . . I have compiled a list of new and terrifying weapons announced by the War and Navy Departments, and of other stories originating there which are boastful or threatening. The total effect was bound to produce a popular reaction, and I really feel that you and [Secretary of War] Bob Patterson ought to look very seriously into this business.

Pro and con letters were soon published in *The Washington Post* and *Time*. One from an ex-infantryman observed, "On Armistice Day I was thinking of so many charming variations of this theme. We could have darling little cakes made in the shape of coffins, and the cutest little crosses pressed of angel-puffs. And a few drops of cherry extract could be—you guessed it—drops of blood."

General Groves faced his own potential controversy in the press. A staffer for famed muckraking columnist Drew Pearson had paid a visit to his office to give him a chance to refute an item his boss was about to distribute. It would reveal a fact that had only been hinted at in the press previously: that Groves had received a cushy $10,000 to allow himself to be Hollywoodized in *The Beginning or the End*—and that this fee allegedly violated a federal statute prohibiting such payments to any government official for movie portrayals. No mention would be made of Groves serving as official adviser, with veto power, for the film.

Groves told the Pearson staffer that he was not aware of any such statute and further that the War Department did not exercise any control over such matters. This seemed to be questionable, for the next day he wrote a two-page memo to a General F.L. Parks, director of the Pentagon's public relations division, explaining that the previous December he had asked his aide W.A. Consodine to contact that bureau to find out if accepting money from MGM (he would sign his contract within weeks) was ethically acceptable. The bureau had signed off on it then and now he asked General Parks to contact Pearson's office and confirm that it had no issue with Groves taking the money.

The Pearson item, for whatever reason, never appeared.

# 19

## Truman, Take Two

The firing of Roman Bohnen from *The Beginning or the End* had now gone public, and was attributed directly to the White House, surely a first in Hollywood history. At least the extraction of Lionel Barrymore from the same movie was promoted not by a sitting president but by a former First Lady. *The New York Times* on November 22 reported the latest, in revealing that the major script revision on Truman's decision to drop the bomb also came at the "request of the White House." Bohnen's replacement by Art Baker "was suggested by the White House secretaries" after the recent screening.

The rather dubious reason? They felt that Bohnen's bearing "was not sufficiently erect and military to duplicate the president's," according to Sam Marx, who claimed the firing was not "mandatory." The script change for the Potsdam scene was necessary, however, because the decision to use the bomb had been "telescoped" too greatly.

The *Los Angeles Times* produced a wonderful headline: "Even President Not Exempt from Retakes!" The Potsdam scene was said by MGM, falsely, to be based on "verbatim material . . . culled from the diary of his secretary, Charles Ross." *Variety* quoted an MGM release directly: "In order to include hitherto undisclosed details of President Truman's historic decision" and "in a further effort to attain accuracy and dramatic effect, the studio is eliminating one scene concerning Mr. Truman with the frank admission that it was

made with customary dramatic license, but with erroneous historical emphasis." For the new scene "details were made available to
MGM by Mr. Ross, at the studio's request."

A few days later the *Times* carried a longer report opening with:
"The atom bomb has proved to be almost as difficult a problem for
Metro-Goldwyn-Mayer as it has for the United Nations." Since
the movie portrays so many famous men it "has been subject to
nearly as many vetoes as a peace treaty." It then explored the two
latest hurdles. One involved Niels Bohr's stubborn refusal to be
depicted. (In fact, unknown to the *Times*, Bohr's attorney had just
informed MGM that his client's "objections are fundamental and
he cannot be dissuaded from this viewpoint," and hinted at legal
action if this was not honored.) The other issue, of course, was the
mandated retake with Truman at Potsdam and the mysterious firing of Roman Bohnen.

Unmentioned was the sad fate of another planned retake: the
visually spectacular depiction of women, workers, and soldiers
getting vaporized in Hiroshima. Not surprisingly, it had been
rejected. It would now be left not only to Matt Cochran's imagination, as in John Lee Mahin's rejected scenario, but everyone
else's.

When he learned that he was being replaced in the MGM movie, Roman Bohnen wrote to President Truman from his North
Hollywood home. It was a polite but slyly critical letter. He noted
Truman's concerns about the depiction of his decision to "send the
atom bomb thundering into this troubled world," adding that he
could "well imagine the emotional torture you must have experienced in giving that fateful order, torture not only then, but now—
perhaps even more so." So he could "understand your wish that the
scene be re-filmed in order to do fuller justice to your anguished
deliberation in that historic moment."

Then he offered a suggestion. People would be talking about his decision for a hundred years, he observed, "and posterity is quite apt to be a little rough" on Truman "for not having ordered that very first atomic bomb to be dropped *outside* of Hiroshima with other bombs poised to follow, but praise God never to be used." His suggestion: Truman should play himself in the film! If he believed in his decision so strongly, why not reenact it himself? "If I were in your difficult position," Bohnen wrote, "I would insist on so doing. Unprecedented, yes—but so is the entire circumstance, including the unholy power of that monopoly weapon." Perhaps to show that he was serious about all of this, Bohnen indicated that he was sending a copy of the letter to Louis B. Mayer "in the sincere hope that he will invite you to play yourself in the retakes," although the tone of his letter might also destroy his chances for any more work at MGM. He signed it: *Respectfully, Roman Bohnen.*

Ten days later, Truman responded warmly, apparently missing, or ignoring, Bohnen's sarcasm. He thanked the actor for "suggesting to Mr. Mayer of MGM that I become a movie star." But he admitted that he didn't have "the talent to be a movie star."

Truman then took time to defend in some detail the decision to use the bomb, revealing much more about his emotional attitude than he usually did. He explained that what he had objected to in the film was that it pictured his decision as a "snap judgment," while in reality "it was anything but that." After the weapon was tested, and the Japanese given "ample warning," the bomb was used against two cities "devoted almost exclusively to the manufacture of ammunition and weapons of destruction" (the usual distortion). He had no qualms "about it whatever for the simple reason that it was believed the dropping of not more than two of these bombs would bring the war to a close. The Japanese in their conduct of the war had been vicious and cruel savages and I came to the conclusion that if 250,000 young Americans could be saved from slaughter the bomb should be dropped, and it was.

"As I said before," Truman concluded, "the only objection to the film was that I was made to appear as if no consideration had been given to the effects of the result of dropping the bomb—that is an absolutely wrong impression." There is little in the historical record or in Truman's letters and diaries, however, to indicate that he did give strong consideration to the human toll in the Japanese cities, the wide release of radiation—or letting the nuclear genie out of the bottle in an act of war.

The Potsdam scene was not the only retake ordered by James McGuinness and Sam Marx. With more time for special effects magic, the blowing up and burning of the city as viewed from above must look even more spectacular. The reaction of the *Enola Gay* crew, as well, continued to be revised, as the studio attempted to find the proper balance between prideful awe and recognition of what their fellow humans might be experiencing down below. This was all the more important because every scene written in the past year showing Japanese civilians before, during, or after the bombing had been excised. And Nagasaki no longer carried any weight whatsoever, not even a footnote in cinema history.

The presumed final retake with the actors in the cabin of the *Enola Gay* was drafted by Frank Wead, then tweaked by McGuinness and Marx. It focused on close-ups of Jeff Nixon and Capt. Parsons, just before the bomb drop.

Nixon: "A city waking—people going to work—and the lightning of the universe hits them in one bolt. . . . They'll never know what hit them."

Parsons: "They've had leaflets warning of this for ten days now—and that's exactly ten days more notice than they gave us at Pearl Harbor!"

This was at least the third reference in the script to the leaflets but the first mention of Pearl Harbor, yet another strained attempt at justification. With John Hersey's *New Yorker* article now published in book form and drawing raves and massive sales—while the Book of the Month Club distributed tens of thousands of copies for no charge—this was all the more vital. Perhaps that's also why, in the MGM footage, one of the four B-29s that took part in the Hiroshima mission now bore the name *Necessary Evil* scrawled in clear view on its front end. (At the time of the mission it was known simply as "No. 91" and gained that evocative nickname only later.)

To make the crew members appear more courageous, and the mission riskier, the (fictional) heavy flak that greeted them near the target now exploded in black clouds with loud bangs just outside their windows. Also given added emphasis: a Geiger counter sat amid the crew, clicking its warning of radiation leaking from the bomb on board, though it never quite reached the danger zone. Another addition to the script arrived after the *Enola Gay* circled back for a brief look, with Nixon observing, "A city as big as Dallas, Texas—it's all in flames at once like striking a match. . . . Now I understand what Matt feared. If ever there is another war, it won't be cities burning one at a time, but the whole world on fire, eating itself to ashes." Pilot Tibbets finally pulls away, saying, "Let's get out of here—I feel like we're over a dead world."

A third retake would put the finishing touches on another scene that had gone through numerous rewrites—the reading of Matt Cochran's farewell letter to his wife at the Lincoln Memorial. Jettisoning at last the idea of superimposing the faces of world statesmen and Manhattan Project leaders in the clouds, MGM had settled on this: Matt reading most of his letter off screen, before he sits down, ghost-like, next to his wife, Lincoln looming behind them, as he finishes reciting the following:

> We stand now where the early savages stood, when they
> ceased running away from fire, and began to use it well.

If these primitives learned to use fire, we of an enlightened century can learn to use atomic energy construc-
tively. God has not shown us a new way to destroy ourselves. Atomic energy is the hand he has extended to
lift us from the ruins of war and lighten the burdens
of peace.

Anne, you and our boy will see the day when the
atoms in a cup of water will heat and light your home,
when the power in a pasteboard railroad ticket will drive
trains across great continents, when the energy in a
blade of grass will send planes to distant lands. We have
found a path so filled with promise, that when we walk
down it we will know that everything that went before
the discovery of atomic energy was the Dark Ages. . . .
You, the giver of new life, must know that what we have
unleashed is not the end. With all my love, I tell you
this, my dear: men will learn to use this new knowledge
well. They won't fail. For this is the timeless moment
that gives all of us a chance to prove that human beings
are made in the image and likeness of God.

---

Leslie Groves was still being sent "final" scripts as they were
revised, and revised again. Now he had been shown an actual
print of the current version of the movie. After that screening, his
latest, and perhaps last, critique delivered to MGM included the
following:

—A huge conference room, Groves complained, "looks like
   Mussolini set-up."
—Even after so many Groves complaints the film con-
   tinued to showcase Robert Walker's "un-Army-like,

smart-alecky foreknowledge." Also, Walker should display a shorter military haircut! Groves further objected to Walker wearing an unmanly apron in a kitchen scene with his girlfriend.

—In the scene with Matt's farewell letter it should be claimed that in halting a possible explosion he did not merely save forty thousand on Tinian but "hundreds of thousands of Americans on the beaches of Japan"—as if that claim had not already been made a half dozen times in the script. Groves even hit the acting in that closing scene: "Matt's wife does unconvincing job." (This was one indisputable assertion.)

—Overall: "Strained attempts at comedy ruin what could be a really good picture."

A few days later, MGM's Barron responded. James K. McGuinness, he reported, wished to assure Groves that the studio felt most of his criticism was "well-founded." They had cut the "somewhat ridiculous" apron scene but they could not fix Robert Walker's hair because he was presently shooting a costume movie and had let his hair grow very long. But with "judicious editing" they had moderated some of Walker's jokey moments along with a "smart-alecky" exchange featuring Audrey Totter. Elsewhere: a scene at Columbia University, rewritten by Leo Szilard, that Groves felt really dragged—the studio agreed but it was "insisted on by Professor Einstein as a condition of his giving permission to being represented in the picture." Still, Groves mainly got what he wanted, as usual.

A letter to Groves from his friend Albin E. Johnson, who had also seen the film, spelled out its pros and cons. Johnson had earned fame as a European correspondent during World War II and now served as a member of the American delegation to the U.N. Atomic

Energy Commission. He felt the MGM movie's overall effect on the public probably would be "negligible," as it "doesn't deal with international control or the outlawry of the weapon." Another favorable point: "By passing over very lightly the 'atrocity aspects' of the atomic bomb—the horrors of Hiroshima and Nagasaki which were capitalized by Hershey [*sic*]—the film doesn't arouse any mass fear or mass revulsion so there can be no criticism along that line. From our standpoint this is all to the good because our goal is to appeal to reason and common sense rather than to fear and emotions in bringing about international control of atomic energy."

Then, donning his cineaste hat, he predicted it wouldn't gain many rave reviews. In places it seemed downright "corny." The finale at the Lincoln Memorial was "rather over-played." But the film was meant to be an entertainment so if it gave the military and Manhattan Project a "well-deserved pat on the back" along the way that would be swell. In any case, "it could have been a lot worse."

Before finally signing his release, Vannevar Bush paid a visit to Charlie Ross at the White House to detail his enduring qualms about the film. His aide Fred Fassett, after attending a screening, had informed Sam Marx that he was "impressed" by the film and felt he should be "congratulated," but concerns about tone and accuracy remained. After receiving Fassett's review, Bush wrote his friend James Conant, noting that further edits in the movie were "up to others and particularly up to the White House." He also alerted Conant that according to Fassett "the chap who depicts you is not a prepossessing looking individual. . . . If I were in your place and that chap that depicts you is a moth-eaten looking individual, I would just not sign" a release. Bush reserved his harshest comments for the film's focus on another character: "Of course

the whole thing blows up Groves, and this did not happen by accident. . . . As a matter of fact, it may be the last straw that breaks
the camel's back in the Army, but I believe he has no career there
anyway."

Now, in Bush's latest visit to the White House, Charles Ross outlined his dealings with MGM going back to the beginning. Again
he insisted that the White House had never officially "approved"
the picture but merely stated it would have no objections if Truman
himself was treated properly. After considerable revisions, this now
seemed to be the case.

Hearing all this, Bush notified his friend Conant that he would
likely submit his permission letter. He added that Ross "quite
appropriately took the point of view, I feel, that censorship on the
part of the White House should certainly be avoided as far as possible." (That line had obviously been crossed, however.) This closed
the matter for Bush, and he was left feeling that the melding of the
bomb to a celluloid romance was deeply regrettable but might not
do any harm in this country "where we are used to such things."

Despite this, James Conant, one of the few who still refused to
sign the waiver, remained concerned about the MGM opus as the
film's opening approached. It was no longer a matter of "accuracy."
Conant, the refined president of Harvard, worried more about the
trivialization of the bomb and the bomb-makers. So now, belated-
ly, he tried to prevent the film from being released in any form. He
wrote to Bernard Baruch, asserting that he agreed with Lippmann
that the film could have a "bad effect" on how other countries
viewed the United States and "endanger the international solution of the atomic energy problem." Conant pressed Baruch to find
some way of having the film "held up and kept out of circulation."
Baruch agreed to look into it, but it is unclear what steps, if any, he
took in this regard.

———

The new Frank Capra picture, *It's a Wonderful Life*, opened in New York just before Christmas to so-so reviews. Donna Reed did draw good notices, however, in the role of wife of George Bailey (Jimmy Stewart). Lionel Barrymore played the evil banker. Bosley Crowther, lead critic for *The New York Times*, judged that "the weakness of this picture . . . is the sentimentality of it—its illusory concept of life. Mr. Capra's nice people are charming, his small town is a quite beguiling place and his pattern for solving problems is most optimistic and facile. But somehow they all resemble theatrical attitudes, rather than average realities." The RKO movie got off to a slow start at the box office as well.

The FBI, reviewing the film for Communist influence for its files, would complain that the "Scrooge-like" banker was "the most hated man" in the picture, to sway audiences against his type. This was a "common trick" used by Communists, the bureau's movie critic decided. Besides that, the two writers, Albert Hackett and Frances Goodrich, while not quite CP members, were observed during the movie shoot "eating luncheon daily with such Communists as Lewis Cole, screen writer, and Earl Robinson, screen writer."

The same week, William Wyler's *The Best Years of Our Lives* was released, and also drew brickbats from the FBI reviewer. Once again the screenwriter, in this case Robert Sherwood, was identified as a known evildoer for giving "aid and comfort" to Communists, and may have let the Reds massage the script without credit. Its star, Fredric March, was said to be a known Communist, as was supporting actor Roman Bohnen. (One can only imagine what the FBI would have thought about Bohnen playing America's current president in the MGM film.) Bankers, again, came off badly, the FBI reviewer complained.

In a final tweak to *The Beginning or the End*, MGM inserted a notice at its start, perhaps in response to various complaints about accuracy and chronology. It informed viewers that what they were about to see was "basically a true story," though with some "re-arrangement of chronology and fictionalization" that was "necessary" for "dramatic license and security purposes," a clear dodge. Rejecting "Deke" Parsons's complaint, however, they did not specifically point to Matt Cochran's radiation accident as pure fabrication.

The movie premiere was still two months off, but that did not stop MGM from preparing a costly rollout of publicity, advertising, and promotion. After a terrific year for the studio, with more than twenty high-grossing releases—and its latest, *The Yearling*, certain to join them—MGM would spare no expense. A pair of lively newspaper ads were prepped. One was headed, "MGM Presents the Scoop of the Century! The Greatest Hush-Hush Secret of All Time!" The silhouette of a young woman was emblazoned with the words, "The only girl who knew the world's most terrifying secret." Next to it was a small drawing of a couple in an embrace, titled "*THE LAST KISS.*" The movie was a LIFE STORY, a LOVE STORY, a MYSTERY STORY. Six small profile shots of the lead actors, none of them exactly a Tracy or Hepburn, stood in the corner, secondary in this pitch.

The second ad immodestly compared the film to previous classics, including *Birth of a Nation*, *Gone with the Wind*, and *The Good Earth*, where "Great Themes" met "Great Entertainments." And now comes "for the first time on the screen, the inside personal story of those who lived, loved and shared the mysteries of the creation of the terrifying atom bomb!" Donlevy and Walker shared top billing but were not pictured.

The studio also prepared a lavish twenty-page booklet for the press with eight "chapters" of text along with more than a dozen stills. Chapter 1 touted the script approval by Truman and the War Department, as if this could only be viewed in a positive light. Chapter 2 was titled "The Beginning . . . A Letter That Startles Hollywood." This creation story starred "a pretty girl, a high school student" and "a young professor, her chemistry teacher." Who could have guessed that "a high school friendship in Iowa" could "result in a motion picture being filmed that has been labeled by government officials, military leaders and scientists as the most important undertaking in Hollywood history"? Even by Hollywood standards the corn ran high here. The booklet concluded with MGM congratulating itself for presenting this movie as "a duty to mankind" executed with "unique attention to authenticity."

Several new press photos had been art-directed. One carried a tacked-on sign poorly covering a "top secret" object that no one was supposed to see—at least until the movie came out and tickets purchased! An image of a crowd of actors around a purported bomb being assembled in a tent in the desert carried a prominent "*Censored*" label over it. "Even the film appearance of the atom bomb, America's 'top secret,' is closely guarded," the caption read, "and will be until the picture is released." Also circulated were black-and-white landscapes (sometimes tinted sepia, blue, or red), with stars of the film in various combinations posing in their movie outfits with artful depictions of a frightening mushroom cloud rising behind them. The caption for one of them read: "The timeless moment that gives all of us a chance to prove that human beings are made in the image and likeness of God." Far less classy was a collection of head shots of eight actors and actresses surrounding a crude black-and-white drawing of a mushroom cloud, almost as if they had just been rudely expelled from it. Perhaps it was a metaphor for the movie itself.

# 20

# Stimson to the Rescue

When MGM screened its near-final cut of *The Beginning or the End* in Chicago, the atomic scientists in attendance greeted it with yawns when they weren't openly mocking it. Leo Szilard had fled the scene rapidly to hide out and perhaps repent in the back seat of chemist Harrison Brown's car. An aide to Leslie Groves who attended a similar screening advised the general, however, that no matter what anyone thought of the finished film its effect on the public and national policy would likely be minimal because it would bomb, as it were, at the box office. But MGM's Carter Barron cabled the studio back in Culver City, "Seldom have we experienced more enthusiasm for the dramatic entertainment of a film than that demonstrated by small preview groups. . . . It appears to be a daringly strong audience picture."

Louella Parsons reported than an MGM executive had taken a print to D.C. for "official approval." Walter Lippmann, who was critical of the previous edit of the film, got to see the final cut at the Pentagon and found it somewhat improved. He informed his friend James Conant that it was "still embarrassingly vulgar, but it is not so dangerously bad as it was." Conant, who had dragged his feet on signing a release for so long, was no longer identified by name in the film. Lippmann informed him that along with Bohr and Meitner he had "made an effective getaway." Conant replied that he could only "rejoice" with this news.

Art Baker, meanwhile, wrote to Charlie Ross, identifying himself as the actor who had been picked to play the president in the retake and (in stark contrast to Roman Bohnen) expressed warm feelings for Truman. Ross replied six days later in a note marked "Personal and Confidential," inviting Baker to Washington. "I suppose you know that the first sequence on President Truman was, as we thought here, pretty bad because it gave the impression that he made a snap decision to drop the bomb on Hiroshima," Ross confirmed. "The new scene puts over the idea—the true idea—that this decision was only taken after the most prayerful decision and upon the advice of all his leading military advisers." As we'll see, Truman himself later embraced that claim of a "snap decision."

Ross had received another fawning thank-you note from James K. McGuinness, as the studio exec returned a few photographs borrowed from the White House files. "For that, and the many other courtesies you extended to me," McGuinness wrote, "and particularly for the favorable support you lent to the atom bomb picture, I want to express my deep gratitude."

As the weeks since publication of John Hersey's "Hiroshima" article ticked by, a certain normalization had settled in. Popular culture made its usual contributions in this regard, extending even to appeals to children. At least 750,000 of them (or their parents) had mailed to General Mills fifteen cents and a Kix cereal box top in exchange for an "Atomic Bomb Ring," with which a kid could purportedly "see genuine atoms SPLIT to smithereens!" On a more serious note, the Henry L. Stimson article, proposed by James Conant to combat the Hersey and Cousins articles—and partly drafted by General Groves and McGeorge Bundy—was published by *Harper's*. It was boosted by a cover line that promised this would explain "Why We Used the Atomic Bomb."

Despite his doubts, the former secretary of war had carried on, reinforced when Truman again asked him to write such an article since Stimson knew "the facts of whole situation better than any-body." (He might know the facts better than Truman, at least. In his letter to Stimson, Truman confessed he could not recall each name among the three he had appointed to advise him on using the bomb—and actually there were *eight* members of that com-mittee. Truman also could not remember through which country, Switzerland or Sweden, he had sent the ultimatum to Japan to sur-render.) Stimson had replied to Truman that he hoped the article would answer the "Chicago scientists" and "satisfy the doubts of the rather difficult class of the community which will have charge of the education of the next generation."

Now, published by *Harper's* in a report that filled eleven pages, Stimson's dispassionate treatise drew wide attention partly because it revealed for the first time some of the key dates, meetings, memos, and individuals surrounding the decision to drop the bomb. Commentators on radio and in print treated it not so much as advocacy but as a statement of facts, much as Conant had hoped. Many newspapers, including *The Washington Post*, reprinted the entire article—*Harper's* made it available to any outlet for no fee—and others quoted from it at length, often on their front pages. Some focused on Stimson's estimate of over 1 million American casualties saved, the highest number (if wildly exaggerated) yet offered. *The New York Times*, where editorials over the preceding eighteen months occasionally raised questions about the use of the bomb, now endorsed Truman's decision completely. It found the reasoning expressed by Stimson "irrefutable," the justifications "unchallengeable."

The New York *Herald Tribune* went even further in deciding the case was closed with these words: "So much for the past."

The article detailed how the decision was made by Truman only after the Interim Committee recommended that the weapon be used as soon as possible and without specific warning against a "dual" target—some sort of military installation surrounded by enough houses ("enough" meaning many thousands) to show off its pure and deadly power. A demonstration shot was judged "impractical" and risky; it might be a "dud," making the U.S. position worse. Japan's surrender terms were always "vague," so Truman really had no choice. Stimson stated repeatedly that the bomb and the bomb alone had ended the war. That meant failing to highlight Russia's critical entry into the conflict against Japan on August 8, or whether U.S. concerns about the Soviet threat in the postwar years played any role in the decision to use the bomb. He ignored Acting Secretary of State Joseph Grew's attempts to end the war by modifying surrender terms (which Stimson for a time supported). Nor did he disclose that a leading argument for using the bomb expressed by many insiders, from Conant to Groves, was that it was the only way to awaken the world to the necessity of abolishing war altogether. It was Stimson himself who had stated that view, although not in his *Harper's* article.

With the Stimson essay a sensation, Truman informed him that he had clarified the issue "very well." Dean Acheson told him it "was badly needed and . . . superbly done." McGeorge Bundy joked that the article had reduced certain annoying "chatterers to silence." In a letter to Stimson, James Conant expressed a heretofore hidden reason why the piece was so important: he was now firmly convinced that the Russians would agree to American proposals in the atomic field "provided they are convinced that we would have the bomb in quantity and would be prepared to use it without hesitation in another war." On the other hand, "if the propaganda against the use of the atomic bomb had been allowed to grow unchecked, the strength of our military position by virtue of having the bomb would have been correspondingly weakened."

This pointed to perhaps the prime reason for shoring up the Hiroshima narrative: not merely to provide the "correct" message for future Americans but to impart the proper lesson to the Soviets.

Praise for the *Harper's* article ran so wide and deep that Conant was shocked when he received a letter from a lawyer friend in Chicago who confessed that Stimson had not convinced him of the morality of extinguishing 200,000 human beings. Dropping the bomb on cities, he wrote, violated "every human instinct of many civilized people." The Chicago scientists, he declared, still agreed with this sentiment.

Conant, alarmed, asked Robert Oppenheimer to investigate that assertion. "As you know," Conant wrote, in a profound understatement, "I feel a great deal turns on this point in regard to the future." Oppenheimer, ever conflicted, would later report to him that concerning the Hiroshima decision the majority of the scientists "feel about things very much as you and I do."

One former high-level official was willing to tell Stimson directly that he was still not fully on board with his defense of the bombing. This was Joseph Grew, who had raised many questions about the need to use the bomb in the weeks before Hiroshima. Grew had a unique perspective, as an authority on Japan and as the U.S. ambassador to that country at the time of Pearl Harbor—who was interned there for nine months after that. Now he reiterated in a letter to Stimson that "in the light of available evidence I myself and others felt" that if a "categorical statement" allowing the Japanese to keep their emperor had been issued in May 1945 "the surrender-minded elements in the Government might well have been afforded by such a statement a valid reason and the necessary strength to come to an early clear-cut decision. . . . If surrender could have been brought about in May, 1945, or even in June or July, before the entrance of Soviet Russia into the [Pacific] war and the use of the atomic bomb, the world would have been the gainer."

In other words, in his expert view, wishing and waiting to use the new weapon might have actually cost, not saved, thousands of American lives. Years later, John J. McCloy, hardly a "dove," would affirm a similar opinion, which he had expressed to Stimson in real time before the atomic attacks. "I am absolutely convinced," he declared, "that had we said they could keep the Emperor, along with the threat of the atomic bomb, they would have accepted and we would never have had to drop the bomb." McGeorge Bundy would later admit this was indeed "an open question."

Shortly after the *Harper's* article appeared, the new Atomic Energy Commission gathered for one of its first meetings. Discussions ensued about the relative importance of focusing on strictly energy/reactor issues versus military/bomb applications, "with rather general final agreement that weapons were of first priority," according to the minutes of the meeting. Maximum effort would be thus directed to reviving Los Alamos, conducting more weapons tests, increasing the production of raw materials for atomic bombs—and developing new devices, such as the hydrogen bomb. Robert Oppenheimer, who had been elected chairman of the AEC's advisory committee, and argued for a focus on peaceful uses, nevertheless went along quietly, telling the assembled: "It seems to me the heart of the problem has been reached with surprising speed: The making of atomic weapons is something to which we are committed."

Leo Szilard now believed only a "miracle" from God could save the day—and the dangerous era ahead. He started referring to himself as a possible "war criminal."

Would the discussion and debate over the Stimson article spark additional interest in *The Beginning or the End*? MGM in any case pressed ahead with its promotional efforts for the movie, now set to finally debut in Washington, D.C., in mid-February. Front and center was a highly unusual five-minute trailer to be shown in theaters. It was based on an obviously fake—although it might have fooled some in the audience—*Inquiring Reporter* format, set in the lobby of a grand old theater where a preview had just been screened. Audience members performing the studio's script were played by little-known actors from the ranks of Hollywood veterans and hopefuls.

Responding to the nosy reporter, a mother (with two kids in tow) exclaimed, "I was tremendously impressed—and deeply moved. . . . Frankly, it's the most important picture I've ever seen." Husband: "I agree. And it took a lot of courage to make this picture. You people should be very proud." Teenage daughter: "I thought the love story was simply wonderful, and so sad." Kid brother: "That love stuff wasn't so hot, but those B-29s sure were." A Catholic priest said he enjoyed "every minute of it. It's a great picture and presents a real challenge for the young people of today," although "faith" and "goodwill" may save the day. With that, a handsome young man interjected that goodwill may be swell, but he liked the parts about the men who made it "and how they kept it a secret."

Suddenly a man in a pencil-thin moustache—a stereotypical movie villain—declared, "facts or no facts, some things are better left unsaid." This was countered by a pleasant-looking woman claiming "the truth never hurt anybody." (This was actress Barbara Billingsley, later Beaver Cleaver's mom but then taking uncredited roles in MGM B-movies.) Other happy attendees chimed in: "True or not it's a great love story." "Inspiring." "Frightening!" "Amazing!" The theater manager, recognized by some as character actor Morris Ankrum, revealed that he'd previewed movies for many years but "I've never seen an audience react like this one. They were with it every inch of the way. . . . You just can't ignore it."

The second half of the trailer provided the more traditional assembly of scenes from the movie and breathless narration. One title card declared: "MGM Daringly Presents The Most

Timely Production in Motion Picture History." Another: "The Secret Story of History's Greatest Undercover Job." Finally: "FACTUAL! AUTHENTIC! THE MEN . . . THE MAGIC . . . THE MACHINES." It closed with Cronyn as Oppenheimer in the film's prologue declaring that he knew the beginning, but "only you, the audience of tomorrow, can know the end." One can only guess how many viewers in the theaters might have wondered why he was talking over their heads to some unseen audience down the road.

Sam Marx, meanwhile, told a reporter for the L.A. *Daily News* that if his movie managed to earn back its costs the studio would bankroll scholarships for would-be physicists at the University of California. This was to show appreciation for not one of the atomic scientists insisting on money for their cooperation with the picture. The studio did cut one man out of the movie, Marx revealed, after he demanded a fee (allegedly $15,000)—this was economist Alexander Sachs, who delivered Einstein's famous letter to FDR that eventually got the bomb project going.

MGM, in any case, appeared to face little further trouble with the Production Code office. Joe Breen had sent over to Louis B. Mayer its formal approval of the finished film, his censors having viewed all the retakes. But Breen felt compelled to add this P.S. at the bottom of the official notification, flagging that one line about radiation exposure that had not been deleted despite his repeated warnings: "This certificate is issued on the understanding that you have deleted the line, *Is it true that if you fool around with that stuff you don't care for girls?*"

# 21

## "Hokum" and "Imbecility"

Well behind schedule and fifteen months after Sam Marx and Tony Owen flew to Oak Ridge to meet Dr. Edward Tompkins, MGM at last "locked" its atomic bomb film, ending the editing process. The final cut came in at a tidy 112 minutes. According to official MGM records, *The Beginning or the End* had been made on a budget of $2.6 million (equivalent to $33 million today). Now publicity efforts were accelerated, advertising readied, screenings announced for film critics, and theater openings booked. The gala world premiere in Washington was set for February 19 and invitations mailed.

To assist the big push, MGM's own magazine, *Lion's Roar*, widely distributed to the press, featured the movie in a ten-page spread, along with coverage of other new releases, including *The Yearling* and *Love Laughs at Andy Hardy*. The headline continued the promo theme that had been building since the previous summer: "Now It Can Be Told: The biggest, best-kept secret in the history of the world—disclosed at last!" And a sub-head: "*The Secret of the Future That Blasts the Screen Asunder!*" All under a large, crossed-out "CENSORED" sign. And on the facing page: "The story that's 5,000,000 times more powerful than TNT!" Technical adviser H.T. Wensel contributed a separate piece titled "No Fiction Writer Could Create Such Excitement, Suspense and Drama."

A new worry had emerged for MGM. Eleanor Roosevelt, silent since her objections forced Lionel Barrymore out of the picture, now let it be known—through her attorney—that she was "sickened" (in the words of columnist Leonard Lyons) that her late husband was portrayed in the movie, at length, in "full face." She claimed that MGM's overseer, Nicholas Schenck, had assured her that FDR would only be filmed from the back, as done with Truman, even though this Hollywood courtesy was generally only granted to living presidents. This threat soon passed when she revealed that she would not sue to halt the release, feeling that would only drive publicity for the movie.

As the premiere neared, *The Washington Post* reported that the "nation's atomic elite" would see themselves on the screen in "the most distinguished event of its kind in Washington's theatrical history." All of the prominent characters in the movie were invited for the big night, but few would attend, due to distance from the event or other factors. Robert Oppenheimer declined. (MGM had set up a private screening for Oppie in San Francisco six days before the D.C. event, to which he invited a few friends, such as E.O. Lawrence. The FBI phone tap found him complaining of a cold as the preview neared and it's not known if he attended.) President Truman was in town but gave it a pass. The Soviet ambassador also was a no-show, which drew wide press coverage.

The pre-screening party would be held in the Mayflower Hotel's lavish Chinese Room with its ornate, recessed ceiling dome. The dessert table held a large cake bedecked with roses and the words "The Beginning or the End," but sanity (and fear of a publicity backlash) prevented any sort of mushroom cloud ornament. General Groves showed up in his Army uniform and medals. A photograph captured him conversing with DuPont's W.S. Carpenter, as he did in the movie. Tom Drake chatted with General Carl Spatz and Senator Tom Connolly, but seemed more entranced by Groves's attractive daughter-in-law. Others in attendance: Truman aide Charles Ross, MGM's Carter Barron, Senators Millard

Tydings and Brien McMahon, W.A. Consodine, David Lilienthal, H.T. Wensel, General Thomas Ferrell, Sumner Pike of the Atomic Energy Commission, former FDR secretary Grace Tully, and the ambassador from Italy.

Then they all left for the Loew's Palace to watch the movie, set to screen at 8:30, passing a line of paying patrons that wound around the block. Now all that was left was to await the verdict of the nation's film critics.

On the positive side, *Variety* would call it "moving" and "tip-top entertainment," with a script and production values "achieving a stature far beyond the average celluloid standards." *Variety* also praised its "aura of authenticity and special historical significance." Hume Cronyn "expertly" impersonated Oppenheimer, and "Brian Donlevy is capital as General Groves, eclipsed only by Godfrey Tearle's extraordinary personation of President Roosevelt. It's to the sum credit of everybody concerned that the documentary values are sufficiently there without becoming static."

The New York *Daily News* viewed it as "far more thrilling and suspenseful" than average and recommended that every man, woman, and child see it. The reviewer for the liberal New York daily *PM* found the film's moral message, whatever it was, "reassuring." *Science Illustrated* claimed that viewers "can be sure that the film is reasonably accurate within the limits of security," and it published photos of Oppenheimer with Cronyn on the set. Bob Considine, never shy about boosting the movie in his Hearst column, now hailed Frank Wead's "brilliant" script—to which *he* had contributed so much.

In the most over-the-top review, Jack Moffitt (a veteran Hollywood screenwriter) in *Esquire* hailed it as a "great film" that "stresses moral values rather than military triumphs. . . . The picture leaves you with the feeling that we may, indeed, be on the threshold of a millennium when the human spirit can produce so intelligent and responsible a breed of men." Hume Cronyn was "great as the irre-pressible Dr. J. Robert Oppenheimer who, in spite of all his intel-ligent misgivings, can't suppress a sort of baseball fan excitement." Director Taurog, a "master of gentle human comedy . .·. had the good taste to pass up 'comedy relief' even when it was accurate." And Taurog wisely focused exclusively on the bomber crew during the Hiroshima attack (as opposed to, say, showing anyone on the ground or anything of Nagasaki). As for the ending: "At first you may feel that the producer has gone a little overboard in playing the final episode in front of the Lincoln Memorial in Washington." But as Matt's wife reads his letter, telling her of the wonderful gifts the atomic age will offer humanity, "the setting seems more and more appropriate."

In *The New York Times*, Bosley Crowther, chief critic since 1940, called the picture "creditable," a fair "re-enactment." Crowther also praised how it handled the moral issues in portraying the bomb as "a necessary evil," falsely claiming that MGM had "taken no obvious sides in the current atomic contentions." As for the actors, Donlevy as Groves made for a "pretty snappy sparkplug." Even so, Crowther was far from thrilled. He found the film marred by "silly" or mawkish sentiment and "hackneyed" romances. Citing the "brashly deceptive" time capsule prologue, he declared that the studio seemed less impressed with its subject than its own heroic efforts in bringing it to the screen. The filmmakers "actually think that they have made history. . . . It is a slightly ridiculous conceit."

In a sense, however, one might say that the film—in exagger-ating, glorifying, and even fabricating key events—*did* "make" history.

Stronger rebukes soon arrived. *Time* magazine laughed at the film's "cheery imbecility." It called on Hollywood to please regard their audiences as "capable of facing facts, even problems which may prove unsolvable," and stop treating them "as if they were spoiled or not-quite bright children." The unnamed reviewer: James Agee, who had a dog in this fight. Agee also wrote regularly for *The Nation*, and there he elaborated: "You learn less about atomic fission from this film that I would assume is taught by now in the more progressive nursery schools; you learn even less than that about the problems of atomic control; and you learn least of all about morals." All in all, he added, the movie provided "a horrifying example" of a coming state-controlled American cinema. Agee wrote this knowing very little about what actually had transpired with the dozens of deletions, revisions, and retakes ordered by the military and the White House.

*Life* magazine appeared to do the studio's bidding by preparing in its oversized format a lavish five-page spread with fourteen stills from the movie. Unfortunately for MGM the text often took a hilariously mocking tone. In its subtitle on the first page it asserted that the long-awaited movie about the bomb had now exploded—"with pseudoscientific pap." It was saddled with a "stale" love story in which a young scientist has to explain to his wife "that he'd be home for dinner more often if it weren't so darn hard to figure out this chain-reaction stuff." Nuclear physics was often simplified "to the level of an Erector set." Actors delivered dialogue about the implications of creating the bomb with "a far-away look in the eyes." While MGM's special effects were awesome, the movie had "destroyed itself by an overdose of what Hollywood considers 'popular appeal.'"

But it was in the captions where Henry Luce's *Life* staff had some real fun. Under photos of the time capsule scene: "Fake authenticity is assumed . . . when it opens with fake newsreel." Commenting on a still with an MGM "censored" label over the bomb: "Phony secrecy . . . keynotes the manner in which *The Beginning or the End* is being sold to the public. Actually moviegoers, presumably including any spies, will see MGM's bomb. It looks like any other."

Elsewhere they described the movie's atomic device as looking like a prop from a Flash Gordon serial. (Actually it looked more like a torpedo than a bomb.) The Fermi pile in the film's lengthy reenactment was surrounded by "enough phony instruments to outfit a laboratory for Dr. Frankenstein."

The final page delivered the death blow, with three stills under the heading, "IT HAS PLENTY OF MOVIE HOKUM." We see Matt Cochran's wife showing him some leg, but he "is always too busy with plutonium to pay much attention to her." Then Matt schools Jeff Nixon on physics, but the latter "prefers to think about girls." Finally we see Matt's wife at the Lincoln Memorial reading his letter "full of flossy but trite hopes for a better world. On this depressing note the movie ends." Reading this, one imagines Louis B. Mayer calling Sam Marx: "You told me all publicity was good publicity!"

Harrison Brown, the Oak Ridge chemist still appalled by the Chicago screening he attended with Leo Szilard in January, took a slightly more evenhanded approach after viewing the movie a second time. Writing in the newly founded *Bulletin of the Atomic Scientists*, he affirmed that the film was still of "poor quality" overall and gave the wrong impression of how scientists work. He continued to lament the "horrible falsification of history" in its depiction of those warning leaflets "showered" over Hiroshima. Still, he felt it should be seen by every American, for *The Beginning or the End* at least gave the public "some feeling as to what atomic bombs are, what they can do, and what they may mean in the society in which they live." Ultimately, in the movie "they are not given any clue as to what they, as individuals, can do about it."

As his finder's fee for helping to bring the movie to MGM, Tony Owen had been promised a reported $40,000 by Louis B. Mayer. When that was slow to materialize, his wife, Donna Reed (her career back on track with *It's a Wonderful Life*), reportedly marched into Mayer's office and demanded payment.

Movie fans, meanwhile, did not exactly storm the 165 theaters across the country where MGM claimed it was screening its "mighty melodrama." This did not stop the studio from taking out an ad in the trades boasting, "They've Been Atom Bombarding the Box Office!" In smaller type: "The way they've been coming is like a chain reaction—there's no stopping it!" By arrangement with MGM, the new FAS-linked National Committee for Atomic Information was allowed to set up information tables in some of the theaters showing the film. The movie did do well at the thousand-seat Grove Theater in Oak Ridge, where the marquee outside touted "The Story of the Atomic Bomb and Oak Ridge."

Devoid of major stars, released later than MGM foresaw, and suffering from mixed reviews, *The Beginning or the End* would earn only $1.2 million (equivalent to $15.5 million in 2019) at the box office in the United States and Canada, and $720,000 abroad, resulting in a loss to MGM of $1.6 million, according to official records. Several dozen 1947 movies banked more proceeds than this drama that was once expected to be—as no less than Louis B. Mayer predicted—"the most important" movie ever made. MGM had survived far bigger flops, but this was disappointing, given the wide promotion and those original hopes. It kicked off a relatively poor year for the studio at the box office, thus contributing to Mayer's weakening hold on his top position (which he would lose just four years later).

In the broader society, however, the crisis for proponents of a nuclear buildup appeared over. With the orchestrated publication of the Stimson article in *Harper's* and the denuding of *The Beginning or the End*, they had surmounted the temporary threat posed by John Hersey's popular article and book and the impassioned critiques by Norman Cousins, theologians, scientists, certain journalists and military brass. "The vast majority of public opinion still stood firmly behind U.S. atomic policy and its decision to use the weapons on Japan," James Hershberg would observe in his biography of James Conant. Truman's image was secured as "careful, informed, and deliberate in his decision to use the bomb."

With that established, the scientists' movement went into a steep spiral. Robert Oppenheimer would lament that now there was a "surprising lack, both quantitatively and in discernment, in the public discussion of atomic energy." A 1947 poll of FAS members found most supporting further production of atomic bombs, by 242–174. With any challenges to developing bigger and better nuclear weapons set aside, American scientists, led by Edward Teller, plunged deeper into trying to create a mega-device, the hydrogen bomb. The Soviets would frantically work on their own atomic and hydrogen devices. The arms race, with its promise of thousands of nuclear warheads in the world, was on. With the atomic attacks on Japan now drawing only muted criticism, each superpower enshrined a dangerous "first-strike" policy for the nuclear era.

Hiroshima and Nagasaki, all the while, sank deeper into what the writer Mary McCarthy called "a hole in human history." The poet Randall Jarrell informed a friend that he felt "so rotten about the country's response" to the atomic bombings that he wished he could become "a naturalized cat or dog." Instead he penned a poem he titled "Losses," in which he wrote: "In bombers named for girls, we burned / The cities we had learned about in school . . ." And in "1945: The Death of the Gods," he pondered the end of the world, "when the rockets rise like stars/and earth is blazing with a thousand suns."

The decision to destroy Hiroshima and Nagasaki, and its aftermath, would remain America's raw nerve, for years, for decades, and still, today.

# 22
# Aftermath, 1947–2020

To the surprise of almost no one, *The Beginning or the End* failed to win any major awards, not even for its groundbreaking special effects in depicting the Trinity and Hiroshima explosions (so lifelike the U.S. Army later used the footage in training films). *March of Time*'s "Atomic Power" film, however, would earn an Academy Award nomination in 1947 for best film short. So maybe MGM should have planned its movie as a feature documentary from the get-go, as some portrayed in the film had suggested.

*The Beginning or the End* would also fail to find a large audience overseas, not even in the UK despite the script distortions that emphasized the Brits' role in creating the bomb. Of course, in most countries abroad, the use of the bomb against two cities was far less popular than in America. Before approving the release of the movie in Spain, for example, Joe Breen's Production Code office ordered MGM to "Delete Chaplain's invocation for crew before taking off to drop atom bomb on Hiroshima." The United States, in addition, was widely criticized abroad for aiming to secure atomic secrets for itself now and forever, as if it was all right for them to use the killer bomb in war but wrong for anyone else to even consider it.

General Groves's prime responsibility for nuclear weapons production was handed over to the Atomic Energy Commission in 1947. He then took the helm of the military overseer, the Armed Forces Special Weapons Project. But General Eisenhower, the Army chief of staff, denied him the position he most wanted, chief of engineers. In his performance review, delivered in person, Eisenhower blasted Groves for arrogance, rudeness, contempt for the rules, and pushing for a promotion out of turn. Three days later, Groves announced he would leave the Army. He wrote a book about the bomb project, *Now It Can Be Told*, and became vice president at Sperry Rand, the giant electronics company. It didn't seem possible, but he grew even more conservative in his later years. He wanted the United States to withdraw from the U.N. and expressed vehemently anti-union views. Responding to race riots during the 1960s he said, "The trouble really started soon after Roosevelt was elected President and he and his wife started to curry favor of the negro population, and encouraged the philosophy that it was all right to be lawless if you thought your cause was a just one."

President Truman's prediction, when he met Robert Oppenheimer, that the Russians would "never" be able to create their own atomic weapons proved rather far off the mark. The Soviets set off their first atomic explosion just four years later. This was then topped by the successful U.S. thermonuclear test in 1952. The Soviets (aided by information from Los Alamos spy Klaus Fuchs) soon developed their own hydrogen bomb, as the frightful, in so many ways, nuclear arms race raged. Each of the superpowers would eventually stock tens of thousands of nuclear warheads in their arsenals. The cost to the United States treasury alone: an estimated $5.8 trillion dollars. Throughout, the United States maintained its "first-use" policy—reserving the right to respond with nuclear warheads to any attack with conventional weaponry (such as the Soviets invading Western Europe or in a crisis with Iran)—which was initiated on August 6, 1945. It remains in place today.

The first one hundred natives forced out of the Bikini Atoll for the U.S. bomb tests returned to their contaminated paradise in

1970. Ten years later, however, they were forced to evacuate again after high levels of strontium 90 were discovered in their well water and cesium 137 in their blood. Only scientists, divers, and the occasional tourist would visit in the decades that followed.

The White House had successfully challenged the way the script for *The Beginning or the End* pictured President Truman making his decision to use his revolutionary new weapon against Japan. Truman and aide Charles Ross wanted to convey that he gave this due deliberation, although they cut a line where he admitted to losing sleep over it. They also wanted to make sure the audience understood that there was, really, no other option (we would call it a "slam dunk" today), thus suggesting he would never entertain any second thoughts, let alone feel any pangs of guilt.

So how did that work out for Truman for the rest of his life? In 1947 he cheered Henry Stimson's avid defense in *Harper's*, adding, "I didn't have any doubt" about the wisdom of the decision—unlike those he labeled "Monday morning quarterbacks." Repeatedly, he claimed that the Soviets decided to get in on the "kill" only after the Hiroshima bombing, ignoring his own successful lobbying of Stalin at Potsdam to declare war on Japan around that time. This would establish that argument as a talking point by defenders of Truman's decision, to this day.

In October 1949, U.S. Senator Brien McMahon wrote to the Truman aide, Matt Connelly, imploring the president to meet briefly two months hence with himself, Norman Cousins, John Hersey and a main character in the latter's *Hiroshima*, Rev. Kiyushi Tanimoto. They wanted to submit a petition signed by 108,000 residents of Hiroshima asking Truman to take the lead in setting up a new world organization dedicated to preventing war. Connelly referred the matter to the State Department, where a high official advised against it, asserting that meeting with Tanimoto was surely only a publicity gimmick designed to "have the effect of directing Japanese public attention to the fact that the A-bomb was dropped by the United States." When McMahon was informed of this refusal, he asked if the president would meet with them if Tanimoto was excluded. Again the reply came: No.

After leaving the White House and asked about dropping the bomb, Truman in 1956 was quoted saying "I'd do it again" and nine years later "I would not hesitate." On one occasion he snapped his fingers to indicate how quickly he made up his mind to drop the bomb—quite a contrast to his insistence on radical changes in the MGM script to suggest he had deliberated for quite some time. In an interview he cited the Japanese soldiers as vicious fighters and "I thought that wiping out complete cities with the bomb would be better." Truman misled another correspondent, echoing the false *The Beginning or the End* claims about explicit U.S. warnings: "There had been a statement by me that we had this most powerful explosive in the history of the world and the best thing for them to do was to surrender."

In 1959 he declared (not for the last time) that "I never lost any sleep over my decision," perhaps the line most associated with Truman and the bomb. But Truman went further: he didn't want *anyone* to lose any sleep over this. In private he had instructed *Enola Gay* pilot Paul Tibbets, "Don't you ever lose any sleep over the fact that you planned and carried out that mission. It was my decision. You had no choice." Yet in the same period he would admit, "You have got to understand this is not a military weapon. It is used to wipe out women and children and unarmed people." He met with a group of Japanese *hibakusha* (bomb survivors) visiting the United States and later said he would be willing to travel to Hiroshima for a television special if asked—"but I won't kiss their ass." This visit never materialized.

And then this revealing episode. When the Hiroshima City

Council sent him a very polite but firm letter of protest over his latest statement that he felt "no compunction whatever" about ordering the use of the bombs, he replied with a fervent defense, blaming Japan for starting the war (the United States was "shot in the back"), for which they had to pay with the "sacrifice" of Hiroshima and Nagasaki. Truman was so anxious to get this message to the Japanese he ordered his secretary to "send it airmail." The Hiroshima council replied by acknowledging the evil of Pearl Harbor, then asked if he truly believed that the slaughtering of 200,000, mainly women and kids, was really a "humane" act? Truman did not respond.

To the end, Truman kept a file of letters hailing or hitting his decision, and sometimes replied to them. He accused one writer of "misplaced sentiment" and called another protester "Just an ignorant Cluck" (this was the man's last name). The file was titled "The Jap Bomb Affair."

The one president who disputed the Hiroshima decision did so both before and after residing in the White House. Dwight D. Eisenhower first made his views public in his 1948 memoir, *Crusade in Europe*, asserting that he "disliked seeing the United States take the lead in introducing into war something as horrible and destructive as this new weapon." Fifteen years later he charged that "Japan was already defeated and . . . dropping the bomb was completely unnecessary." Ike firmly believed "We shouldn't have hit them with that awful thing." He had told Stimson, and possibly Truman, about his "feeling of depression" and "grave misgivings" in the weeks leading up to the dropping of the bomb. Stimson grew "deeply perturbed" and tried to refute his reasoning. Much later, Leslie Groves launched a fruitless personal investigation into whether Eisenhower, in fact, actually expressed that view back in 1945.

How did Eisenhower's attitude about Hiroshima affect his view of nuclear weapons after he entered the White House? It did not prevent him from overseeing an enormous nuclear buildup and aggressive hydrogen bomb testing in Nevada during the 1950s, which put at grave risk many of the tens of thousands of soldiers who experienced the blasts and residents living downwind.

In 1964, four years before he was elected president, Richard Nixon visited Hiroshima and like many foreign dignitaries laid a wreath at the main memorial and offered a silent prayer. But what impression did that make on Nixon? He strongly defended Truman's use of the bomb for the rest of his life and, as president, seriously considered employing nuclear weapons himself on one or more occasions.

Jimmy Carter, out of office, also visited Hiroshima. Ronald Reagan, who presided over another massive nuclear buildup (begun under Carter), told a reporter in 1980 that the bomb "ended a great war and probably saved, well, it's been estimated 2 million casualties, in what would have eventually been the invasion of Japan." Later, Reagan said the biblical Armageddon might be at hand— and that a passage in Revelations specifically foretold Hiroshima, describing a plague where "the eyes are burned from the head and the hair falls from the body and so forth."

When a television reporter asked President George H.W. Bush whether the United States should apologize for dropping the atomic bombs, he replied: "Not from this president. I was fighting over there." Bush expressed not only the enduring influence of the official Hiroshima narrative but the understandable emotions of a World War II veteran who had lost friends in the fighting. Bill Clinton, far too young to have served in that war, preemptively cut off any calls for a U.S. apology. He announced that he agreed with Truman's decision, which "we did not believe then and I do not believe now was the wrong one."

After several years in office, Barack Obama (as he had done in many other areas) finally broke the mold. He sent the U.S. ambassador for Japan to the memorial ceremony in Hiroshima in August 2011, the first time this had occurred. Two years later the attendee was Ambassador Caroline Kennedy. Then, in 2016, he became the first president, sitting or past, to attend the Hiroshima ceremony himself. This produced scare stories in conservative American media suggesting he would apologize for Truman dropping the bomb, which of course did not happen. Obama was photographed embracing one of the survivors and he issued a general statement on avoiding the use of nuclear weapons in the future. Nothing very bold, but at least he was there. Donald Trump, then the presumptive Republican nominee for president, tweeted, "Does President Obama ever discuss the sneak attack on Pearl Harbor while he's in Japan?"

When Trump took office it was a return to threatening the use of the bomb against enemies real and imagined, and the modernizing of the U.S. nuclear arsenal to make the weapons more tactical and "useable." The hands on the famous Doomsday Clock managed by the *Bulletin of the Atomic Scientists* moved forward to two minutes to midnight—for the first time since 1953. When Senator Elizabeth Warren, during a Democratic presidential debate, dared endorse a "no-first-use" policy for the United States, she was slammed by many Republicans and some in her own party. Representative Liz Cheney demanded to know "which American cities and how many American citizens are you willing to sacrifice with your policy of forcing the U.S. to absorb a nuclear attack before we can strike back?"

And what of those who had a hand in creating MGM's *The Beginning or the End* or the competing project at Paramount?

Norman Taurog went on to direct more than two dozen films,

including eight for Elvis Presley (among them *Blue Hawaii* and *G.I. Blues*), the most any director could claim, if they wished to. Among the many B-movies he churned out was 1965's *Dr. Goldfoot and the Bikini Machine*. He would remain the youngest Oscar winner for best director until Damien Chazzelle took the prize in 2017. Hal B. Wallis produced several of the Elvis films that Taurog directed, but he also helmed more distinguished projects, including *True Grit*, *Barefoot in the Park*, *Becket*, and *The Rose Tattoo*. Frank "Spig" Wead passed away at the age of fifty-two a few months after the film was released. Bob Considine penned his final Hollywood script, *The Babe Ruth Story*, in 1948, then found a lucrative career, while still on the Hearst payroll, in co-writing or ghostwriting books, including *The Red Plot Against America* (1949) for Robert Stripling.

Among the stars of the film, poor Robert Walker suffered the cruelest fate. Four years after *The Beginning or the End* he landed his greatest role, in Hitchcock's *Strangers on a Train*. By then, however, he suffered from alcoholism and mental illness, aggravated by the aftermath of his high-profile divorce from Jennifer Jones and then a short-lived marriage to the daughter of director John Ford. He died in 1951 at the age of thirty-two when a combination of drinking and drugs caused him to stop breathing.

Hume Cronyn would go on to a long and distinguished life in the theater (sometimes teamed with his wife, Jessica Tandy, as in *The Gin Game*), on television, and in movies, where he enjoyed a surprising late-career boost as one of the geezers in the hit film *Cocoon*. Audrey Totter became a film noir "It" girl. Brian Donlevy sank further into supporting roles in movies, though his lead performance in two sci-fi "Quartermass" features, produced by Britain's Hammer Studios, has endeared him to film historians and genre fans. He became a familiar star in TV productions during the 1950s.

Roman Bohnen, after getting fired from playing Harry Truman, continued gaining character roles for a short while—for example, as Joan of Arc's uncle—but, like others associated with the Group Theatre, worked under the cloud of alleged Communist connections. He was called to testify before a California senate committee investigating the "Red menace" but refused to answer questions. Under strain from various political and personal troubles, he collapsed on stage and died in 1949 at the age of forty-eight. Bohnen didn't live long enough to be blacklisted but was posthumously named as a Communist Party member by the actor Lloyd Bridges.

Sam Marx would claim that James K. McGuiness acted "with such partiality to his own pet people that I wound up using people I didn't want and couldn't reject" for *The Beginning or the End*. His career as a movie producer never took off, and he switched to TV series in the mid-1950s. Marx wrote a pair of memoirs on his early years in Hollywood and, in *Deadly Illusions*, the alleged suicide—or unsolved murder—of Jean Harlow's husband Paul Bern. (He would claim that his old MGM bosses, Thalberg and Mayer, conspired to cover up the murder to save Harlow's career.) Marx died in 1992 at ninety, shortly after I interviewed him for my book on Upton Sinclair's wild and influential 1934 race for governor of California, *The Campaign of the Century*.

James K. McGuinness became one of the first, and most friendly, witnesses before the House Unamerican Activities Committee (HUAC) in the autumn of 1947, and played a prominent role in the early blacklist era. The man McGuinness tried hardest to please in revising *The Beginning or the End*, Charlie Ross, died at his desk in the White House in 1950 from a coronary. Truman aide Matthew J. Connelly was convicted in 1956 of accepting a bribe during his tenure in the White House and served six months in federal prison.

The drawn, gray, haunted visage of J. Robert Oppenheimer in his later years came to symbolize a true expression of the atomic age and the decision to make, and then use, a revolutionary new weapon against two cities. His face appeared mask-like, but as always it was impossible to tell what was behind the mask, what was hidden or most deeply felt.

The investigations of his security lapses, begun even before Trinity, came to fruition as the Red Scare swept America and top-level resentment of Oppenheimer's lukewarm reaction to developing the hydrogen bomb festered. His security clearance (for which Leslie Groves once stuck out his neck) was finally revoked in 1953, a decision sustained after a contentious hearing the following year. Oppenheimer was likely doomed when he admitted that he had lied a decade earlier about his friend Haakon Chevalier approaching him to find out if he might pass secrets to the Soviets. He had behaved like "an idiot" then, he admitted. Among those who testified against him were Leslie Groves, Edward Teller, and E.O. Lawrence. Continuing past policy, the FBI tapped his telephone in Princeton and listened in on his frequent conferences with his attorneys.

Stripped of the clearance, he managed to stay active lecturing and writing, but the heart seemed to go out of him. He did not join the nuclear control efforts of Einstein and others, though he was by no means hostile to them. His views on making and using the bomb against Japan remained maddeningly inconsistent when they weren't impossible to decipher (which is probably what he preferred). He said, "There is no doubt we were hideously uncomfortable about being associated with such slaughter," yet later declared, "About the making of the bomb and Trinity, I have no remorse." He confessed that physicists had "known sin," but also "I understand why it happened and appreciate with what nobility those men with whom I'd worked so closely made their decision." Even his opposition to the hydrogen bomb was far from clear and forthright.

Shortly before his death he told *The New York Times*, "I never regretted, and do not regret now, having done my part of the job. . . . I also think that it was a damn good thing that the bomb was developed, that it was recognized as something important and new, and that it would have an effect on the course of history." It could have been an excerpt from a second Matt Cochran letter to his *The Beginning or the End* widow. Urged by Oppenheimer's friends, and Edward Teller, to signal some measure of rehabilitation, John F. Kennedy in 1963 awarded Oppenheimer the Enrico Fermi Award, which came with a $50,000 check. It was presented to him after the president died (his widow, Jackie, went out of her way to attend and asked to meet Oppenheimer). He died four years later, at the age of sixty-two, after a bout with throat cancer.

*The Beginning or the End* would eventually reach a much wider audience, via television, but this property of Turner Entertainment is rarely aired (and a DVD version was not released until recently). Because of its quasi-documentary form, its depiction of history is no doubt accepted by most viewers. Movie guides rarely question its accuracy. Some have hailed it as an important and very early example of a "docu-drama."

After the box office failure of *The Beginning or the End* there would not be another Hiroshima-related movie for more than six years. Once again MGM would be its sponsor, and its message was the same. The idea had come from General Curtis "Mad Bomber" LeMay, who had directed the burning of dozens of Japanese cities before becoming head of the new Strategic Air Command. *Above and Beyond* explored the story of Hiroshima from the perspective of pilot Paul Tibbets (played by Robert Taylor). To show the blast effects of the bomb the producers simply inserted footage from MGM's previous film. This saved MGM money but did little to expand the audience's awareness of what an atomic weapon could do. In the climactic scene, Tibbets releases the Hiroshima bomb and, surveying a city on fire, radios his report. "Results good," he says. Then he repeats it, this time grimly, more aware of the words. This was not in the original script, but was added later, probably to humanize the men who dropped the bomb. Tibbets, in any case, slammed that scene when it came out. Bosley Crowther of *The New York Times* criticized some aspects of the movie but, as he had done with *The Beginning or the End*, praised the "substance and plausibility" of its handling of dropping the bomb.

Repeatedly the film underlined its theme—deploying a bomb that can kill tens of thousands in an instant is dirty work but someone's got to do it. As in *The Beginning or the End*, saving hundreds of thousands of American lives is the main message, although Truman is not a key character here. And like the earlier film, *Above and Beyond* did not light up the box office.

Hollywood would not produce another film on the subject of Hiroshima and Nagasaki for decades, leaving the field to postapocalypse fantasies (*On the Beach*), nuclear thrillers such as *Fail-Safe*, the absurdist masterpiece *Dr. Strangelove*, and the frightening docu-drama *The War Game*. The movie industry's failure to reexamine the subject with a fresh eye contributed "to the larger cultural process," historian Paul Boyer observed, "by which Hiroshima and Nagasaki gradually sank, unconfronted and unresolved, into the deeper recesses of American awareness."

Finally, in 1989, Roland Joffe's *Fat Man and Little Boy* appeared, with good guy Paul Newman as Groves and relative unknown Dwight Schultz as Oppenheimer. So you know who had the audience's attention and sympathy, even though this was far from the director's intention. (Mrs. Groves had wanted Clark Gable for the role of her husband in *The Beginning or the End*. Now she finally got her handsome leading man.) John Cusack played a young scientist who suffered a Matt Cochran–type radiation accident. Joffe, who had directed *The Killing Fields*, tried to create a complex picture

that questioned the official Hiroshima narrative, while emphasiz-
ing the qualms of the scientists who made the bomb. But Newman's Groves would dominate the film, riding roughshod over
Oppenheimer at every turn. The film received a mixed reception
from critics. Vincent Canby of *The New York Times* observed that
with Groves expressing his views so much more persuasively than
anyone else the film was "stunningly ineffective" in promoting
Joffe's obvious anti-bomb sentiments.

The Showtime channel in 1995 attempted an ambitious, three-
hour docu-drama to mark the fiftieth anniversary of the dropping
of the bombs, titled simply *Hiroshima*, with no major stars but co-
directed by Hollywood veteran Roger Spottiswoode. Generally
sympathetic to the use of the new weapon against Japan, it nevertheless pictured Truman spending barely a minute, after learning
that the first bomb was ready, to scribble a note authorizing its use.
This time he was no longer alive and in the White House to order
a radically different take.

That same year saw a surge in news coverage for the fiftieth-
anniversary commemoration of the opening of the atomic era.
Nearly all of the TV reports backed the decision to use the bomb,
except for a Peter Jennings special for ABC, which drew wide criticism for daring to question Truman's actions—some objecting
that Jennings, as a native of Canada, was obviously biased. Even
more revealing was the gutting of the exhibit surrounding the
Smithsonian's display of the rebuilt front section of the *Enola Gay*
at its National Air and Space Museum in Washington, D.C. The
original script for the extensive, well-balanced exhibit was strongly criticized by some veterans' groups, pundits, and members of
Congress. They bullied the curators into painting a decidedly pro-
bomb picture with little or no mention of the case against dropping the bomb or the 200,000 who died, not unlike that offered by

*The Beginning or the End.* Ultimately, the exhibit was killed entirely and the bomber was simply put on self-glorifying display.

A well-intentioned and quality television series, *Manhattan*, debuted from one of the smaller streaming/cable upstarts, WGN, in 2014. It focused on fictional scientists at Los Alamos, although Oppie occasionally made an appearance, and included ethical debates. Rachel Brosnahan played the lead scientist's bisexual wife, but this was before her awards and popularity from *The Marvelous Mrs. Maisel*, and the series died after just two seasons—with the Trinity test.

Ayn Rand would write only one other screenplay for Hal Wallis, and it went unproduced. Her script for *The Fountainhead* did reach fruition, however, when Warner Bros. released the movie directed by King Vidor in 1949. It starred Gary Cooper and Patricia Neal. Vidor had planned on hiring liberals Humphrey Bogart and Lauren Bacall, but Rand insisted on conservative Cooper. She also successfully objected to the trimming of Howard Roark's courtroom speech—it had been reduced partly because Cooper said he did not understand it. The film was neither a critical nor a commercial hit.

As she continued writing her follow-up, *Atlas Shrugged*, she appeared as a "friendly witness" before HUAC warning about Communist propaganda in movies. She also composed a pamphlet for the Motion Picture Alliance, where James K. McGuinness remained a major player, entitled *Screen Guide for Americans.* "The purpose of the Communists in Hollywood is *not* the production of political movies openly advocating Communism," she warned. "Their purpose is *to corrupt our moral premises by corrupting non-political movies*—by introducing small, casual bits of propaganda into innocent stories—thus making people absorb the basic principles of Collectivism *by indirection and implication*. The principle of free speech . . . does not require that we furnish the Communists with the means to preach their ideas, and does not imply that we owe them jobs and support to advocate our own destruction at our own expense." Among the films she cited that contained hidden pro-Communist messages was *The Best Years of Our Lives*. Another group she was allied with put *It's a Wonderful Life* in the same category.

*Atlas Shrugged* was published in 1957 and would become her most popular and influential novel. She portrayed its character largely based on Robert Oppenheimer, named Robert Stadler, as the brilliant chairman of the physics department at Patrick Henry University. Then he accepts the directorship of the State Science Institute, which, he later discovers, was run by a man who secretly planned to use science to promote political power. This leads Stadler to attempt a "Project X" and a shattering "ultrasonic" weapon, but he would die for his sins.

Critics vied in mocking the novel. Granville Hicks in *The New York Times Book Review* judged that it was "written out of hate." *Time* magazine asked: "Is it a novel? Is it a nightmare? Is it Superman—in the comic strip or the Nietzschean version?" Even some conservatives blasted it. Whittaker Chambers, settling at the *National Review* after the Alger Hiss controversy, called *Atlas Shrugged* "remarkably silly" and "sophomoric," adding that it could be called a novel "only by devaluing the term." But one of Rand's admirers, Alan Greenspan, wrote a complaining letter to *The New York Times Book Review* calling the novel "a celebration of life and happiness. Justice is unrelenting. . . . Parasites who persistently avoid either purpose or reason perish as they should."

Rand stayed true to her "Objectivist" calling into the 1970s until her health and income declined. Going against her steely principles, she filed for Social Security and Medicare benefits. When she died in 1974 she was buried in Valhalla, New York, with a six-foot floral arrangement in the shape of a dollar sign nearby. Alan Greenspan attended the funeral.

Almost forty years after the MGM project, as the editor of *Nuclear Times* magazine, I had a chance to interview Paul Tibbets. All these years after dropping the bomb, did he feel any regrets whatsoever? "I've got a standard answer on that," he informed me, without missing a beat, "I felt nothing about it." He said he was "sorry" for all those "who got burned up down there, but I felt sorry for those who died at Pearl Harbor, too. . . . People get mad when I say this, but—it was as impersonal as could be. There wasn't anything personal as far as I'm concerned, so I had no personal part in it.

"It wasn't my decision to make morally, one way or another. I did what I was told—I didn't invent the bomb, I just dropped the damn thing. It was a success, and that's where I've left it." (He was no "crybaby pilot.") Then, echoing Truman, "I can assure you that I sleep just as peacefully as anybody can sleep." When August 6 rolls around each year "sometimes people have to tell me. To me it's just another day." In fact, he wrote in his autobiography, *The Tibbets Story*, that when Truman instructed him not to lose any sleep over it, he appreciated the message but found it "unnecessary."

In 1976, as a retired brigadier general, he reenacted the Hiroshima mission at an air show in Texas, with a smoke bomb set off to simulate a mushroom cloud. He intended to do it again elsewhere, but international protests forced a cancellation. He told a *Washington Post* reporter, "For awhile in the 1950s, I got a lot of letters condemning me . . . but they faded out." On the other hand, "I got a lot of letters from women propositioning me."

A decade after talking with Tibbets, and spending a month in Hiroshima and Nagasaki, I met another adviser for *The Beginning or the End*, Charles Sweeney, pilot of the aircraft that released its deadly cargo over Nagasaki. We were in the green room at CNN and about to appear together on Larry King's popular prime-time program. With rather too much apparent pleasure, he offered a stout defense of the decision to drop the second bomb, which he repeated on-air, along with false historical claims, such as contending (echoing the popular myth promoted by Truman) the Soviets had not agreed to attack Japan until after the Nagasaki raid.

And what of the couple who provided the original crucial connection for the MGM atomic bomb movie? Tony Owen would become a longtime independent producer of B-movies, proudly proclaiming, "I am no genius, I just wanted to make commercial films." His wife, Donna Reed, meanwhile established herself as a rising star after *It's a Wonderful Life*. She won the Academy Award for best supporting actress for the memorable role of Montgomery Clift's girlfriend (a classy hostess/maybe prostitute) in *From Here to Eternity*, which climaxed with the Japanese attack on Pearl Harbor.

When her movie career stalled, she would gain her greatest fame with the long-running TV series *The Donna Reed Show*. On a segment of the popular program *This Is Your Life*, one of the associates from her past who offered a testimonial was Dr. Edward Tompkins. She remained married to Tony Owen until 1971, when they divorced. A longtime Republican, she became an anti–Vietnam war activist, after supporting Senator Eugene McCarthy's insurgent campaign for president in 1968, and chaired the Beverly Hills chapter of Another Mother for Peace, best known for popularizing the slogan *War is not healthy for children and other living things*.

Reed also came to oppose nuclear power. "If nuclear power plants are safe, let the commercial insurance industry insure them," she advised. "Until these most expert judges of risk are willing to gamble with their money, I'm not willing to gamble with the health and safety of my family." She also explained, "I'm not really a leader of causes. Some people think that I have been active in women's lib. I haven't. But perhaps I have contributed to the movement by urging women to speak out on matters that concern them." She would die from cancer in 1986 at the age of sixty-four.

There is no record that Reed ever viewed or commented on *The Beginning or the End*.

———

> *O! it is excellent to have a giant's strength,*
> *but it is tyrannous to use it like a giant.*
>
> —Shakespeare, *Measure for Measure*

Three-quarters of a century after the atomic attacks on Hiroshima and Nagasaki, and the genesis of *The Beginning or the End*, why does the decision to drop the bomb, and the enduring defense of that in Hollywood, matter today? After all, that decision, and the more than 200,000 deaths that followed—not to mention more than forty years of a costly and dangerous arms race with the Soviets—cannot be undone.

Perhaps the strongest reason is this: Most American media commentators, military leaders, and top elected officials continue to endorse the "first strike" of the bomb against Japan. This remains true despite new evidence surrounding that decision that has emerged over several decades. Little has changed abroad—where in most countries dropping the two bombs has been roundly condemned. Indeed, American support for our use of the bomb in 1945 gives us little moral standing in arguing that other nations should not develop nuclear weapons, nor consider using them before an enemy attacks (that's official U.S. "first-use" policy, remember). Recall Einstein's warning in 1946: "The American decision may have been a fatal error, for men accustom themselves to thinking that a weapon that was used once can be used again."

So it all goes back to Hiroshima and Nagasaki.

The self-justifying "Hiroshima narrative" has been handed down to generations of Americans, and clearly matters today as much as it ever has, in the era of Donald J. Trump. From the start of the atomic age, top policymakers and pundits have wisely emphasized, "We must try to never use nuclear weapons again," yet they inevitably endorse the two times the weapon *already* has been used in a deadly first strike. To make these exceptions, however atrocious and unique the conditions in 1945 after years of slaughter, means exceptions can be made in the future—to "end a war" or "save American lives" (or, for that matter, intimidate a potential aggressor).

Now, under President Trump, "policies equating cyberthreats to nuclear threats, or raising the profile of nuclear weapons in our conventional defenses . . . makes nuclear use more likely," warn former national security advisers Richard A. Clarke and Steve Andreasen. An article in *Military Times* in July 2019 revealed that new policies for the Pentagon promote use of tactical nuclear weapons to create "decisive results and the restoration of strategic stability" thereby allowing commanders to go for a "win."

A month later, the United States withdrew from the Intermediate-Range Nuclear Forces (INF) Treaty with the Russians, a 1987 accord that banned the possession of ground-launched ballistic and cruise missiles with a range of 310 to 3,420 miles. Two weeks after that the Defense Department test-fired a cruise missile that would have violated the treaty. It was intended "less as a technology assessment than as a political statement" to put China and Russia on the defensive, observed Michael T. Klare, a longtime arms control expert. "Unless halted by Congress, this drive will almost certainly spark a dangerous new arms race and dramatically narrow the 'firebreak' between conventional and nuclear war."

And what is the cost of even a limited first-strike beyond immediate civilian casualties? Environmental scientists at Rutgers University recently concluded that even a brief exchange of several dozen weapons could create a "mini-nuclear winter." Effects could last two or three years and create climate change leading to tens of millions of deaths from starvation due to the collapse of grain crops.

Ariel Dorfman in the *New York Review of Books* posed what he called "the question" not long ago: "To what extent does Americans' belief in the rightness of President Truman's fateful decision in 1945 provide moral support for the brimstone rhetoric of nuclear conflagration that President Trump is deploying today?" He cited a recent Stanford study that suggested six in ten Americans would approve a nuclear first-strike against Iran that might save the lives of 20,000 U.S. soldiers even at the cost of two million civilian lives. The study concluded that the so-called "nuclear taboo" for Americans was "shallow and easily overcome by the pressures of war."

What Dorfman called "the question" has been hanging in the air since World War II, regularly ignored but at times re-emerging in a dramatic way. In June 1965, for example, nearly nineteen years after his "Hiroshima" article threatened a president's defense of deploying two massively powerful bombs, John Hersey appeared at the White House. This came just as another president was under attack for targeting other sites in Asia, this time in Vietnam, with thousands of smaller explosives. At a much-publicized celebration of the arts, Hersey and other famous writers had the opportunity to read a short selection from one of their works. While most of the authors, such as Saul Bellow, were opposed to Lyndon B. Johnson's Vietnam policies, they chose not to use this venue for protest, especially with the president's wife, Lady Bird, sitting in the front row.

Hersey, however, decided to read an extract from "Hiroshima," introducing it with a pointed, almost poetic comment as relevant today as it was then. "Let these words be a reminder," he implored the audience. "The step from one degree of violence to the next is imperceptibly taken, and cannot easily be taken back. We cannot for a moment forget the truly terminal dangers in these times of miscalculation, of arrogance, of accident, of reliance not on moral strength but on mere military power."

The line against using nuclear weapons has been drawn, but it has been drawn in shifting sand. And America drew it there. Hiroshima was the beginning, but we are not yet safely at its end.

# ACKNOWLEDGMENTS

I would like to thank all of the archivists at numerous sites who have immeasurably aided my often difficult and confounding research related to the atomic bombings since the early 1990s, starting with a grant from the Truman Library in Independence, MO. For this book extensive research was carried out with much vital assistance at the Library of Congress in Washington, D.C.; the National Archives and Records Administration in College Park, MD; the Motion Picture Academy's Margaret Herrick Library in Beverly Hills, CA; the University of California's Cinematic Arts Library in Los Angeles; The University of Chicago Library; and the Harvard University Archives in Cambridge, MA.

A special thank you to Kristine Krueger at the Herrick Library, and to Satu Haase-Webb for her usual vital research work at the Library of Congress and at the National Archives.

Michael Barson provided some key images. My agent Gary Morris stuck with this book idea when the going got rough and editor Carl Bromley provided strong guidance and support. Martin J. Sherwin reviewed the Oppenheimer passages, and Alex Wellerstein examined the entire manuscript. Also thanks to Emily Albarillo and Liana Krissoff at The New Press for their attentive editing. I will always be indebted to my mentor in this general field of research and writing, Robert Jay Lifton, as well as to my wife, Barbara Bedway, for her close read of the manuscript and other loving support on this subject (and others) going back years, decades.

# NOTES

## Archives Cited

**HARV-Conant:** Papers of James B. Conant in Harvard University Archives, Cambridge, MA.

**HST-OF:** Harry S. Truman Presidential Library, Official File, Independence, MO.

**HST-PPF:** Harry S. Truman Presidential Library, Post-Presidential File, Independence, MO.

**HST-Press Secy:** Harry S. Truman Presidential Library, President's Secretary's File, Independence, MO.

**HST-Ross:** Papers of Charles Ross at Harry S. Truman Presidential Library, Independence, MO.

**LOC-Bush:** Papers of Vannevar Bush, Box 172, Atomic Energy, at the Library of Congress, Washington, D.C.

**LOC-Opp:** Papers of J. Robert Oppenheimer, Box 11, Atomic Bomb, Films, at the Library of Congress, Washington, D.C.

**LOC-Sherwin:** Martin J. Sherwin collection, FBI files, Box 11, 12, 17, Library of Congress, Washington, D.C.

**LSP-UC:** Leo Szilard Papers, University of California (San Diego).

**MPA-Hopper:** Hedda Hopper Correspondence, Motion Picture Academy, Margaret Herrick Library, Beverly Hills, CA.

**MPA-Mannix Ledger:** Records of MGM executive Eddie Mannix, Motion Picture Academy, Margaret Herrick Library, Beverly Hills, CA.

**MPA-MGM:** Turner/MGM Scripts and Related (produced), Motion Picture Academy, MGM "The Beginning or the End" Files, Margaret Herrick Library, Beverly Hills, CA.

**MPA-Prod Code:** Motion Picture Association of America: Production Code Administration Records, Motion Picture Academy, Margaret Herrick Library, Beverly Hills, CA.

**MPA-Wallis:** Hal Wallis Papers, Correspondence with Ayn Rand 1944–1948, Motion Picture Academy, Margaret Herrick Library, Beverly Hills, CA.

**NARA-Groves RG 200:** Papers of General Leslie R. Groves, National Archives and Records Administration, College Park, MD. Correspondence 1941–1970s, Box 11, Movies.

**UC-AOR:** University of Chicago, Papers of the Association of Oak Ridge Engineers and Scientists, Boxes 5, 7, and 20.

## 1: The Donna Reed Show

1    Tompkins letter to Owen/Reed, Oct. 26, 1945 (UC-AOR).

1    Donna Reed's background: Fultz, *In Search of Donna Reed*.

1    "I think anyone that had him for a teacher": *Bulletin Review* (Denison, Iowa), March 30, 2012.

3    "Re-creation of the bombing": Lifton and Mitchell, *Hiroshima in America*.

3    "Seldom, if ever": Murrow, *In Search of Light*.

5    Second Tompkins letter to Reed: Oct. 29, 1945 (UC-AOR).

5    Tompkins calls Reed: Memo, Nov. 1, 1945 (UC-AOR).

6    Owen and Marx meet: Marx chapter in Goldstein and Konigsberg, eds., *The Movies*; his report, Nov. 27, 1945 (MPA-MGM B-747).

6    Barron phoned and wrote: Mick Broderick chapter in Jacobs, *Filling the Hole in the Nuclear Future*.

7    "Anatomic Bomb" in *Life* magazine: Boyer, *By the Bomb's Early Light*.

8    "Most important movie": Marx chapter in Goldstein and Konigsberg, eds., *The Movies*; his report, Nov. 27, 1945 (MPA-MGM B-747).

8    "Let's call President Truman": Marx chapter in Goldstein and Konigsberg, eds., *The Movies*.

9    Owen-Tompkins phone call: Memo, Nov. 1, 1945 (UC-AOR).

9    Marx background: Marx, *Mayer and Thalberg* and *A Gaudy Spree*.

11    "We are very happy": Marx chapter in Goldstein and Konigsberg, eds., *The Movies*; his report, Nov. 27, 1945 (MPA-MGM B-747).

11    Ayn Rand background: Heller, *Ayn Rand and the World She Made*; Branden, *The Passion of Ayn Rand*.

12    Essex House dispute: Manager to Wallis, Sept. 21, 1945; Wallis replies Sept. 26, 1945 (MPA-Wallis).

## 2: From Oak Ridge to the Oval Office

13    Scientists warn: *Time*, Nov. 5, 1945; Einstein, *The Atlantic Monthly*, November 1945.

14    Sturgeon's letter: Boyer, *By the Bomb's Early Light*.

14    Oak Ridge visit: Marx chapter in Goldstein and Konigsberg, eds., *The Movies*; his report, Nov. 27, 1945 (MPA-MGM B-747).

15    FAS office in D.C.: Marx chapter in Goldstein and Konigsberg, eds., *The Movies*; his report, Nov. 27, 1945 (MPA-MGM B-747); Smith, *A Peril and a Hope*.

16    "The office is a dumpy suite": Smith, *A Peril and a Hope*.

16    Meeting with Groves: Marx chapter in Goldstein and Konigsberg, eds., *The Movies*; his report, Nov. 27, 1945 (MPA-MGM B-747); Anonymous Memo on visit, Nov. 14, 1945 (UC-AOR).

17    "destroy its capacity": Norris, *Racing for the Bomb*.

17    Scientists' newsletter on visit: Box 20, Folder 1 (UC-AOR).

17    D.C. visit continued: Marx chapter in Goldstein and Konigsberg, eds., *The Movies*; his report, Nov. 27, 1945 (MPA-MGM B-747).

18    "Defiled": *Commonweal*, Aug. 24 and 31, 1945.

18    Spellman to Marx: Marx chapter in Goldstein and Konigsberg, eds., *The Movies*; his report, Nov. 27, 1945 (MPA-MGM B-747).

19    Lawrence comment: *U.S. News*, Aug. 17 and 31, 1945.

19    Gallup poll: Boyer, *By the Bomb's Early Light*.

19    Truman and Oppenheimer meet: Bird and Sherwin, *American Prometheus*; McCullough, *Truman*; Rhodes, *The Making of the Atomic Bomb*.

20    Marx and Owen meet with Truman: Marx chapter in Goldstein and Konigsberg, eds., *The Movies*; his report, Nov. 27, 1945 (MPA-MGM B-747).

21    "Gracious" chat: Barron to Truman, Nov. 21, 1945 (HST-Press Secy).

21    Truman replies to Barron, Nov. 26, 1945 (HST-Pres Secy).

21    Marx meets with Oppenheimer, and the party: Marx chapter in Goldstein and Konigsberg, eds., *The Movies*; his report, Nov. 27, 1945 (MPA-MGM B-747).

24    Groves on radiation: Lifton and Mitchell, *Hiroshima in America*.

24    Groves testified to Congress: *New York Times*, Nov. 29, 1945.

24    Groves's involvement with bomb: Groves, *Now It Can Be Told*; Lifton and Mitchell, *Hiroshima in America*; Rhodes, *The Making of the Atomic Bomb*.

## 3: The Race for the Bomb (Film)

26  "The genesis of the Paramount opus": Cohn letter to Hopper, MPA-Hopper Correspondence, March 25, 1947.

27  Cohn to friend Connelly on movie: Nov. 9, 1945 (HST-OF).

27  Connelly replied: Nov. 14, 1945 (HST-OF).

28  Cohn notified Connelly, aware of MGM now: Nov. 29, 1945 (HST-OF).

28  Rand contract with Wallis: July 5, 1944 (MPA-Wallis).

28  "From the Waldorf": Nov. 30, 1945 (UC-AOR).

29  "Now MGM" announced: *New York Times*, Dec. 10, 1945.

29  "Less than a week later": *New York Times*, Dec. 16, 1945.

30  Beatty draft for Wallis: Undated (MPA-MGM B-753).

31  Marx movie scenario: Nov. 27, 1945 (MPA-MGM B-747).

31  Oak Ridge movie scenario: Undated, circa Dec. 1945 (UC-AOR).

32  Mead and Bateson: Richard D. Present to S.G. English, Dec. 11, 1945 (UC: AOR).

32  Mead and bomb: Margaret Mead and the Power of Culture, Library of Congress site, https://www.loc.gov/exhibits/mead/oneworld-learn.html.

## 4: The FBI vs. Oppie

34  Rand's San Fernando house: Heller, *Ayn Rand and the World She Made*.

35  Rand memo to Wallis: Jan. 2, 1946, Harriman, ed., *Journals of Ayn Rand*; also MPA-Wallis.

36  Oppenheimer left Los Alamos: Bird and Sherwin, *American Prometheus*.

36  "If atomic bombs are to be added": Bird and Sherwin, *American Prometheus*.

36  Farewell address: Bird and Sherwin, *American Prometheus*.

36  To Ernest O. Lawrence: Smith and Weiner, eds., *Robert Oppenheimer*.

37  Hoover circulated Oppenheimer file: Bird and Sherwin, *American Prometheus*.

38  Considine's treatment for MGM: December 1945 (MPA-MGM B-749).

38  Considine and weeping scientist: His Hearst INS column, Feb. 28, 1947.

41  James M. Cain on McGuinness and McGuinness career: Schwartz, *The Hollywood Writers' Wars.*

41  McGuinness names Wead writer, and Marx's view: Marx chapter in Goldstein and Konigsberg, eds., *The Movies.*

## 5: Saboteurs and Bridge-Playing Wives

43  Wead's memo: Dec. 31, 1945 (MPA-MGM B-754).

44  Groves's background: Groves, *Now It Can Be Told*; Rhodes, *The Making of the Atomic Bomb.*

46  Nichols on Groves: Nichols, *The Road to Trinity.*

46  Groves and Kyoto: Groves, *Now It Can Be Told*; Lifton and Mitchell, *Hiroshima in America.*

47  Groves and Marshall: Lifton and Mitchell, *Hiroshima in America.*

47  Groves and Nagasaki: Lifton and Mitchell, *Hiroshima in America*; Groves, *Now It Can Be Told.*

47  Groves's MGM contract: Dec. 31, 1945 (NARA-Groves).

48  Wead's outline: Jan. 4, 1946 (MPA-MGM B-755).

50  Daghlian radiation incident: Lifton and Mitchell, *Hiroshima in America*; Rhodes, *The Making of the Atomic Bomb.*

51  FDR and the bomb: Lifton and Mitchell, *Hiroshima in America*; Rhodes, *The Making of the Atomic Bomb.*

## 6: The Rand Report

53  Troops go to Hiroshima and Nagasaki: Lifton and Mitchell, *Hiroshima in America.*

54  Photographs and footage seized: Mitchell, *Atomic Cover-up.*

54  Mark Hatfield recalls: Lifton and Mitchell, *Hiroshima in America.*

54  "Atom Bowl" in Nagasaki: Mitchell, *Atomic Cover-up.*

56  Rand's 16-pager for Wallis: Jan. 19, 1946 (MPA-MGM B-762).

57  New Year's party: Bird and Sherwin, *American Prometheus.*

58  Marx set his sights on Oppie: Letter to Oppenheimer, Jan. 7, 1946 (LOC-Opp).

58  Rand's interview with Oppenheimer: Harriman, ed., *Journals of Ayn Rand.*

59  Tompkins memo to colleagues: Undated, circa Jan. 1946 (LOC-Opp).

**60**  Tompkins letter to Enrico Fermi: Jan. 16, 1946 (LOC-Opp).

**61**  Cousins hosts party and then Marx letter: Jan. 10, 1946 (UC-AOR).

**62**  Adding some sex: Virginia MacPherson, United Press, Jan. 11, 1946.


## 7: Nobody Can Harness Man

**63**  Rand interviews Oppenheimer again, plus Groves and others: Harriman, ed., *Journals of Ayn Rand*; Heller, *Ayn Rand and the World She Made*.

**65**  "Philosophic Notes": Harriman, ed., *Journals of Ayn Rand*.

**65**  Wead script: Jan. 16, 1946 (MPA-MGM B-759).

**67**  Tompkins reviews Wead script: Jan. 23, 1946 (MPA-MGM B-766).

**68**  "very cagey": Paul Tompkins to Edward Tompkins, Jan. 10, 1946 (UC-AOR).

**69**  "I know you will not want to lend": Richard Present to Einstein, Jan. 30, 1946, Albert Einstein Archives, The Hebrew University of Jerusalem, Israel.

**69**  "I think that most of the men": Nickson to Tompkins, Jan. 22, 1946 (UC-AOR).

**69**  Groves and that $10,000 fee: *Newsweek*, Feb. 11, 1946.

**70**  $5,000 check as "hot potato": For example, Tompkins to Henshaw, Jan. 24, 1946; R.D. Present telegram to atomic scientists group in Chicago, Feb. 6, 1946 (UC-AOR).

**70**  Rand's new outline: March 2, 1946 (MPA-MGM B-774 and B-777).


## 8: Ticking Clocks and Time Capsules

**73**  New Smith sketch for Wallis: MPA-MGM B-748.

**74**  Smith outline for Wallis: MPA-MGM B-766.

**75**  "I'm doing everything here": Tompkins to Nickson, Jan. 30, 1946 (UC-AOR).

**76**  Marx's view of Norman Taurog: Marx chapter in Goldstein and Konigsberg, eds., *The Movies*.

**76**  Taurog description: Goldstein and Konigsberg, eds., *The Movies*.

**77**  New "prologue" for script: Feb. 6, 1946 (MPA-MGM B-771).


## 9: The End of the Beginning

**80**  Operation Crossroads: Boyer, *By the Bomb's Early Light*; Lifton and Mitchell, *Hiroshima in America*; Miller, *Under the Cloud*.

82   "One hell of a good sales job": *Time*, April 1, 1946.

82   Roger Angell short story: *New Yorker*, April 13, 1946.

83   Tompkins-Marx blowout: Ed Tompkins to Paul Tompkins, Feb. 13 and 16, 1946 (UC-AOR).

84   Tompkins and McGuinness meet: Tompkins to Tompkins, Feb. 13, 1946 (UC-AOR).

85   Playing the tapes of calls for studio execs: Smith, *A Peril and a Hope*.

85   Revised Wead script: Mainly March 1946 (MPA-MGM B-779, B-782, B-784, B-785).


## 10: Enter General Groves

88   Groves and radiation: Lifton and Mitchell, *Hiroshima in America*.

89   "I am working now": Berliner, ed., *Letters of Ayn Rand*.

90   Rand's script for Wallis: Feb.–March 1946 (MPA-MGM B-773).

91   Siemes eyewitness article: *Time*, Feb. 11, 1946.

92   Tompkins memo to Marx: Feb. 10, 1946, did not send and then met (UC-AOR).

93   Tompkins meets Rosten: His letter to Paul Tompkins, and Rosten's reply "the following day": Feb. 13, 1946.(UC-AOR).

94   Nickson memo: Feb. 23, 1946 (UC-AOR).

94   Consodine reviews script: March 7, 1946 (NARA-Groves).

96   Breen office comments on script: March 7, 1946 (MPA-Prod Code).

98   Groves critique of script: March 4 and 12, 1946 (NARA-Groves).

99   Consodine's play-by-play on script: March 4, 1946 (NARA-Groves).


## 11: "Top Secret" Is Out

101  Wallis caves to MGM: *New York Times*, March 23, 1946.

102  Rand to Wallis complaint: March 19, 1946 (MPA-Wallis).

103  Cohn also angry: Letter to Hopper, March 25, 1947 (MPA-Hopper correspondence F-280).

103  Federal Council of Churches report: *New York Times*, March 6, 1946.

104  Sheen hits atomic attack: *New York Times*, April 8, 1946.

105  Latest Wead script: MPA-MGM B-779.

106  Allison on Nagasaki: Lifton and Mitchell, *Hiroshima in America*.

107  Nagasaki history and the bomb: Southard, *Nagasaki*; Lifton and Mitchell, *Hiroshima in America*.

**108** Telford Taylor on war crime: Taylor, *Nuremberg and Vietnam.*

**109** Gillespie and special effects money: Gillespie Special Effects Collection, *The Beginning or the End* (MPA-MGM).

**109** MGM casting: Marx chapter in Goldstein and Konigsberg, eds., *The Movies.*

**110** Actors' credits: IMDb.com.

## 12: Dinner with the Oppenheimers

**112** Marx plans to meet: Letter to Oppenheimer, April 18, 1946 (LOC-Opp).

**112** Marx and the dinner: Oppenheimer to Nickson, circa May 1946 (LOC-Opp).

**114** FBI surveillance: Hoover to attorney general, April 26, 1946 (LOC-Sherwin).

**114** Marx revises script: Letter to Oppenheimer, April 24, 1946 (LOC-Opp).

**115** MGM's memo of requests to military: April 16, 1946 (NARA-Groves).

**117** Military approves: April 24 and 27, 1946 (NARA-Groves).

**117** Agee's background: Lifton and Mitchell, *Hiroshima in America*; Boyer, *By the Bomb's Early Light*; Bergreen, *James Agee, a Life.*

**118** "Dedication Day" story: Agee, *The Collected Short Prose of James Agee*; Lifton and Mitchell, *Hiroshima in America*; Boyer, *By the Bomb's Early Light.*

**118** Agee and Chaplin: Bergreen, *James Agee, a Life.*

**119** Song lyrics: Boyer, *By the Bomb's Early Light.*

**119** Hawkins's background: Bird and Sherwin, *American Prometheus.*

**119** Hawkins telegram to Oppie: April 26, 1946 (LOC-Opp).

**119** Oppenheimer aide replies to Hawkins: April 29, 1946 (LOC-Opp).

**120** "There they watched in amusement": Smith, *A Peril and a Hope.*

**120** FBI and Hawkins: Teletypes from "Fletcher" to D.C. bureau, May 20 and May 21, 1946 (LOC-Sherwin).

**120** Cronyn letter to Oppie: April 30, 1946 (LOC-Opp).

**121** Kitty/Robert phone call: FBI transcript, May 14, 1946 (LOC-Sherwin).

**122** Oppenheimer comments to Nickson: circa May 1946 (LOC-Opp).

## 13: Those Japanese A-Bombs

**124** White House reviews script: Barron to Ros, April 19, 1946; Ross replies to Barron, April 19, 1946 (HST-OF 692 Misc.).

**125** Latest Wead script: MPA-MGM, B-783, B-784, B-785.

**127** Teller and Super conference, Fuchs and Greenglass: Bird and Sherwin, *American Prometheus*; Rhodes, *The Making of the Atomic Bomb*.

**128** The Slotin accident: Lifton and Mitchell, *Hiroshima in America*; Rhodes, *The Making of the Atomic Bomb*; Wellerstein, "The Demon Core and the Strange Death of Louis Slotin."

**130** Donna Reed and *It's a Wonderful Life*: Fultz, *In Search of Donna Reed*.

**131** Eleanor Roosevelt and Barrymore: Considine, Hearst INS news service, June 19, 1946; *New York Times*, Nov. 15, 2000; Hoberman, *Army of Phantoms*.

**133** Hughes film with Jane Russell: *New Republic*, June 17, 1946.

**133** Latest Breen review of script: MPA-Prod Code.

**134** Groves critiques latest script: April 16, 1946 (NARA-Groves).

**135** Groves to Barron on script, April 16, 1946 (NARA-Groves).


## 14: Dr. Einstein, I Presume?

**136** Einstein telegram: Isaacson, *Einstein*.

**136** Einstein interview: *New York Times*, June 23, 1946.

**137** Einstein's FBI surveillance: Jerome, *The Einstein File*; https://www.theblackvault.com.

**138** Einstein to Mayer, June 24, 1946; Marx to Einstein, July 1, 1946; Einstein to Marx, July 8, 1946; Marx to Einstein, July 16, 1946; McGuiness to Mayer, July 16, 1946; Mayer replies to Einstein: July 18, 1946 (Albert Einstein Archives, Tel Aviv, 57/152–164). Also: Isaacson, *Einstein*.

**139** Szilard and signing release: Szilard telegram to Einstein and Einstein okay, July 27, 1946: Lanouette, *Genius in the Shadows*.

**139** Szilard's 1945 petition: Lanouette, *Genius in the Shadows*.

**140** Szilard and the FBI: Lanouette, *Genius in the Shadows*.

**140** Letter to Hoover: From Lt. Col. Charles Banks, June 4, 1946 (LSP-UC).

**140** "One of the many reports": Chicago FBI File #100.18133 (LSP-UC).

**140** Groves and the Jews: Interview, Jan. 5, 1965, Voices of the Manhattan Project, https://www.manhattanprojectvoices.org.

**140** Rabinowitz speaking out: Letter to *New York Times*, June 28, 1971.

**141** Szilard at MGM studio: Lanouette, *Genius in the Shadows*.

**141** Marx writes Einstein for support: Lanouette, *Genius in the Shadows*.

**141** Szilard tells Einstein he will sign: Lanouette, *Genius in the Shadows*.

**141** Hersey and Hiroshima: Treglown, *Mr. Straight Arrow*; Yavenditti, "John Hersey and the American Conscience."

**143** Marx assures Bush: April 24, 1946; Bush replies April 26, 1946 (LOC-Bush).

**144** Truman's "incendiary" message on strike: McCullough, *Truman*.

**144** Bush still concerned: Letter to Ross, May 20, 1946; Ross replies, May 21, 1946 (LOC-Bush).

**146** Bush fires off note to Groves: May 22, 1946; Groves replies June 3, 1946 (LOC-Bush).

## 15: A Possible "Prophylactic"

**147** First major piece on film: *Los Angeles Times*, June 30, 1946.

**148** Press photos: Photo files, *The Beginning or the End*, 3 boxes (MPA-MGM).

**149** "After that photo op": Marx chapter in Goldstein and Konigsberg, eds., *The Movies*.

**150** Oppenheimer and Chevalier: Bird and Sherwin, *American Prometheus*.

**150** USSBS report on bombings: *U.S. News*, July 5, 1946; Lifton and Mitchell, *Hiroshima in America*.

**153** Oppenheimer won't attend: Bird and Sherwin, *American Prometheus*; Oppenheimer letter to Truman, May 3, 1946 (HST-OF).

**154** Truman response on "crybaby": Letter to Acheson, May 7, 1946 (HST-OF).

**154** Missing pages of script: *The Herald-News* (Passaic, NJ), Feb. 22, 1947.

**154** Cousins report on test: "The Standardization of Catastrophe," *Saturday Review*, Aug. 10, 1946.

**155** Considine observed test: Weisgall, *Operation Crossroads*.

**155** The second "Baker" test: *New York Times*, Aug. 6, 1946; Weisgall, *Operation Crossroads*.

**156** MGM short: "Bikini: The Atom Island" (watch it: https://youtu .be/zri2knpOSqo)

**156** *March of Time* background: Fielding, *The March of Time*.

**157** Oppie gets word on film short: Telegram, July 9, 1946 (LOC-Opp).

**157** Bush informs Conant: July 18, 1946 (LOC-Bush).

**158** Rand correspondence and letter to agent: Berliner, ed., *Letters of Ayn Rand*.

## 16: John Hersey and the End of "Whoopee"

**160** *March of Time*: "Atomic Power" film short vol. 12, no. 13, Aug. 9, 1946.

**161** *Time* reviews short: Aug. 12, 1946.

**161** Japanese and American footage seized: Mitchell, *Atomic Cover-up*.

**163** Publicity photos: Photo files, *The Beginning or the End*, 3 boxes (MPA-MGM).

**164** Owen's proposed radio series: Smith, *A Peril and a Hope*.

**164** Hersey piece appears: *New Yorker*, Aug. 31, 1946.

**165** Reaction to Hersey article: *Time*, Sept. 9, 1946; *New York Times*, Sept. 8, 1946; Lifton and Mitchell, *Hiroshima in America*; Treglown, *Mr. Straight Arrow*; Yavenditti, "John Hersey and the American Conscience."

**165** *New York Times* editorial: Aug. 30, 1946.

**167** "Water over the dam": *BAS*, May 1, 1946.

**167** Second *New York Times* editorial on Hersey: Sept. 19, 1946.

**167** Macdonald response to Hersey: *Politics* magazine, Oct. 1946.

**168** McCarthy letter on Hersey: *Politics* magazine, Nov. 1946.

**168** Cousins article on Hersey: "The Literacy of Survival," *Saturday Review*, Sept. 14, 1946.

**169** Wilkerson and that priest: *Hollywood Reporter*, Nov. 19, 2012. Overview: https://www.hollywoodreporter.com/features/blacklist-thr-add resses-role-65-391931.

**169** Wilkerson column naming names: *Hollywood Reporter*, July 29, 1946.

**170** Oppie and FBI: Bird and Sherwin, *American Prometheus*.

## 17: Preview in Pomona

**172** Barron informed Groves with news: Sept. 27, 1946. (NARA-Groves).

**172** Mahin's new sequence in Hiroshima: Sept. 24, 1946 (MPA-MGM B-794).

**175** Lang and "Cloak and Dagger": Hoberman, *Army of Phantoms*; Willmetts, *In Secrecy's Shadow*.

**176** Breen analysis of overall movie: MPA-Prod Code.

**176** Lyons item on Truman: *New York Post*, Oct. 7, 1946.

**177** Ross-Ross exchanges: H. Ross to C. Ross, Oct. 9, 1946; C. Ross to H. Ross, Oct. 14, 1946; H. Ross to C. Ross, Oct. 17, 1946; C. Ross to H. Ross, Oct. 22, 1946; H. Ross to C. Ross, Oct. 29, 1946 (all HST-OF).

**178** Conant takes action to counter Hersey: Hershberg, *James B. Conant*; Lifton and Mitchell, *Hiroshima in America*.

**179** Oswald C. Brewster and Stimson: His letter, May 24, 1945 (HST-OF); Wyden, *Day One*; Lifton and Mitchell, *Hiroshima in America*.

**181** Pomona screening and response: Marx to Oppenheimer, with attachments on screening, Oct. 16, 1946 (LOC-Opp).

**183** Marx to Oppie and invite: Oct. 16, 1946 (LOC-Opp).

**184** FBI records call: Summary to bureau, Sept. 28, 1946, (LOC-Sherwin).

**184** Parsons takes complaint on movie to MGM: Oct. 21, 1946 (NARA-Groves).

**185** Parsons takes complaint to Groves: Dec. 12, 1946 (NARA-Groves).

## 18: "A Problem with the President's Scene"

**186** D.C. screening: Hershberg, *James B. Conant*; Broderick, *Hibakusha Cinema*.

**186** Lippmann warning letter to Aydelotte: Oct. 28, 1946 (LOC-Opp).

**188** Aydelotte informs Oppie on Lippmann: Nov. 5, 1946 (LOC-Opp).

**188** Lippmann complains to Conant: Oct. 28, 1946 (HARV-Conant).

**189** Ross to Barron: Oct. 29, 1946 (HST-OF 692 Misc.).

**189** Lifton: Lifton and Mitchell, *Hiroshima in America*.

**189** Groves on Truman "noninterference": Lamont, *Day of Trinity*.

**189** Groves on Truman as "boy on a toboggan": *Look* magazine, Aug. 13, 1963.

**190** McGuinness to Lippmann on response to complaints: Nov. 1, 1946 (LOC-Opp).

**190** McGuinness to Ross on new shooting: Nov. 1, 1946 (HST-Ross).

**190** New scene in script sent to White House: Nov. 1, 1946 (HST-Ross).

**192** McGuinness to Ross on Bohnen: Nov. 1, 1946 (HST-Ross).

**193** Ross edits new scene in script: Nov. 8, 1946 (HST-Ross).

**194** McGuinness thanks Ross: Nov. 18, 1946 (HST-Ross).

**195** Truman quotes that were omitted: Lifton and Mitchell, *Hiroshima in America.*

**196** Blandy and cake controversy: *New York Times*, Nov. 11, 1946; Boyer, *By the Bomb's Early Light.*

**197** Lippmann writes to Forrestal on cake controversy: Boyer, *By the Bomb's Early Light.*

**198** Groves and Pearson item: Memo to General Parks, Nov. 14, 1946 (NARA-Groves).

## 19: Truman, Take Two

**200** Bohnen is fired: *New York Times*, Nov. 22, 1946; *Variety*, Dec. 9, 1946; *Los Angeles Times*, Dec. 9, 1946.

**201** Longer *New York Times* piece on Bohnen, etc.: Dec. 1, 1946.

**201** Bohnen writes to Truman: Dec. 2, 1946 (HST-PSF).

**202** Truman replies to Bohnen: Dec. 12, 1946 (HST-PSF).

**203** Final revise of scene with crew in cabin: MPA-MGM B-794.

**204** Retake of final scene of movie: Oct. 10, 1946 (MPA-MGM B-795).

**205** Groves's latest critique: Nov. 15 and 19, 1946 (NARA-Groves).

**206** Barron responds to Groves: Dec. 4, 1946 (NARA-Groves).

**206** Johnson to Groves on movie: Undated, circa Dec. 1946 (NARA-Groves).

**207** Fassett to Marx on movie: Oct. 26, 1946; Bush to Conant: Nov. 4, 1946 (LOC-Bush).

**207** Bush and Ross: Bush letter to Conant, Dec. 6, 1946 (LOC-Bush).

**208** Bush to Conant on latest feelings on movie: Nov. 4 and 27, 1946 (LOC-Bush).

**208** Conant tries to get Baruch involved in stopping movie: Dec. 20, 1946 (HARV-Conant); Hershberg, *James B. Conant.*

**209** FBI reviews films: *Chicago Tribune*, Dec. 21, 2017.

**210** MGM ads and booklet on movie: MPA-MGM.

**211** New publicity photos: Photo files, *The Beginning or the End*, 3 boxes (MPA-MGM).

## 20: Stimson to the Rescue

**212** Szilard at Chicago screening: Lanouette, *Genius in the Shadows*; Smith, *A Peril and a Hope*.

**212** Groves aide comments and Barron assures studio: Reingold, "MGM Meets the Bomb."

**212** Louella Parsons syndicated column: Jan. 8, 1947.

**212** Lippmann assures Conant: Jan. 10, 1947 (HARV-Conant).

**212** New actor Baker writes: Jan. 7, 1947, Ross replies Jan. 13, 1947 (HST-PSF).

**213** McGuinness thanks Ross: Jan. 14, 1947 (HST-Ross).

**213** Stimson article: *Harper's*, Feb. 1947; Truman comments to Stimson and Stimson replies: Hershberg, *James B. Conant*; Lifton and Mitchell, *Hiroshima in America*.

**214** *Herald-Tribune* on Stimson article: Jan. 28, 1947.

**214** Response to article by *New York Times*, Truman, Acheson, Bundy, Conant: Wittner, *One World or None*; Lifton and Mitchell, *Hiroshima in America*.

**216** Letter to Conant from lawyer on Stimson article: Hershberg, *James B. Conant*.

**216** Conant to Oppenheimer on scientists: Hershberg, *James B. Conant*.

**216** Grew critique of bombing: Lifton and Mitchell, *Hiroshima in America*.

**217** McCloy to Stimson on bombing: Hershberg, *James B. Conant*.

**217** "open question": Bundy interviewed by Peter Jennings for ABC news special, "Hiroshima," July 1995.

**217** AEC and Oppenheimer's feelings: Bird and Sherwin, *American Prometheus*.

**217** Movie trailer: See https://youtu.be/DqnQ1U3_Qt4.

**219** Marx tells reporter: *New York Times*, Jan. 12, 1947.

**219** Latest from Breen on movie: MPA-Prod Code.

## 21: "Hokum" and "Imbecility"

**220** Budget for movie: MPA-Mannix Ledger.

**220** *Lion's Roar*: MPA-MGM.

**220** Eleanor protests: Earl Wilson syndicated column, Feb. 20, 1947; Leonard Lyons column, Feb. 21, 1947.

**221** Oppie screening: Memos in FBI file, Jan. 25, 1947 and Feb. 9, 1947 (LOC-Sherwin).

**221** The big party: Photo files, *The Beginning or the End*, 3 boxes (MPA-MGM).

**222** Reviews: *Variety*, Feb. 19, 1947; *Science Illustrated*, Oct. 1946; *Esquire*, May 1947; *New York Times*, Feb. 21, 1947; *Time*, February 24, 1947; *Life*, March 17, 1947.

**222** Considine hails: Feb. 27, 1947.

**225** Harrison Brown review: *Bulletin of the Atomic Scientists*, March 1947.

**225** Tony Owen's money: Fultz, *In Search of Donna Reed*.

**226** Film's losses: MPA-Mannix Ledger.

**227** "The vast majority," Hershberg, *James B. Conant*.

**227** 1947 poll of FAS: Buyer, *By the Bomb's Early Light*.

## 22: Aftermath, 1947–2020

**228** Production Code and Spain: MPA-Prod Code.

**229** Groves retires: *New York Times*, Feb. 2, 1948.

**229** Ike critiques and denies Groves: Norris, *Racing for the Bomb*.

**229** "The trouble really started": Norris, *Racing for the Bomb*.

**230** Truman's responses to using bomb over the years: Lifton and Mitchell, *Hiroshima in America*; HST-OF, HST-PPF, HST-Press secy.

**230** The Tanimoto affair: McMahon to Connelly, Oct. 26, 1949; State Department memo, R.D. Muir to Connelly, Oct. 27, 1946; McMahon to Connelly, Nov. 2, 1946 and Connelly reply to him, Nov. 7, 1946. All in HST-PSF.

**232** Other presidents' responses to bombing: Lifton and Mitchell, *Hiroshima in America*.

**234** Obama in Hiroshima: *New York Times*, May 27, 2016.

**234** Trump tweets on Obama: CNN.com, May 29, 2016.

**234** Liz Cheney on Warren's first-use comment: *Politico*, Aug. 2, 2019.

**236** Oppenheimer's later years: Bird and Sherwin, *American Prometheus*; Lifton and Mitchell, *Hiroshima in America*.

**237** Oppenheimer on use of bomb to *New York Times*: Aug. 1, 1965.

**238** Other Hollywood films: Appendix in Lifton and Mitchell, *Hiroshima in America*.

**241** Rand's later years: Heller, *Ayn Rand and the World She Made*; Branden, *The Passion of Ayn Rand*.

**242** Reviews of novel and Greenspan: Heller, *Ayn Rand and the World She Made*.

**243** Tibbets and Sweeney look back on bombing: Mitchell, *Atomic Cover-up*.

**244** Reed's later years: Fultz, *In Search of Donna Reed*.

**246** Cyberattacks and first-strike: "With nuclear weapons, we're getting too comfortable thinking the unthinkable," *Washington Post*, Jan. 30, 2018.

**246** Article in *Military Times*: July 10, 2019.

**246** Klare on INF treaty withdrawal: *The Nation*, Aug. 30, 2019.

**247** Dorfman article: "Nuclear Apocalypse Now," *New York Review of Books*, Sept. 22, 2017.

**247** Hersey at White House: Treglown, *Mr. Straight Arrow*.

# BIBLIOGRAPHY

Agee, James. *The Collected Short Prose of James Agee*. London: Calder and Boyers, 1972.

Bergreen, Laurence. *James Agee, a Life*. New York: Dutton, 1984.

Berliner, Michael S., ed. *Letters of Ayn Rand*. New York: Plume, 1997.

Bird, Kai, and Martin J. Sherwin. *American Prometheus: The Triumph and Tragedy of J. Robert Oppenheimer*. New York: Vintage, 2005.

Boyer, Paul. *By the Bomb's Early Light*. New York: Pantheon, 1985.

Branden, Barbara. *The Passion of Ayn Rand*. New York: Anchor, 1987.

Broderick, Mick. *Hibakusha Cinema*. New York: Routledge, 2009.

Cronyn, Hume. *A Terrible Liar*. New York: William Morrow, 1991.

Evans, Joyce A. *Celluloid Mushroom Clouds*. Boulder: Westview Press, 1998.

Fielding, Raymond. *The March of Time 1935–1951*. New York: Oxford University Press, 1978.

Fultz, Jay. *In Search of Donna Reed*. Iowa City: University of Iowa Press, 1998.

Goldstein, Laurence, and Ira Konigsberg, eds. *The Movies*. Ann Arbor: University of Michigan Press, 1996.

Groves, Leslie R. *Now It Can Be Told*. New York: Harper, 1962.

Harriman, David, ed. *Journals of Ayn Rand*. New York: Dutton, 1997.

Heller, Anne C. *Ayn Rand and the World She Made*. New York: Anchor Books, 1999.

Herken, Gregg. *Brotherhood of the Bomb*. New York: Henry Holt and Co., 2002.

Hershberg, James, *James B. Conant*. New York: Knopf, 1993.

Hoberman, J. *Army of Phantoms: American Movies and the Making of the Cold War*. New York: The New Press, 2011.

Isaacson, Walter. *Einstein: His Life and Universe*. New York: Simon & Schuster, 2007.

Jacobs, Robert. *Filling the Hole in the Nuclear Future*. Lanham, MD: Lexington Books, 2010.

Jerome, Fred. *The Einstein File*. New York: St. Martin's, 2002.

Lamont, Lansing. *Day of Trinity*. New York: Signet, 1966.

Lanouette, William. *Genius in the Shadows*. New York: Scribner's, 1992.

Leahy, William D. *I Was There*. New York: Whittlesey House, 1950.

Lifton, Robert, and Greg Mitchell. *Hiroshima in America: Fifty Years of Denial*. New York: Putnam, 1995.

Marx, Samuel. *Mayer and Thalberg*. New York: Random House, 1975.

———. *A Gaudy Spree: Literary Hollywood When the West Was Fun*. New York: Franklin Watts, 1987.

McCullough, David. *Truman*. New York: Simon & Schuster, 1992.

Mitchell, Greg. *Atomic Cover-up*. New York: Sinclair Books, 2012.

Murrow, Edward R. *In Search of Light*. New York: Knopf, 1967.

Nichols, Kenneth D. *The Road to Trinity*. New York: William Morrow, 1987.

Norris, Robert S. *Racing for the Bomb: General Leslie R. Groves, the Manhattan Project's Indispensable Man*. South Royalton, VT: Steerforth Press, 2014.

Rhodes, Richard. *The Making of the Atomic Bomb*. New York: Simon and Schuster, 1986.

———. *Dark Sun*. New York: Simon & Schuster, 1995.

Rosenblatt, Roger. *Witness: The World Since Hiroshima*. New York: Little, Brown, 1985.

Schwartz, Sheila. *The Hollywood Writers' Wars*. New York: McGraw-Hill, 1983.

Smith, Alice Kimball. *A Peril and a Hope*. Chicago: University of Chicago Press, 1965.

Smith, Alice Kimball, and Charles Weiner, eds. *Robert Oppenheimer: Letters and Recollections*. Stanford: Stanford University Press, 1980.

Southard, Susan. *Nagasaki: Life After Nuclear War*. New York: Penguin, 2015.

Taylor, Telford. *Nuremberg and Vietnam: An American Tragedy*. New York: Bantam, 1971.

Treglown, Jeremy. *Mr. Straight Arrow: The Career of John Hersey*. New York: Farrar, Straus and Giroux, 2019.

Wallis, Hal, and Charles Higham. *Starmaker*. New York: Macmillan, 1980.

Weisgall, Jonathan, *Operation Crossroads*. Annapolis, MD: Naval Institute Press, 1994.

Willmetts, Simon. *In Secrecy's Shadow*. Edinburgh: Edinburgh University Press, 2016.

Wellerstein, Alex. "The Demon Core and the Strange Death of Louis Slotin," *New Yorker*, May 21, 2016.

Wittner, Lawrence S. *One World or None*. Stanford: Stanford University Press, 1993.

Wyden, Peter. *Day One*. New York: Simon & Schuster, 1989.

Yavenditti, Michael J. "John Hersey and the American Conscience," *Pacific Historical Review*, Feb. 1974.

# INDEX

# ABOUT THE AUTHOR

**Greg Mitchell**'s books include *The Tunnels: Escapes Under the Berlin Wall and the Historic Films the JFK White House Tried to Kill*; *The Campaign of the Century: Upton Sinclair's Race for Governor of California and the Birth of Media Politics*, winner of the Goldsmith Book Prize and finalist for the *Los Angeles Times* Book Prize; *Tricky Dick and the Pink Lady*, a *New York Times* Notable Book; *So Wrong for So Long: How the Press, the Pundits—and the President—Failed on Iraq*; and, with Robert Jay Lifton, *Hiroshima in America* and *Who Owns Death?* He is the former editor of *Nuclear Times* and *Editor & Publisher*. He spent a month in Hiroshima and Nagasaki in 1984 on a journalism grant. Mitchell co-produced the recent documentary film, *Following the Ninth*. He lives in the New York City area.

# PUBLISHING IN
# THE PUBLIC INTEREST

Thank you for reading this book published by The New Press. The New Press is a nonprofit, public interest publisher. New Press books and authors play a crucial role in sparking conversations about the key political and social issues of our day.

We hope you enjoyed this book and that you will stay in touch with The New Press. Here are a few ways to stay up to date with our books, events, and the issues we cover:

- Sign up at www.thenewpress.com/subscribe to receive updates on New Press authors and issues and to be notified about local events
- Like us on Facebook: www.facebook.com/newpress books
- Follow us on Twitter: www.twitter.com/thenewpress

Please consider buying New Press books for yourself; for friends and family; or to donate to schools, libraries, community centers, prison libraries, and other organizations involved with the issues our authors write about.

The New Press is a 501(c)(3) nonprofit organization. You can also support our work with a tax-deductible gift by visiting www.thenewpress.com/donate.